IS

A 2004 Update
and Practical Guide

to the International Ship and
Port Facility Security Code

EDITED AND COMPILED BY:
PETER MOTH

Foreshore
Publications

ISBN 1 901630 02 1

This publication contains material originating from the International Maritime Organization, The United States Coast Guard and the Commission of the European Communities

**Published by
Foreshore
Publications
Maritime Centre
Northney Marina
Hayling Island
Hants
PO11 0NH**

E-Mail:
foreshore@mail.com
**Tel: +44 (0)23 92
460111
Fax: +44 (0)23 92
460123**

**Edited
and Compiled by:**

Peter Moth

**Production and
Sales Manager:**

**Peter Webb
Marine Media
Marketing**

**ISBN:
1 901630 02 1**

**Printed by
SG Design
Havant, England**

**Front cover:
mv Limburg attacked
by terrorists off the
Yemeni coast.
October 2002**
Photo: courtesy
AP

Readers are advised that *all* text entered in tinted or bordered frames, e.g.

| Port Facility Security .... | Port Facility Security .... |

and,
all advertisements, *all* page headings, *all* illustrations, *all* photographs and the Keyword Index do NOT form part of official texts unless specifically indicated as such.

In keeping with the style of the original text, the nomenclature use of the International English "ize" idiom, rather than the British English "ise" idiom, has been used throughout this publication, as and where appropriate

Inclusion of advertisements in the publication as a whole, or in sections thereof, does not imply or confirm approval, endorsement or recommendation by the Publishers or any other body of that product or service so promoted.

ISPS Code
2004 Update – A Practical Guide
© 2004 Foreshore Publications

Foreshore Publications and Foreshore Media are imprints of Maritime Intelligence Ltd, Maritime Centre, Northney Marina, Hayling Island, Hants PO11 0NH, England

ISPS CODE
2004 UPDATE
A PRACTICAL GUIDE

contains

THE INTERNATIONAL SHIP & PORT FACILITY SECURITY CODE
(Part A and Part B)

AMENDMENTS TO SOLAS 1974
– amendments to SOLAS Chapters V and XI
– new SOLAS Chapter XI2

IMO CONFERENCE RESOLUTIONS
– pertaining to the enhancement of maritime security

KEYWORD INDEX
– to the ISPS Code

EUROPEAN COMMISSION REGULATION
– on Enhancing Ship and Port Facility Security (Proposal)

EUROPEAN COMMISSION DIRECTIVE
– on Enhancing Port Security (Proposal)

US MARITIME STRATEGY FOR HOMELAND SECURITY

CONTENTS

CONTENTS

Part B

**Part B
(Guidance)**

CONTENTS

Amendments to SOLAS 1974

Other Conference Resolutions

**Part B (guidance)
contd.**

**SOLAS Amendments
Resolution No 1**

**Conference
Resolutions
Nos 3–11**

CONTENTS

IMO Guidance

European Proposals

US Maritime Strategy

.

"I urge early implementation of maritime security measures"

"The devastating news of recent atrocities should serve as a grim reminder of the vulnerability of all modes of transport to acts of terrorism. As far as we, servants of the maritime mode are concerned, we should mobilize all our resources to protect our industry, the international trade and the global economy from those whose motives and acts have nothing at all to do with all that the civilized world stands for.

"I urge all parties concerned, be they Administrations, designated authorities, port authorities, companies, recognized security organizations, training institutions or others, to intensify their efforts to meet the entry-into-force deadline for the new security regime specified in SOLAS chapter XI-2 and the International Ship and Port Facility Security Code.

"I might even go one step further by urging all parties concerned, in particular SOLAS Contracting Governments and port organizations, to implement the new measures as early as possible, as far as ships entitled to fly their flags and port facilities under their jurisdiction are concerned.

"My argument, in so doing, is simple. While the 1st July deadline constitutes a pact among Governments doing business in a civilized manner under the mutually binding provisions of a treaty instrument, this deadline means nothing to terrorists who may decide to strike wherever and whenever such an act might suit their evil purposes – and, have no doubt, they will do so if they assess that our defences are low or, to put it in a different manner, when they think that our defences are not high enough to prevent and deter them from committing any atrocities they may have in mind to commit against our industry, the international trade and the world economy."

Mr Efthimios E Mitropoulos

IMO Secretary-General

March 2004

INTRODUCTION

A new, comprehensive security regime for international shipping is set to enter into force on 1 July 2004 following the adoption by the International Maritime Organization (IMO) of a series of measures to strengthen maritime security and to prevent and suppress acts of terrorism against shipping.

The Maritime Security Conference, held at the London headquarters of the IMO between 9 and 13 December 2002, was of crucial significance not only to the international maritime community but the world community as a whole, given the pivotal role shipping plays in the conduct of world trade. The measures adopted at the Conference represent the culmination of just over a year's intense work by IMO's Maritime Safety Committee and its Intersessional Working Group since the terrorist atrocities in the United States in September 2001.

The Conference adopted a number of amendments to the 1974 Safety of Life at Sea Convention (SOLAS), the most far-reaching of which enshrines the new International Ship and Port Facility Security Code (ISPS Code).

The Code contains detailed security-related requirements for Governments, port authorities and shipping companies in a mandatory section (Part A), together with a series of guidelines about how to meet these requirements in a second, non-mandatory section (Part B). The Conference also adopted a series of resolutions designed to add weight to the amendments, encourage the application of the measures to ships and port facilities not covered by the Code and pave the way for future work on the subject.

In essence, the Code takes the approach that ensuring the security of ships and port facilities is basically a risk management activity and that to determine what security measures are appropriate, an assessment of the risks must be made in each particular case.

The purpose of the Code is to provide a standardized, consistent framework for evaluating risk, enabling governments to offset changes in threat with changes in vulnerability, for ships and port facilities.

To begin the process, each Contracting Government will conduct Port Facility Security Assessments. Such assessments will have three essential components. First, they must identify and evaluate important assets and infrastructures that are critical to the port facility as well as those areas or structures that, if damaged, could cause significant loss of life or damage to the port facility's economy or environment.

Then, the assessment must identify the actual threats to those

Introduction and General Explanation of the ISPS Code

Essence and purpose of the ISPS Code

Security Assessments – the three essential components

INTRODUCTION

critical assets and infrastructure in order to prioritise security measures.

Finally, the assessment must address vulnerability of the port facility by identifying its weaknesses in physical security, structural integrity, protection systems, procedural policies, communications systems, transportation infrastructure, utilities, and other areas within a port facility that may be a likely target. Once this assessment has been completed, Contracting Governments can accurately evaluate risk.

This risk management concept will be embodied in the Code through a number of minimum functional security requirements for ships and port facilities.

Security requirements for:

Ships

For **ships**, these requirements will include:
- ✔ ship security plans
- ✔ ship security officers
- ✔ company security officers
- ✔ certain onboard equipment

Port facilities

For **port facilities**, the requirements will include:
- ✔ port facility security plans
- ✔ port facility security officers
- ✔ certain security equipment

Ships and port facilities

The Port Facility:

In addition the requirements for **ships and for port facilities** include:
- ✔ monitoring and controlling access
- ✔ monitoring the activities of people and cargo
- ✔ ensuring security communications are readily available.

Because each ship (or class of ship) and each port facility present different risks, the method in which they will meet the specific requirements of this Code will be determined and eventually be approved by the Administration or Contracting Government, as the case may be.

Security levels 1, 2 and 3

In order to communicate the threat at a port facility or for a ship, the Contracting Government will set the appropriate security level. Security Levels 1, 2, and 3 correspond to normal, medium, and high threat situations, respectively. The security level creates a link between the ship and the port facility, since it triggers the implementation of appropriate security measures for the ship and for the port facility.

Reducing vulnerability

The preamble to the Code states that, as threat increases, the only logical counteraction is to reduce vulnerability. The Code provides several ways to reduce vulnerabilities. Ships will be subject to a system of survey, verification, certification, and control to ensure that their security measures are implemented. This system will be based on a considerably expanded control system as stipulated in the 1974 Convention for Safety of Life at Sea (SOLAS). Port facilities will also be required to report certain security related information to the Contracting Government concerned, which in turn will submit a list of approved port facility security plans, including location and contact details to IMO.

Under the terms of the Code, shipping companies will be required to designate a Company Security Officer for the Company and a Ship Security Officer for each of its ships. The Company Security Officer's responsibilities include ensuring that a Ship Security Assessment is properly carried out, that Ship Security Plans are prepared and submitted for approval by (or on behalf of) the Administration and thereafter is placed on board each ship.

The Company and the Ship:

– Security Officers

The Ship Security Plan should indicate the operational and physical security measures the ship itself should take to ensure it always operates at Security Level 1. The plan should also indicate the additional, or intensified, security measures the ship itself can take to move to and operate at Security Level 2 when instructed to do so. Furthermore, the plan should indicate the possible preparatory actions the ship could take to allow prompt response to instructions that may be issued to the ship at Security Level 3.

– Ship Security Plan

Ships will have to carry an International Ship Security Certificate indicating that they comply with the requirements of SOLAS Chapter XI-2 and part A of the ISPS Code. When a ship is at a port or is proceeding to a port of Contracting Government, the Contracting Government has the right, under the provisions of regulation XI-2/9, to exercise various control and compliance measures with respect to that ship. The ship is subject to port State control inspections but such inspections will not normally extend to examination of the Ship Security Plan itself except in specific circumstances.

– International Ship Security Certificate

– port State control inspections

The ship may, also, be subject to additional control measures if the Contracting Government exercising the control and compliance measures has reason to believe that the security of the ship has, or the port facilities it has served have, been compromised.

Each Contracting Government has to ensure completion of a Port Facility Security Assessment for each port facility within its territory that serves ships engaged on international voyages. The Port Facility Security Assessment is fundamentally a risk analysis of all aspects of a port facility's operation in order to determine which parts of it are more susceptible, and/or more likely, to be the subject of attack. Security risk is seen a function of the threat of an attack coupled with the vulnerability of the target and the consequences of an attack.

The Port Facility:

– Security Assessment

INTRODUCTION

– Port Facility
Security Officer

– Port Facility
Security Plan

– port State Control
inspections

Responsibilities of
Contracting
Governments

Amendments to
SOLAS 1974

Modifications to
SOLAS Chapter V

On completion of the analysis, it will be possible to produce an overall assessment of the level of risk. The Port Facility Security Assessment will help determine which port facilities are required to appoint a Port Facility Security Officer and prepare a Port Facility Security Plan. This plan should indicate the operational and physical security measures the port facility should take to ensure that it always operates at Security Level 1. The plan should also indicate the additional, or intensified, security measures the port facility can take to move to and operate at Security level 2 when instructed to do so. It should also indicate the possible preparatory actions the port facility could take to allow prompt response to the instructions that may be issued at Security Level 3.

In addition to port State control inspections and additional control measures, the relevant authorities may request the provision of information regarding the ship, its cargo, passengers and ship's personnel prior to the ship's entry into port. There may be circumstances in which entry into port could be denied.

Contracting Governments have various responsibilities, including setting the applicable Security Level, approving the Ship Security Plan and relevant amendments to a previously approved Plan, verifying the compliance of ships with the provisions of SOLAS chapter XI-2 and part A of the ISPS Code and issuing the International Ship Security Certificate, determining which port facilities located within their territory are required to designate a Port Facility Security Officer, ensuring completion and approval of the Port Facility Security Assessment and the Port Facility Security Plan and any subsequent amendments; and exercising control and compliance measures. It is also responsible for communicating information to the International Maritime Organization and to the shipping and port industries.

Contracting Governments can designate, or establish, Designated Authorities within Government to undertake their security duties and allow Recognised Security Organisations to carry out certain work with respect to port facilities, but the final decision on the acceptance and approval of this work should be given by the Contracting Government or the Designated Authority.

The Conference adopted a series of Amendments to the 1974 SOLAS Convention. Among other things, these amendments create a new SOLAS chapter dealing specifically with maritime security, which in turn contains the mandatory requirement for ships to comply with the ISPS Code.

Modifications to Chapter V (Safety of Navigation) contain a new timetable for the fitting of Automatic Identification Systems (AIS). Ships, other than passenger ships and tankers, of 300 gross tonnage and upwards but less than 50,000 gross tonnage, will be required to fit AIS not later than the first safety equipment survey after 1 July 2004 or by 31 December 2004, whichever occurs earlier. Ships fitted with AIS shall maintain AIS in operation at all times except where international agreements, rules or standards provide for the protection of navigational information.

The existing SOLAS Chapter XI (Special measures to enhance maritime safety) has been re-numbered as Chapter XI-1. Regulation XI-1/3 is modified to require ships' identification numbers to be permanently marked in a visible place either on the ship's hull or superstructure. Passenger ships should carry the marking on a horizontal surface visible from the air. Ships should also be marked with their ID numbers internally.

SOLAS Chapter XI

Ship's Identification Number

And a new regulation XI-1/5 requires ships to be issued with a Continuous Synopsis Record (CSR) which is intended to provide an on-board record of the history of the ship. The CSR shall be issued by the Administration and shall contain information such as the name of the ship and of the State whose flag the ship is entitled to fly, the date on which the ship was registered with that State, the ship's identification number, the port at which the ship is registered and the name of the registered owner(s) and their registered address. Any changes shall be recorded in the CSR so as to provide updated and current information together with the history of the changes.

Continuous Synopsis Record (CSR)

A brand-new Chapter XI-2 (Special measures to enhance maritime security) is added after the renumbered Chapter XI-1. This chapter applies to passenger ships and cargo ships of 500 gross tonnage and upwards, including high speed craft, mobile offshore drilling units and port facilities serving such ships engaged on international voyages.

Regulation XI-2/3 of the new chapter enshrines the International Ship and Port Facilities Security Code (ISPS Code). Part A of this Code will become mandatory and part B contains guidance as to how best to comply with the mandatory requirements.

The regulation requires Administrations to set Security Levels and ensure the provision of Security Level information to ships entitled to fly their flag. Prior to entering a port, or whilst in a port, within the territory of a Contracting Government, a ship shall comply with the requirements for the Security Level set by that Contracting Government, if that Security Level is higher than the Security Level set by the Administration for that ship.

Setting security levels

Regulation XI-2/4 confirms the role of the Master in exercising his professional judgement over decisions necessary to maintain the security of the ship. It says he shall not be constrained by the Company, the charterer or any other person in this respect.

Role of the Master

INTRODUCTION

Ship Security Alert System

Regulation XI-2/5 requires all ships to be provided with a Ship Security Alert System, according to a strict timetable that will see most vessels fitted by 2004 and the remainder by 2006. When activated the Ship Security Alert System shall initiate and transmit a ship-to-shore security alert to a competent authority designated by the Administration, identifying the ship, its location and indicating that the security of the ship is under threat or it has been compromised. The system will not raise any alarm on-board the ship. The ship security alert system shall be capable of being activated from the navigation bridge and in at least one other location.

Regulation XI-2/6 covers requirements for port facilities, providing among other things for Contracting Governments to ensure that Port Facility Security Assessments are carried out and that Port Facility Security Plans are developed, implemented and reviewed in accordance with the ISPS Code.

Information to IMO

Other regulations in this chapter cover the provision of information to IMO, the control of ships in port, (including measures such as the delay, detention, restriction of operations including movement within the port, or expulsion of a ship from port), and the specific responsibility of Companies.

Resolutions adopted by the Conference

The Conference adopted 11 resolutions:.
- **Conference resolution 1** (Adoption of amendments to the annex to SOLAS 1974, as amended)
- **Conference resolution 2** (Adoption of the International Ship and Port Facility Security (ISPS) Code)
- **Conference resolution 3** (Further work by the IMO pertaining to the enhancement of maritime security)
- **Conference resolution 4** (Future amendments to Chapters XI-1 and XI-2 of the 1974 SOLAS Convention on special measures to enhance maritime safety and security)
- **Conference resolution 5** (Promotion of technical co-operation and assistance)
- **Conference resolution 6** (Early implementation of the special measures to enhance maritime security)
- **Conference resolution 7** (Establishment of appropriate measures to enhance the security of ships, port facilities, mobile offshore drilling units on location and fixed and floating platforms not covered by chapter XI-2 of SOLAS 1974)
- **Conference resolution 8** (Enhancement of security in co-operation with the International Labour Organization)
- **Conference resolution 9** (Enhancement of security in co-operation with the World Customs Organization)
- **Conference resolution 10** (Early implementation of long-range ships' identification and tracking)
- **Conference resolution 11** (Human element-related aspects and shore leave for seafarers)

ABBREVIATIONS USED IN THE ISPS CODE AND ANNEXES	
AIS	Automatic Identification System
CSO	Company Security Officer
CSR	Continuous Synopsis Record
CTU	Cargo Transport Unit
DoC	Document of Compliance (ISM Code)
DoS	Declaration of Security
ILO	International Labour Organization
ISSC	International Ship Security Certificate
MOU	Memorandum of Understanding
PFSA	Port Facility Security Assessment
PFSO	Port Facility Security Officer
PFSP	Port Facility Security Plan
RSO	Recognized Security Organization
SoCPF	Statement of Compliance of a Port Facility
SSA	Ship Security Assessment
SSO	Ship Security Officer
SSP	Ship Security Plan
WCO	World Customs Organization

List of Abbreviations

(Note: this list is not part of the official text)

Overview

OBJECTIVES OF THE ISPS CODE

Detect Security Threats and Implement Security Measures: to establish an international framework involving co-operation between Contracting Governments, Government agencies, local administrations and the shipping and port industries to detect security threats and take preventive measures against security incidents affecting ships or port facilities used in international trade

Roles for Government, maritime administrations, shipping companies and the ports industry: to establish the respective roles and responsibilities of the Contracting Governments, Government agencies, local administrations and the shipping and port industries, at the national and international level for ensuring maritime security

Collation and promulgation of security-related information: to ensure the early and efficient collection and exchange of security-related information

Plans and procedures: to provide a methodology for security assessments so as to have in place plans and procedures to react to changing security levels

Instil confidence: to ensure confidence that adequate and proportionate maritime security measures are in place.

TIMETABLE

Consultation	during 2002
IMO Agreement	12 December 2002
SOLAS Amendments accepted	1 January 2004
ISPS Code enters into force	**1 July 2004**

STRUCTURE

The Code is in two parts:
Part A which is mandatory
Part B which is recommendatory

Minimum requirements are:

For ships:	**For port facilities:**
ship security assessment	port facility security assessment
ship security plans	port facility security plans
ship security officers	port facility security officers
company security officers	certain security equipment
certain onboard equipment	

In addition, **for ships *and* for port facilities**:
monitoring and controlling access
monitoring the activities of people and cargo
ensuring security communications are readily available.

Elements of the ISPS Code

Ship Security Plan (SSP) means a plan developed to ensure the application of measures on board the ship designed to protect persons on board, cargo, cargo transport units, ship's stores or the ship from the risks of a security incident.

Port Facility Security Plan (PFSP) means a plan developed to ensure the application of measures designed to protect the port facility and ships, persons, cargo, cargo transport units and ship's stores within the port facility from the risks of a security incident.

Ship Security Officer (SSO) means the person on board the ship, accountable to the master, designated by the Company as responsible for the security of the ship, including implementation and maintenance of the Ship Security Plan and for liaison with the Company Security Officer and Port Facility Security Officers.

Company Security Officer (CSO) means the person designated by the Company for ensuring that a Ship Security Assessment is carried out; that a Ship Security Plan is developed, submitted for approval, and thereafter implemented and maintained and for liaison with Port Facility Security Officers and the Ship Security Officer.

Port Facility Security Officer (PFSO) means the person designated as responsible for the development, implementation, revision and maintenance of the Port Facility Security Plan and for liaison with the Ship Security Officers and Company Security Officers.

Security Level 1 means the level for which minimum appropriate protective security measures shall be maintained at all times.

Security Level 2 means the level for which appropriate additional protective security measures shall be maintained for a period of time as a result of heightened risk of a security incident.

Security Level 3 means the level for which further specific protective security measures shall be maintained for a limited period of time when a security incident is probable or imminent, although it may not be possible to identify the specific target.

**Not official text
For general
reference only**

Checklist

SHIP SECURITY ASSESSMENT

Basic Elements:
A Ship Security Assessment should address the following elements on board or within the ship:

- ❑ physical security;
- ❑ structural integrity;
- ❑ personnel protection systems;
- ❑ procedural policies;
- ❑ radio and telecommunication systems, including computer systems and networks; and
- ❑ other areas that may, if damaged or used for illicit observation, pose a risk to persons, property, or operations on board the ship or within a port facility.

Expert Assistance
Those involved in a Ship Security Assessment should be able to draw upon expert assistance in relation to:

- ❑ knowledge of current security threats and patterns;
- ❑ recognition and detection of weapons, dangerous substances and devices;
- ❑ recognition, on a non-discriminatory basis, of characteristics and behavioural patterns of persons who are likely to threaten security;
- ❑ techniques used to circumvent security measures;
- ❑ methods used to cause a security incident;
- ❑ effects of explosives on ship's structures and equipment;
- ❑ ship security;
- ❑ ship/port interface business practices;
- ❑ contingency planning, emergency preparedness and response;
- ❑ physical security;
- ❑ radio and telecommunications systems, including computer systems and networks;
- ❑ marine engineering; and
- ❑ ship and port operations

Checklist

The Company Security Officer should obtain and record the information required to conduct a Ship Security Assessment, including:

❏ the general layout of the ship;

❏ the location of areas which should have restricted access, such as navigation bridge, machinery spaces of category A and other control stations as defined in chapter II-2, etc.;

❏ the location and function of each actual or potential access point to the ship;

❏ changes in the tide which may have an impact on the vulnerability or security of the ship;

❏ the cargo spaces and stowage arrangements;

❏ the locations where the ship's stores and essential maintenance equipment is stored;

❏ the locations where unaccompanied baggage is stored;

❏ the emergency and stand-by equipment available to maintain essential services

❏ the number of ship's personnel, any existing security duties and any existing training requirement practices of the Company;

❏ existing security and safety equipment for the protection of passengers and ship's personnel;

❏ escape and evacuation routes and assembly stations which have to be maintained to ensure the orderly and safe emergency evacuation of the ship;

❏ existing agreements with private security companies providing ship/waterside security services; and

❏ existing security measures and procedures in effect, including inspection and, control procedures, identification systems, surveillance and monitoring equipment, personnel identification documents and communication, alarms, lighting, access control and other appropriate systems

Ship Security Assessment (SSA) (contd)

Not official text For general reference only

Checklist

SHIP SECURITY PLAN

Content

The content of each individual Ship Security Plan should vary depending on the particular ship it covers.

The Ship Security Assessment (SSA) will have identified the particular features of the ship and the potential threats and vulnerabilities. The preparation of the SSP will require these features to be addressed in detail. Administrations may prepare advice on the preparation and content of a SSP.

All Ship Security Plans should:

- ☐ detail the organizational structure of security for the ship;

- ☐ detail the ship's relationships with the Company, port facilities, other ships and relevant authorities with security responsibility;.

- ☐ detail the communication systems to allow effective continuous communication within the ship and between the ship and others, including port facilities;

- ☐ detail the basic security measures for Security Level 1, both operational and physical, that will always be in place;

- ☐ detail the additional security measures that will allow the ship to progress without delay to Security Level 2 and, when necessary, to Security Level 3;

- ☐ provide for regular review, or audit, of the SSP and for its amendment in response to experience or changing circumstances; and

- ☐ reporting procedures to the appropriate Contracting Governments contact points.

Preparation of an effective SSP should rest on a thorough assessment of all issues that relate to the security of the ship, including, in particular, a thorough appreciation of the physical and operational characteristics, including the voyage pattern, of the individual ship.

All SSPs should be approved by, or on behalf of, the Administration.

If an Administration uses a Recognized Security Organization (RSO) to review or approve the SSP, the RSO should not be associated with any other RSO that prepared, or assisted in the preparation of, the plan.

Checklist

COMPANY SECURITY OFFICER

The Company shall designate a Company Security Officer.

A person designated as the Company Security Officer may act as the Company Security Officer for one or more ships, depending on the number or types of ships the Company operates provided it is clearly identified for which ships this person is responsible. A Company may, depending on the number or types of ships they operate designate several persons as Company Security Officers provided it is clearly identified for which ships each person is responsible.

The duties and responsibilities of the Company Security Officer shall include, but are not limited to:

- ❏ advising the level of threats likely to be encountered by the ship, using appropriate security assessments and other relevant information;

- ❏ ensuring that Ship Security Assessments are carried out;

- ❏ ensuring the development, the submission for approval, and thereafter the implementation and maintenance of the Ship Security Plan;

- ❏ ensuring that the Ship Security Plan is modified, as appropriate, to correct deficiencies and satisfy the security requirements of the individual ship;

- ❏ arranging for internal audits and reviews of security activities;

- ❏ arranging for the initial and subsequent verifications of the ship by the Administration or the Recognized Security Organization;

- ❏ ensuring that deficiencies and non-conformities identified during internal audits, periodic reviews, inspections and verifications of compliance are promptly addressed and dealt with;

- ❏ enhancing security awareness and vigilance;

- ❏ ensuring adequate training for personnel responsible for the security of the ship;

- ❏ ensuring effective communication and co-operation between the Ship Security Officer and the relevant Port Facility Security Officers;

- ❏ ensuring consistency between security requirements and safety requirements;

- ❏ ensuring that, if sister-ship or fleet security plans are used, the plan for each ship reflects the ship-specific information accurately; and

- ❏ ensuring that any alternative or equivalent arrangements approved for a particular ship or group of ships are implemented and maintained.

Checklist

SHIP SECURITY OFFICER

A Ship Security Officer shall be designated on each ship.

The duties and responsibilities of the Ship Security Officer shall include, but are not limited to:

- ❑ undertaking regular security inspections of the ship to ensure that appropriate security measures are maintained;

- ❑ maintaining and supervising the implementation of the Ship Security Plan, including any amendments to the plan;

- ❑ co-ordinating the security aspects of the handling of cargo and ship's stores with other shipboard personnel and with the relevant Port Facility Security Officers;

- ❑ proposing modifications to the Ship Security Plan;

- ❑ reporting to the Company Security Officer any deficiencies andnon-conformities identified during internal audits, periodic reviews, security inspections and verifications of compliance and implementing any corrective actions;

- ❑ enhancing security awareness and vigilance on board;

- ❑ ensuring that adequate training has been provided to shipboard personnel, as appropriate;

- ❑ reporting all security incidents;

- ❑ co-ordinating implementation of the Ship Security Plan with the Company Security Officer and the relevant Port Facility Security Officer; and

- ❑ ensuring that security equipment is properly operated, tested, calibrated and maintained, if any.

Checklist

PORT FACILITY SECURITY ASSESSMENT

The Port Facility Security Assessment (PFSA) may be conducted by a Recognized Security Organization (RSO). However, approval of a completed PFSA should only be given by the relevant Contracting Government.

Content

A PFSA should address the following elements within a port facility:

- ❑ physical security;
- ❑ structural integrity;
- ❑ personnel protection systems;
- ❑ procedural policies;
- ❑ radio and telecommunication systems, including computer systems and networks;
- ❑ relevant transportation infrastructure;
- ❑ utilities; and
- ❑ other areas that may, if damaged or used for illicit observation, pose a risk to persons, property, or operations within the port facility.

Expert Assistance

Those involved in a PFSA should be able to draw upon expert assistance in relation to:

- ❑ knowledge of current security threats and patterns;
- ❑ recognition and detection of weapons, dangerous substances and devices;
- ❑ recognition, on a non-discriminatory basis, of characteristics and behavioural patterns of persons who are likely to threaten security;
- ❑ techniques used to circumvent security measures;
- ❑ methods used to cause a security incident;
- ❑ effects of explosives on structures and port facility services;
- ❑ port facility security;
- ❑ port business practices;
- ❑ contingency planning, emergency preparedness and response;
- ❑ physical security measures e.g. fences;
- ❑ radio and telecommunications systems, including computer systems and networks;
- ❑ transport and civil engineering; and
- ❑ ship and port operations.

If a Contracting Government uses a RSO to review or verify compliance of the PFSA, the RSO should not be associated with any other RSO that prepared or assisted in the preparation of that assessment.

Checklist

PORT FACILITY SECURITY PLAN

A Port Facility Security Plan (PFSP) shall be developed and maintained, on the basis of a Port Facility Security Assessment, for each port facility, adequate for the ship/port interface. The plan shall make provisions for the three Security Levels, as defined in the Code.

Subject to provisions, a Recognized Security Organization may prepare the Port Facility Security Plan of a specific port facility.

The Port Facility Security Plan shall be approved by the Contracting Government in whose territory the port facility is located.

Such a plan shall be developed taking into account the guidance given in Part B of this Code and shall be in the working language of the port facility. The plan shall address, at least, the following:

- ❑ measures designed to prevent weapons or any other dangerous substances and devices intended for use against persons, ships or ports and the carriage of which is not authorized, from being introduced into the port facility or on board a ship;
- ❑ measures designed to prevent unauthorized access to the port facility, to ships moored at the facility, and to restricted areas of the facility;
- ❑ procedures for responding to security threats or breaches of security, including provisions for maintaining critical operations of the port facility or ship/port interface;
- ❑ procedures for responding to any security instructions the Contracting Government, in whose territory the port facility is located, may give at Security Level 3;
- ❑ procedures for evacuation in case of security threats or breaches of security;
- ❑ duties of port facility personnel assigned security responsibilities and of other facility personnel on security aspects;
- ❑ procedures for interfacing with ship security activities;
- ❑ procedures for the periodic review of the plan and updating;
- ❑ procedures for reporting security incidents;
- ❑ identification of the Port Facility Security Officer including 24-hour contact details;
- ❑ measures to ensure the security of the information contained in the plan;
- ❑ measures designed to ensure effective security of cargo and the cargo handling equipment at the port facility;
- ❑ procedures for auditing the Port Facility Security Plan;
- ❑ procedures for responding in case the ship security alert system of a ship at the port facility has been activated; and
- ❑ procedures for facilitating shore leave for ship's personnel or personnel changes, as well as access of visitors to the ship including representatives of seafarers' welfare and labour organizations.

Checklist

PORT FACILITY SECURITY OFFICER

A Port Facility Security Officer shall be designated for each port facility. A person may be designated as the Port Facility Security Officer for one or more port facilities.

The duties and responsibilities of the Port Facility Security Officer shall include, but are not limited to:

- ❏ conducting an initial comprehensive security survey of the port facility taking into account the relevant Port Facility Security Assessment;

- ❏ ensuring the development and maintenance of the Port Facility Security Plan;

- ❏ implementing and exercising the Port Facility Security Plan;

- ❏ undertaking regular security inspections of the port facility to ensure the continuation of appropriate security measures;

- ❏ recommending and incorporating, as appropriate, modifications to the Port Facility Security Plan in order to correct deficiencies and to update the plan to take into account of relevant changes to the port facility;

- ❏ enhancing security awareness and vigilance of the port facility personnel;

- ❏ ensuring adequate training has been provided to personnel responsible for the security of the port facility;

- ❏ reporting to the relevant authorities and maintaining records of occurrences which threaten the security of the port facility;

- ❏ co-ordinating implementation of the Port Facility Security Plan with the appropriate Company and Ship Security Officer(s);

- ❏ co-ordinating with security services, as appropriate;

- ❏ ensuring that standards for personnel responsible for security of the port facility are met;

- ❏ ensuring that security equipment is properly operated, tested, calibrated and maintained, if any; and

- ❏ assisting Ship Security Officers in confirming the identity of those seeking to board the ship when requested.

CONFERENCE RESOLUTION 2

**IMO Conference
of Contracting
Governments to
the International
Convention for the
Safety of Life at Sea
(SOLAS), 1974**

**Adoption of the
ISPS Code**

ADOPTION OF THE INTERNATIONAL SHIP AND PORT FACILITY
SECURITY (ISPS) CODE

ADOPTION OF THE RESOLUTIONS AND RECOMMENDATIONS
AND RELATED MATTERS

CONFERENCE RESOLUTION 2 (ADOPTED 12 DECEMBER 2002)

ADOPTION OF THE INTERNATIONAL CODE FOR THE SECURITY
OF SHIPS AND OF PORT FACILITIES

The **Conference,**

Having adopted amendments to the International Convention for the
Safety of Life at Sea, 1974, as amended (hereinafter referred to
as "the Convention"), concerning special measures to enhance
maritime safety and security,

Considering that the new chapter XI-2 of the Convention makes a
reference to an International Ship and Port Facility Security
(ISPS) Code and requires that ships, companies and port
facilities to comply with the relevant requirements of part A of
the International Ship and Port Facility Security (ISPS) Code,
as specified in part A of the ISPS Code,

Being of the opinion that the implementation by Contracting
Governments of the said chapter will greatly contribute to the
enhancement of maritime safety and security and safeguarding
those on board and ashore,

Having considered a draft of the International Code for the Security
of Ships and of Port Facilities prepared by the Maritime Safety
Committee of the International Maritime Organization
(hereinafter referred to as "the Organization"), at its seventy-
fifth and seventy-sixth session, for consideration and adoption
by the Conference,

1. **Adopts** the International Code for the Security of Ships and of
    Port Facilities (hereinafter referred to as "the Code"), the text of
    which is set out in the Annex to the present resolution;

2. **Invites** Contracting Governments to the Convention to note that
    the Code will take effect on 1 July 2004 upon entry into force
    of the new Chapter XI-2 of the Convention;

3. **Requests** the Maritime Safety Committee to keep the Code
    under review and amend it, as appropriate;

4. **Requests** the Secretary-General of the Organization to transmit
    certified copies of the present resolution and the text of the
    Code contained in the Annex to all Contracting Governments to
    the Convention;

5. **Further Requests** the Secretary-General to transmit copies of
    this resolution and its Annex to all Members of the
    Organization, which are not Contracting Governments to the
    Convention.

PREAMBLE

1   The Diplomatic Conference on Maritime Security held in London in December 2002 adopted new provisions in the International Convention for the Safety of Life at Sea, 1974 and this Code* to enhance maritime security. These new requirements form the international framework through which ships and port facilities can co-operate to detect and deter acts which threaten security in the maritime transport sector.

2   Following the tragic events of 11th September 2001, the twenty-second session of the Assembly of the International Maritime Organization (the Organization), in November 2001, unanimously agreed to the development of new measures relating to the security of ships and of port facilities for adoption by a Conference of Contracting Governments to the International Convention for the Safety of Life at Sea, 1974 (known as the Diplomatic Conference on Maritime Security) in December 2002. Preparation for the Diplomatic Conference was entrusted to the Organization's Maritime Safety Committee (MSC) on the basis of submissions made by Member States, intergovernmental organizations and non-governmental organizations in consultative status with the Organization.

3   The MSC, at its first extraordinary session, held also in November 2001, in order to accelerate the development and the adoption of the appropriate security measures established an MSC Intersessional Working Group on Maritime Security. The first meeting of the MSC Intersessional Working Group on Maritime Security was held in February 2002 and the outcome of its discussions was reported to, and considered by, the seventy-fifth session of the MSC in March 2002, when an ad hoc Working Group was established to further develop the proposals made. The seventy-fifth session of the MSC considered the report of that Working Group and recommended that work should be taken forward through a further MSC Intersessional Working Group, which was held in September 2002. The seventy-sixth session of the MSC considered the outcome of the September 2002 session of the MSC Intersessional Working Group and the further work undertaken by the MSC Working Group held in conjunction with the Committee's seventy-sixth session in December 2002, immediately prior to the Diplomatic Conference and agreed the final version of the proposed texts to be considered by the Diplomatic Conference.

4   The Diplomatic Conference (9 to 13 December 2002) also adopted amendments to the existing provisions of the International Convention for the Safety of Life at Sea, 1974 (SOLAS 74) accelerating the implementation of the requirement to fit Automatic

---

* The complete name of this Code is the International Code for the Security of Ships and of Port Facilities. The abbreviated name of this Code, as referred to in regulation XI-2/1 of SOLAS 74 as amended, is the International Ship and Port Facility Security (ISPS) Code or, in short, the ISPS Code.

**Annex
International Code
for the Security of
Ships and Port
Facilities**

**Diplomatic
Conference on
Maritime Security**

**MSC Intersessional
Working Group on
Maritime Security**

**The Code –
abbreviated
definition**

PREAMBLE

Amendments to
existing provisions of
SOLAS:
– AIS
– Ship's
Identification
Number
– Continuous
Synopsis Record

Extension of SOLAS
to cover port
facilities at the
ship/port interface

Compatibility with
STCW 1978 and
ISM Code

Additional burden
on some Contracting
Governments

Continuing
co-operation
between all involved

ISPS Part B and
SOLAS Ch XI-2

Identification Systems and adopted new Regulations in Chapter XI-1 of SOLAS 74 covering marking of the Ship's Identification Number and the carriage of a Continuous Synopsis Record. The Diplomatic Conference also adopted a number of Conference Resolutions including those covering implementation and revision of this Code, Technical Co-operation, and co-operative work with the International Labour Organization and World Customs Organization. It was recognized that review and amendment of certain of the new provisions regarding maritime security may be required on completion of the work of these two Organizations.

5 The provision of Chapter XI-2 of SOLAS 74 and this Code apply to ships and to port facilities. The extension of SOLAS 74 to cover port facilities was agreed on the basis that SOLAS 74 offered the speediest means of ensuring the necessary security measures entered into force and given effect quickly. However, it was further agreed that the provisions relating to port facilities should relate solely to the ship/port interface. The wider issue of the security of port areas will be the subject of further joint work between the International Maritime Organization and the International Labour Organization. It was also agreed that the provisions should not extend to the actual response to attacks or to any necessary clear-up activities after such an attack.

6 In drafting the provision care has been taken to ensure compatibility with the provisions of the International Convention on Standards of Training, Certification and Watchkeeping and Certification for Seafarers, 1978, as amended, the International Safety Management (ISM) Code and the harmonised system of survey and certification.

7 The provisions represent a significant change in the approach of the international maritime industries to the issue of security in the maritime transport sector. It is recognized that they may place a significant additional burden on certain Contracting Governments. The importance of Technical Co-operation to assist Contracting Governments implement the provisions is fully recognized.

8 Implementation of the provisions will require continuing effective co-operation and understanding between all those involved with, or using, ships and port facilities including ship's personnel, port personnel, passengers, cargo interests, ship and port management and those in National and Local Authorities with security responsibilities. Existing practices and procedures will have to be reviewed and changed if they do not provide an adequate level of security. In the interests of enhanced maritime security additional responsibilities will have to be carried by the shipping and port industries and by National and Local Authorities.

9 The guidance given in part B of this Code should be taken into account when implementing the security provisions set out in Chapter XI-2 of SOLAS 74 and in part A of this Code. However, it is recognized that the extent to which the guidance applies may vary

depending on the nature of the port facility and of the ship, its trade and/or cargo.

10 Nothing in this Code shall be interpreted or applied in a manner inconsistent with the proper respect of fundamental rights and freedoms as set out in international instruments, particularly those relating to maritime workers and refugees including the International Labour Organization Declaration of Fundamental Principles and Rights at Work as well as international standards concerning maritime and port workers.

11 Recognizing that the Convention on the Facilitation of Maritime Traffic, 1965, as amended, provides that foreign crew members shall be allowed ashore by the public authorities while the ship on which they arrive is in port, provided that the formalities on arrival of the ship have been fulfilled and the public authorities have no reason to refuse permission to come ashore for reasons of public health, public safety or public order, Contracting Governments when approving ship and port facility security plans should pay due cognisance to the fact that ship's personnel live and work on the vessel and need shore leave and access to shore based seafarer welfare facilities, including medical care.

Fundamental rights and freedoms

Crew shore leave

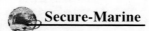

Part A
Mandatory
Requirements
regarding the
Provisions of
Chapter XI-2 of
SOLAS 1974 as
amended

Objectives

Functional
requirements

Definitions

1 GENERAL

1.1 Introduction

This part of the International Code for the Security of Ships and Port Facilities contains mandatory provisions to which reference is made in chapter XI-2 of the International Convention for the Safety of Life at Sea, 1974 as amended.

1.2 Objectives

The objectives of this Code are:

.1 to establish an international framework involving co-operation between Contracting Governments, Government agencies, local administrations and the shipping and port industries to detect security threats and take preventive measures against security incidents affecting ships or port facilities used in international trade;

.2 to establish the respective roles and responsibilities of the Contracting Governments, Government agencies, local administrations and the shipping and port industries, at the national and international level for ensuring maritime security;

.3 to ensure the early and efficient collection and exchange of security-related information;

.4 to provide a methodology for security assessments so as to have in place plans and procedures to react to changing security levels; and

.5 to ensure confidence that adequate and proportionate maritime security measures are in place.

1.3 Functional requirements

In order to achieve its objectives, this Code embodies a number of functional requirements. These include, but are not limited to:

.1 gathering and assessing information with respect to security threats and exchanging such information with appropriate Contracting Governments;

.2 requiring the maintenance of communication protocols for ships and port facilities;

.3 preventing unauthorized access to ships, port facilities and their restricted areas;

.4 preventing the introduction of unauthorized weapons, incendiary devices or explosives to ships or port facilities;

.5 providing means for raising the alarm in reaction to security threats or security incidents;

.6 requiring ship and port facility security plans based upon security assessments; and

.7 requiring training, drills and exercises to ensure familiarity with security plans and procedures.

2 DEFINITIONS

2.1 For the purpose of this part, unless expressly provided otherwise:

.1 *Convention* means the International Convention for the Safety of

Life at Sea, 1974 as amended.

.2 *Regulation* means a regulation of the Convention.

.3 *Chapter* means a chapter of the Convention.

.4 *Ship Security Plan* means a plan developed to ensure the application of measures on board the ship designed to protect persons on board, cargo, cargo transport units, ship's stores or the ship from the risks of a security incident.

.5 *Port Facility Security Plan* means a plan developed to ensure the application of measures designed to protect the port facility and ships, persons, cargo, cargo transport units and ship's stores within the port facility from the risks of a security incident.

.6 *Ship Security Officer* means the person on board the ship, accountable to the master, designated by the Company as responsible for the security of the ship, including implementation and maintenance of the Ship Security Plan and for liaison with the Company Security Officer and Port Facility Security Officers.

.7 *Company Security Officer* means the person designated by the Company for ensuring that a Ship Security Assessment is carried out; that a Ship Security Plan is developed, submitted for approval, and thereafter implemented and maintained and for liaison with Port Facility Security Officers and the Ship Security Officer.

.8 *Port Facility Security Officer* means the person designated as responsible for the development, implementation, revision and maintenance of the Port Facility Security Plan and for liaison with the Ship Security Officers and Company Security Officers.

.9 *Security Level 1* means the level for which minimum appropriate protective security measures shall be maintained at all times.

.10 *Security Level 2* means the level for which appropriate additional protective security measures shall be maintained for a period of time as a result of heightened risk of a security incident.

.11 *Security Level 3* means the level for which further specific protective security measures shall be maintained for a limited period of time when a security incident is probable or imminent, although it may not be possible to identify the specific target.

2.2 The term *ship*, when used in this Code, includes mobile offshore drilling units and high-speed craft as defined in regulation XI-2/1.

2.3 The term *Contracting Government* in connection with any reference to a port facility, when used in sections 14 to 18, includes a reference to the *Designated Authority*.

2.4 Terms not otherwise defined in this part shall have the same meaning as the meaning attributed to them in chapters I and XI-2.

3 APPLICATION

3.1 This Code applies to:

.1 the following types of ships engaged on international voyages:

.1 passenger ships, including high-speed passenger craft;

Definitions

SSP

PFSP

SSO

CSO

PFSO

Security Level 1

Security Level 2

Security Level 3

"Ship"

"Contracting Government"/ "Designated Authority"

Application:

– ship types

.2 cargo ships, including high-speed craft, of 500 gross tonnage and upwards; and

.3 mobile offshore drilling units; and

.2 port facilities serving such ships engaged on international voyages.

3.2 Notwithstanding the provisions of section 3.1.2, Contracting Governments shall decide the extent of application of this Part of the Code to those port facilities within their territory which, although used primarily by ships not engaged on international voyages, are required, occasionally, to serve ships arriving or departing on an international voyage.

3.2.1 Contracting Governments shall base their decisions, under section 3.2, on a Port Facility Security Assessment carried out in accordance with this Part of the Code.

3.2.2 Any decision which a Contracting Government makes, under section 3.2, shall not compromise the level of security intended to be achieved by chapter XI-2 or by this Part of the Code.

3.3 This Code does not apply to warships, naval auxiliaries or other ships owned or operated by a Contracting Government and used only on Government non-commercial service.

3.4 Sections 5 to 13 and 19 of this part apply to Companies and ships as specified in regulation XI-2/4.

3.5 Sections 5 and 14 to 18 of this part apply to port facilities as specified in regulation XI-2/10.

3.6 Nothing in this Code shall prejudice the rights or obligations of States under international law.

4 RESPONSIBILITIES OF CONTRACTING GOVERNMENTS

4.1 Subject to the provisions of regulation XI-2/3 and XI-2/7, Contracting Governments shall set security levels and provide guidance for protection from security incidents. Higher security levels indicate greater likelihood of occurrence of a security incident. Factors to be considered in setting the appropriate security level include:

.1 the degree that the threat information is credible;

.2 the degree that the threat information is corroborated;

.3 the degree that the threat information is specific or imminent; and

.4 the potential consequences of such a security incident.

4.2 Contracting Governments, when they set Security Level 3, shall issue, as necessary, appropriate instructions and shall provide security related information to the ships and port facilities that may be affected.

4.3 Contracting Governments may delegate to a Recognized Security Organization certain of their security related duties under chapter XI-2 and this Part of the Code with the exception of:

.1 setting of the applicable security level;

.2 approving a Port Facility Security Assessment and subsequent amendments to an approved assessment;

.3 determining the port facilities which will be required to designate a Port Facility Security Officer;

.4 approving a Port Facility Security Plan and subsequent amendments to an approved plan;

.5 exercising control and compliance measures pursuant to regulation XI-2/9; and

.6 establishing the requirements for a Declaration of Security.

4.4 Contracting Governments shall, to the extent they consider appropriate, test the effectiveness of the Ship or the Port Facility Security Plans, or of amendments to such plans, they have approved, or, in the case of ships, of plans which have been approved on their behalf.

5 DECLARATION OF SECURITY

5.1 Contracting Governments shall determine when a Declaration of Security is required by assessing the risk the ship/port interface or ship to ship activity poses to persons, property or the environment.

5.2 A ship can request completion of a Declaration of Security when:

.1 the ship is operating at a higher security level than the port facility or another ship it is interfacing with;

.2 there is an agreement on a Declaration of Security between Contracting Governments covering certain international voyages or specific ships on those voyages;

.3 there has been a security threat or a security incident involving the ship or involving the port facility, as applicable;

.4 the ship is at a port which is not required to have and implement an approved Port Facility Security Plan; or

.5 the ship is conducting ship to ship activities with another ship not required to have and implement an approved Ship Security Plan.

5.3 Requests for the completion of a Declaration of Security, under this section, shall be acknowledged by the applicable port facility or ship.

5.4 The Declaration of Security shall be completed by:

.1 the master or the Ship Security Officer on behalf of the ship(s); and, if appropriate,

.2 the Port Facility Security Officer or, if the Contracting Government determines otherwise, by any other body responsible for shore-side security, on behalf of the port facility.

5.5 The Declaration of Security shall address the security requirements that could be shared between a port facility and a ship (or between ships) and shall state the responsibility for each.

5.6 Contracting Governments shall specify, bearing in mind the provisions of regulation XI-2/9.2.3, the minimum period for which Declarations of Security shall be kept by the port facilities located within their territory.

5.7 Administrations shall specify, bearing in mind the provisions of

Port Facility Security Plan

Testing Ship and Port Security Plans

Declaration of Security

– Contracting Governments assessment

– ship request

– persons to complete

– requirements for shared ship/port responsibilities

– minimum period of retention (ports)

ISPS Code – Part A (Mandatory)

– minimum period of retention (ships)

regulation XI-2/9.2.3, the minimum period for which Declarations of Security shall be kept by ships entitled to fly their flag.

Obligations of the Company

6 OBLIGATIONS OF THE COMPANY

6.1 The Company shall ensure that the Ship Security Plan contains a clear statement emphasizing the master's authority. The Company shall establish in the Ship Security Plan that the Master has the overriding authority and responsibility to make decisions with respect to the safety and security of the ship and to request the assistance of the Company or of any Contracting Government as may be necessary.

Master's authority

Support to Master and Security Officers

6.2 The Company shall ensure that the Company Security Officer, the Master and the Ship Security Officer are given the necessary support to fulfil their duties and responsibilities in accordance with Chapter XI-2 and this Part of the Code.

Ship Security:

7 SHIP SECURITY

7.1 A ship is required to act upon the Security Levels set by Contracting Governments as set out below.

– at Security Level 1

7.2 At Security Level 1, the following activities shall be carried out, through appropriate measures, on all ships, taking into account the guidance given in Part B of this Code, in order to identify and take preventive measures against security incidents:

.1 ensuring the performance of all ship security duties;
.2 controlling access to the ship;
.3 controlling the embarkation of persons and their effects;
.4 monitoring restricted areas to ensure that only authorized persons have access;
.5 monitoring of deck areas and areas surrounding the ship;
.6 supervising the handling of cargo and ship's stores; and
.7 ensuring that security communication is readily available.

– at Security Level 2

7.3 At Security Level 2, the additional protective measures, specified in the Ship Security Plan, shall be implemented for each activity detailed in section 7.2, taking into account the guidance given in Part B of this Code.

– at Security Level 3

7.4 At Security Level 3, further specific protective measures, specified in the Ship Security Plan, shall be implemented for each activity detailed in section 7.2, taking into account the guidance given in Part B of this Code.

Ship acknowledging change in security level

7.5 Whenever Security Level 2 or 3 is set by the Administration, the ship shall acknowledge receipt of the instructions on change of the security level.

Ship acknowledging Contracting Government instruction

7.6 Prior to entering a port or whilst in a port within the territory of a Contracting Government that has set Security Level 2 or 3, the ship shall acknowledge receipt of this instruction and shall confirm to the port facility security officer the initiation of the implementation of the appropriate measures and procedures as detailed in the Ship Security Plan, and in the case of Security Level 3, in instructions issued by the Contracting Government which has set Security Level 3.

ISPS Code

ISPS Code – Part A (Mandatory)

The ship shall report any difficulties in implementation. In such cases, the Port Facility Security Officer and Ship Security Officer shall liaise and co-ordinate the appropriate actions.

7.7 If a ship is required by the Administration to set, or is already at, a higher security level than that set for the port it intends to enter or in which it is already located, then the ship shall advise, without delay, the competent authority of the Contracting Government within whose territory the port facility is located and the Port Facility Security Officer of the situation.

7.7.1 In such cases, the Ship Security Officer shall liaise with the Port Facility Security Officer and co-ordinate appropriate actions, if necessary.

7.8 An Administration requiring ships entitled to fly its flag to set Security Level 2 or 3 in a port of another Contracting Government shall inform that Contracting Government without delay.

7.9 When Contracting Governments set security levels and ensure the provision of security level information to ships operating in their territorial sea, or having communicated an intention to enter their territorial sea, such ships shall be advised to maintain vigilance and report immediately to their Administration and any nearby coastal States any information that comes to their attention that might affect maritime security in the area.

7.9.1 When advising such ships of the applicable Security Level, a Contracting Government shall, taking into account the guidance given in the Part B of this Code, also advise those ships of any security measure that they should take and, if appropriate, of measures that have been taken by the Contracting Government to provide protection against the threat.

8 SHIP SECURITY ASSESSMENT

8.1 The Ship Security Assessment is an essential and integral part of the process of developing and updating the Ship Security Plan.

8.2 The Company Security Officer shall ensure that the Ship Security Assessment is carried out by persons with appropriate skills to evaluate the security of a ship, in accordance with this section, taking into account the guidance given in Part B of this Code.

8.3 Subject to the provisions of section 9.2.1, a Recognized Security Organization may carry out the Ship Security Assessment of a specific ship.

8.4 The Ship Security Assessment shall include an on-scene security survey and, at least, the following elements:

.1 identification of existing security measures, procedures and operations;

.2 identification and evaluation of key ship board operations that it is important to protect;

.3 identification of possible threats to the key ship board operations and the likelihood of their occurrence, in order to establish and prioritise security measures; and

.4 identification of weaknesses, including human factors in the

Margin notes

Difficulties of ship in implementing security instructions

Ship at higher security level than port

Ships in foreign port required to set higher security level

Ships operating in territorial waters or on coastal passage

Applying Part B guidance

Ship Security Assessment

– persons with appropriate skills

– on-scene security survey

– identification and evaluation of key onboard operations

– identify weaknesses

Security assessment retained by ship

infrastructure, policies and procedures.

8.5 The Ship Security Assessment shall be documented, reviewed, accepted and retained by the Company.

Ship Security Plan

9 SHIP SECURITY PLAN

9.1 Each ship shall carry on board a Ship Security Plan approved by the Administration. The plan shall make provisions for the three Security Levels as defined in this Part of the Code.

Preparation and review by a recognised security organisation

9.1.1 Subject to the provisions of section 9.2.1, a Recognized Security Organization may prepare the Ship Security Plan for a specific ship.

9.2 The Administration may entrust the review and approval of Ship Security Plans, or of amendments to a previously approved plan, to Recognized Security Organizations.

Conditions

9.2.1 In such cases the Recognized Security Organization, undertaking the review and approval of a Ship Security Plan, or its amendments, for a specific ship shall not have been involved in either the preparation of the Ship Security Assessment or of the Ship Security Plan, or of the amendments, under review.

Submission

9.3 The submission of a Ship Security Plan, or of amendments to a previously approved plan, for approval shall be accompanied by the security assessment on the basis of which the plan, or the amendments, have been developed.

Language

9.4 Such a plan shall be developed, taking into account the guidance given in Part B of this Code and shall be written in the working language or languages of the ship. If the language or languages used is not English, French or Spanish, a translation into one of these languages shall be included. The plan shall address, at least, the following:

Plan to include:

– measures to control weapons and dangerous devices

.1 measures designed to prevent weapons, dangerous substances and devices intended for use against persons, ships or ports and the carriage of which is not authorized from being taken on board the ship;

– identification of restricted areas
– unauthorised access
– security threat response
– procedures for response
– evacuation

.2 identification of the restricted areas and measures for the prevention of unauthorized access to them;

.3 measures for the prevention of unauthorized access to the ship;

.4 procedures for responding to security threats or breaches of security, including provisions for maintaining critical operations of the ship or ship/port interface;

.5 procedures for responding to any security instructions Contracting Governments may give at Security Level 3;

.6 procedures for evacuation in case of security threats or breaches of security;

– duties

.7 duties of shipboard personnel assigned security responsibilities and of other shipboard personnel on security aspects;

–auditing procedures
– training & drills

.8 procedures for auditing the security activities;

.9 procedures for training, drills and exercises associated with the plan;

– interface with port

.10 procedures for interfacing with port facility security activities;

.11 procedures for the periodic review of the plan and for updating;

.12 procedures for reporting security incidents;

.13 identification of the Ship Security Officer;

.14 identification of the Company Security Officer including 24-hour contact details;

.15 procedures to ensure the inspection, testing, calibration, and maintenance of any security equipment provided on board;

.16 frequency for testing or calibration of any security equipment provided on board;

.17 identification of the locations where the ship security alert system activation points are provided; and

.18 procedures, instructions and guidance on the use of the ship security alert system, including the testing, activation, deactivation and resetting and to limit false alerts.

9.4.1 Personnel conducting internal audits of the security activities specified in the plan or evaluating its implementation shall be independent of the activities being audited unless this is impracticable due to the size and the nature of the Company or of the ship.

9.5 The Administration shall determine which changes to an approved Ship Security Plan or to any security equipment specified in an approved plan shall not be implemented unless the relevant amendments to the plan are approved by the Administration. Any such changes shall be at least as effective as those measures prescribed in chapter XI-2 and this Part of the Code.

9.5.1 The nature of the changes to the Ship Security Plan or the security equipment that have been specifically approved by the Administration, pursuant to section 9.5, shall be documented in a manner that clearly indicates such approval. This approval shall be available on board and shall be presented together with the International Ship Security Certificate (or the Interim International Ship Security Certificate). If these changes are temporary, once the original approved measures or equipment are reinstated, this documentation no longer needs to be retained by the ship.

9.6 The plan may be kept in an electronic format. In such a case, it shall be protected by procedures aimed at preventing its unauthorized deletion, destruction or amendment.

9.7 The plan shall be protected from unauthorized access or disclosure.

9.8 Ship security plans are not subject to inspection by officers duly authorized by a Contracting Government to carry out control and compliance measures in accordance with regulation XI-2/9, save in circumstances specified in section 9.8.1.

.1 Administrations may allow, in order to avoid compromising in any way the objective of providing on board the ship security alert system, this information to be kept elsewhere on board in a document known to the Master, the Ship Security Officer and other senior shipboard personnel as may be decided by the Company.

9.8.1 If the officers duly authorized by a Contracting Government

Side notes:

- updates
- reporting procedures
- identification of security officers
- inspection and testing

- location and procedures of security alert system

Independent audit

Approval of changes to the plan

Documenting changes

Plan in electronic format

Protection from unauthorised access

Inspection by Contracting Government's officers:

–storage

ISPS Code – Part A (Mandatory)

have clear grounds to believe that the ship is not in compliance with the requirements of chapter XI-2 or part A of this Code, and the only means to verify or rectify the non-compliance is to review the relevant requirements of the Ship Security Plan, limited access to the specific sections of the plan relating to the non-compliance is exceptionally allowed, but only with the consent of the Contracting Government of, or the Master of, the ship concerned. Nevertheless, the provisions in the plan relating to section 9.4 subsections .2, .4, .5,.7, .15, .17 and .18 of this Part of the Code are considered as confidential information, and cannot be subject to inspection unless otherwise agreed by the Contracting Governments concerned.

10 RECORDS

10.1 Records of the following activities addressed in the Ship Security Plan shall be kept on board for at least the minimum period specified by the Administration, bearing in mind the provisions of regulation XI-2/9.2.3:

.1 training, drills and exercises;

.2 security threats and security incidents;

.3 breaches of security;

.4 changes in security level;

.5 communications relating to the direct security of the ship such as specific threats to the ship or to port facilities the ship is, or has been;

.6 internal audits and reviews of security activities;

.7 periodic review of the Ship Security Assessment;

.8 periodic review of the Ship Security Plan;

.9 implementation of any amendments to the plan; and

.10 maintenance, calibration and testing of any security equipment provided on board including testing of the ship security alert system.

10.2 The records shall be kept in the working language or languages of the ship. If the language or languages used are not English, French or Spanish, a translation into one of these languages shall be included.

10.3 The records may be kept in an electronic format. In such a case, they shall be protected by procedures aimed at preventing their unauthorized deletion, destruction or amendment.

10.4 The records shall be protected from unauthorized access or disclosure.

11 COMPANY SECURITY OFFICER

11.1 The Company shall designate a Company Security Officer. A person designated as the Company Security Officer may act as the Company Security Officer for one or more ships, depending on the number or types of ships the Company operates provided it is clearly identified for which ships this person is responsible. A Company may, depending on the number or types of ships they operate designate several persons as Company Security Officers provided it is

ISPS Code – Part A (Mandatory)

clearly identified for which ships each person is responsible.

11.2 In addition to those specified elsewhere in this Part of the Code, the duties and responsibilities of the Company Security Officer shall include, but are not limited to:

Company Security Officer (contd)

Duties and responsibilities

- .1 advising the level of threats likely to be encountered by the ship, using appropriate security assessments and other relevant information;
- .2 ensuring that Ship Security Assessments are carried out;
- .3 ensuring the development, the submission for approval, and thereafter the implementation and maintenance of the Ship Security Plan;
- .4 ensuring that the Ship Security Plan is modified, as appropriate, to correct deficiencies and satisfy the security requirements of the individual ship;
- .5 arranging for internal audits and reviews of security activities;
- .6 arranging for the initial and subsequent verifications of the ship by the Administration or the Recognized Security Organization;
- .7 ensuring that deficiencies and non-conformities identified during internal audits, periodic reviews, security inspections and verifications of compliance are promptly addressed and dealt with;
- .8 enhancing security awareness and vigilance;
- .9 ensuring adequate training for personnel responsible for the security of the ship;
- .10 ensuring effective communication and co-operation between the Ship Security Officer and the relevant Port Facility Security Officers;
- .11 ensuring consistency between security requirements and safety requirements;
- .12 ensuring that, if sister-ship or fleet security plans are used, the plan for each ship reflects the ship-specific information accurately; and
- .13 ensuring that any alternative or equivalent arrangements approved for a particular ship or group of ships are implemented and maintained.

12 SHIP SECURITY OFFICER

12.1 A Ship Security Officer shall be designated on each ship.

Ship Security Officer

12.2 In addition to those specified elsewhere in this Part of the Code, the duties and responsibilities of the Ship Security Officer shall include, but are not limited to:

Duties and responsibilities

- .1 undertaking regular security inspections of the ship to ensure that appropriate security measures are maintained;
- .2 maintaining and supervising the implementation of the Ship Security Plan, including any amendments to the plan;
- .3 co-ordinating the security aspects of the handling of cargo and ship's stores with other shipboard personnel and with the relevant Port Facility Security Officers;

.4 proposing modifications to the Ship Security Plan;

.5 reporting to the Company Security Officer any deficiencies and non-conformities identified during internal audits, periodic reviews, security inspections and verifications of compliance and implementing any corrective actions;

.6 enhancing security awareness and vigilance on board;

.7 ensuring that adequate training has been provided to shipboard personnel, as appropriate;

.8 reporting all security incidents;

.9 co-ordinating implementation of the Ship Security Plan with the Company Security Officer and the relevant Port Facility Security Officer; and

.10 ensuring that security equipment is properly operated, tested, calibrated and maintained, if any.

13 TRAINING, DRILLS AND EXERCISES ON SHIP SECURITY

13.1 The Company Security Officer and appropriate shore-based personnel shall have knowledge and have received training, taking into account the guidance given in Part B of this Code.

13.2 The Ship Security Officer shall have knowledge and have received training, taking into account the guidance given in Part B of this Code.

13.3 Shipboard personnel having specific security duties and responsibilities shall understand their responsibilities for ship security as described in the Ship Security Plan and shall have sufficient knowledge and ability to perform their assigned duties, taking into account the guidance given in Part B of this Code.

13.4 To ensure the effective implementation of the Ship Security Plan, drills shall be carried out at appropriate intervals taking into account the ship type, ship personnel changes, port facilities to be visited and other relevant circumstances, taking into account the guidance given in Part B of this Code.

13.5 The Company Security Officer shall ensure the effective coordination and implementation of Ship Security Plans by participating in exercises at appropriate intervals, taking into account the guidance given in Part B of this Code.

14 PORT FACILITY SECURITY

14.1 A port facility is required to act upon the security levels set by the Contracting Government within whose territory it is located. Security measures and procedures shall be applied at the port facility in such a manner as to cause a minimum of interference with, or delay to, passengers, ship, ship's personnel and visitors, goods and services.

14.2 At Security Level 1, the following activities shall be carried out through appropriate measures in all port facilities, taking into account the guidance given in Part B of this Code, in order to identify and take preventive measures against security incidents:

.1 ensuring the performance of all port facility security duties;

.2 controlling access to the port facility;

.3 monitoring of the port facility, including anchoring and berthing area(s);

.4 monitoring restricted areas to ensure that only authorized persons have access;

.5 supervising the handling of cargo;

.6 supervising the handling of ship's stores; and

.7 ensuring that security communication is readily available.

14.3 At Security Level 2, the additional protective measures, specified in the port facility security plan, shall be implemented for each activity detailed in section 14.2, taking into account the guidance given in Part B of this Code.

– at Security Level 2

14.4 At Security Level 3, further specific protective measures, specified in the port facility security plan, shall be implemented for each activity detailed in section 14.2, taking into account the guidance given in Part B of this Code.

– at Security Level 3

14.4.1 In addition, at Security Level 3, port facilities are required to respond to and implement any security instructions given by the Contracting Government within whose territory the port facility is located.

14.5 When a Port Facility Security Officer is advised that a ship encounters difficulties in complying with the requirements of Chapter XI-2 or this Part or in implementing the appropriate measures and procedures as detailed in the Ship Security Plan, and in the case of Security Level 3 following any security instructions given by the Contracting Government within whose territory the port facility is located, the Port Facility Security Officer and Ship Security Officer shall liaise and co-ordinate appropriate actions.

Action when ship unable to comply with security level

14.6 When a Port Facility Security Officer is advised that a ship is at a Security Level, which is higher than that of the port facility, the Port Facility Security Officer shall report the matter to the competent authority and shall liaise with the Ship Security Officer and co-ordinate appropriate actions, if necessary.

Action when ship at higher security level than port

15 PORT FACILITY SECURITY ASSESSMENT

15.1 The Port Facility Security Assessment is an essential and integral part of the process of developing and updating the port facility security plan.

Port Facility Security Assessment

15.2 The Port Facility Security Assessment shall be carried out by the Contracting Government within whose territory the port facility is located. A Contracting Government may authorise a Recognized Security Organization to carry out the Port Facility Security Assessment of a specific port facility located within its territory.

15.2.1 When the Port Facility Security Assessment has been carried out by a Recognized Security Organization, the security assessment shall be reviewed and approved for compliance with this section by the Contracting Government within whose territory the port facility is located.

Review and approval

Skills required

Periodic review

Assessment to include:

– identification of assets to protect and of threats

– counter measures

– identification of weaknesses

Covering more than one port facility

Summary and protection from unauthorised access

Port Facility Security Plan

Preparation by a recognised security organisation

Approval

Language

To include: – anti-weapon measures

15.3 The persons carrying out the assessment shall have appropriate skills to evaluate the security of the port facility in accordance with this section, taking into account the guidance given in Part B of this Code.

15.4 The Port Facility Security Assessments shall periodically be reviewed and updated, taking account of changing threats and/or minor changes in the port facility and shall always be reviewed and updated when major changes to the port facility take place.

15.5 The Port Facility Security Assessment shall include, at least, the following elements:

  .1 identification and evaluation of important assets and infrastructure it is important to protect;

  .2 identification of possible threats to the assets and infrastructure and the likelihood of their occurrence, in order to establish and prioritize security measures;

  .3 identification, selection and prioritization of counter measures and procedural changes and their level of effectiveness in reducing vulnerability; and

  .4 identification of weaknesses, including human factors in the infrastructure, policies and procedures.

15.6 The Contracting Government may allow a Port Facility Security Assessment to cover more than one port facility if the operator, location, operation, equipment, and design of these port facilities are similar. Any Contracting Government, which allows such an arrangement shall communicate to the Organization particulars thereof.

15.7 Upon completion of the Port Facility Security Assessment, a report shall be prepared, consisting of a summary of how the assessment was conducted, a description of each vulnerability found during the assessment and a description of counter measures that could be used to address each vulnerability. The report shall be protected from unauthorized access or disclosure.

16 PORT FACILITY SECURITY PLAN

16.1 A Port Facility Security Plan shall be developed and maintained, on the basis of a Port Facility Security Assessment, for each port facility, adequate for the ship/port interface. The plan shall make provisions for the three Security Levels, as defined in this Part of the Code.

16.1.1 Subject to the provisions of section 16.2, a Recognized Security Organization may prepare the Port Facility Security Plan of a specific port facility.

16.2 The Port Facility Security Plan shall be approved by the Contracting Government in whose territory the port facility is located.

16.3 Such a plan shall be developed taking into account the guidance given in Part B of this Code and shall be in the working language of the port facility. The plan shall address, at least, the following:

  .1 measures designed to prevent weapons or any other dangerous substances and devices intended for use against persons, ships or ports and the carriage of which is not authorized, from being introduced into the port facility or on board a ship;

.2 measures designed to prevent unauthorized access to the port facility, to ships moored at the facility, and to restricted areas of the facility;

.3 procedures for responding to security threats or breaches of security, including provisions for maintaining critical operations of the port facility or ship/port interface;

.4 procedures for responding to any security instructions the Contracting Government, in whose territory the port facility is located, may give at Security Level 3;

.5 procedures for evacuation in case of security threats or breaches of security;

.6 duties of port facility personnel assigned security responsibilities and of other facility personnel on security aspects;

.7 procedures for interfacing with ship security activities;

.8 procedures for the periodic review of the plan and updating;

.9 procedures for reporting security incidents;

.10 identification of the Port Facility Security Officer including 24-hour contact details;

.11 measures to ensure the security of the information contained in the plan;

.12 measures designed to ensure effective security of cargo and the cargo handling equipment at the port facility;

.13 procedures for auditing the Port Facility Security Plan;

.14 procedures for responding in case the ship security alert system of a ship at the port facility has been activated; and

.15 procedures for facilitating shore leave for ship's personnel or personnel changes, as well as access of visitors to the ship including representatives of seafarers' welfare and labour organizations.

16.4 Personnel conducting internal audits of the security activities specified in the plan or evaluating its implementation shall be independent of the activities being audited unless this is impracticable due to the size and the nature of the port facility.

16.5 The Port Facility Security Plan may be combined with, or be part of, the port security plan or any other port emergency plan or plans.

16.6 The Contracting Government in whose territory the port facility is located shall determine which changes to the Port Facility Security Plan shall not be implemented unless the relevant amendments to the plan are approved by them.

16.7 The plan may be kept in an electronic format. In such a case, it shall be protected by procedures aimed at preventing its unauthorized deletion, destruction or amendment.

16.8 The plan shall be protected from unauthorized access or disclosure.

16.9 Contracting Governments may allow a Port Facility Security Plan

– prevention of unauthorised access

– security threat and security instructions procedures

–duties of port security personnel

– interfacing with ship security
– review
– reporting
– identification of Port Facility Security Officer
– security of cargo

– audit
– response to ship security alert system

– facilitating shore leave and ship visitors

Independence of auditors

Other port emergency plans

Approval criteria

Electronic format

Unauthorised access

ISPS Code – Part A (Mandatory)

Covering more than
one port facility

Officer

Port Facility Security

Duties to include:

– initial survey

– development,
implementation and
exercising of plan

– incorporating
modifications

– enhancing security
awareness
and training

– reporting

–co-ordination with
other security
officers

– security equipment
monitoring

– identifying identity
of visitors

Support

Training, Drills and
Exercises on Port
Facility Security

to cover more than one port facility if the operator, location, operation, equipment, and design of these port facilities are similar. Any Contracting Government, which allows such an alternative arrangement, shall communicate to the Organization particulars thereof.

17 PORT FACILITY SECURITY OFFICER

17.1 A Port Facility Security Officer shall be designated for each port facility. A person may be designated as the Port Facility Security Officer for one or more port facilities.

17.2 In addition to those specified elsewhere in this Part of the Code, the duties and responsibilities of the Port Facility Security Officer shall include, but are not limited to:

  .1 conducting an initial comprehensive security survey of the port facility taking into account the relevant Port Facility Security Assessment;

  .2 ensuring the development and maintenance of the Port Facility Security Plan;

  .3 implementing and exercising the Port Facility Security Plan;

  .4 undertaking regular security inspections of the port facility to ensure the continuation of appropriate security measures;

  .5 recommending and incorporating, as appropriate, modifications to the Port Facility Security Plan in order to correct deficiencies and to update the plan to take into account of relevant changes to the port facility;

  .6 enhancing security awareness and vigilance of the port facility personnel;

  .7 ensuring adequate training has been provided to personnel responsible for the security of the port facility;

  .8 reporting to the relevant authorities and maintaining records of occurrences which threaten the security of the port facility;

  .9 co-ordinating implementation of the Port Facility Security Plan with the appropriate Company and Ship Security Officer(s);

  .10 co-ordinating with security services, as appropriate;

  .11 ensuring that standards for personnel responsible for security of the port facility are met;

  .12 ensuring that security equipment is properly operated, tested, calibrated and maintained, if any; and

  .13 assisting Ship Security Officers in confirming the identity of those seeking to board the ship when requested.

17.3 The Port Facility Security Officer shall be given the necessary support to fulfil the duties and responsibilities imposed by Chapter XI-2 and this Part of the Code.

18 TRAINING, DRILLS AND EXERCISES ON PORT FACILITY SECURITY

18.1 The Port Facility Security Officer and appropriate port facility security personnel shall have knowledge and have received training, taking into account the guidance given in Part B of this Code.

18.2 Port facility personnel having specific security duties shall understand their duties and responsibilities for port facility security, as described in the Port Facility Security Plan and shall have sufficient knowledge and ability to perform their assigned duties, taking into account the guidance given in Part B of this Code.

Security duties of other personnel

18.3 To ensure the effective implementation of the Port Facility Security Plan, drills shall be carried out at appropriate intervals taking into account the types of operation of the port facility, port facility personnel changes, the type of ship the port facility is serving and other relevant circumstances, taking into account guidance given in Part B of this Code.

Drills

18.4 The Port Facility Security Officer shall ensure the effective coordination and implementation of the Port Facility Security Plan by participating in exercises at appropriate intervals, taking into account the guidance given in Part B of this Code.

Participation in exercises

19 VERIFICATION AND CERTIFICATION FOR SHIPS

19.1 Verifications

19.1.1 Each ship to which this Part of the Code applies shall be subject to the verifications specified below:

Verification and Certification for Ships

.1 an initial verification before the ship is put in service or before the certificate required under section 19.2 is issued for the first time, which shall include a complete verification of its security system and any associated security equipment covered by the relevant provisions of Chapter XI-2, this Part of the Code and the approved Ship Security Plan. This verification shall ensure that the security system and any associated security equipment of the ship fully complies with the applicable requirements of Chapter XI-2 and this Part of the Code, is in satisfactory condition and fit for the service for which the ship is intended;

Initial verification

.2 a renewal verification at intervals specified by the Administration, but not exceeding five years, except where section 19.3 is applicable. This verification shall ensure that the security system and any associated security equipment of the ship fully complies with the applicable requirements of chapter XI-2, this Part of the Code and the approved Ship Security Plan, is in satisfactory condition and fit for the service for which the ship is intended;

Renewal verification

.3 at least one intermediate verification. If only one intermediate verification is carried out it shall take place between the second and third anniversary date of the certificate as defined in regulation I/2(n). The intermediate verification shall include inspection of the security system and any associated security equipment of the ship to ensure that it remains satisfactory for the service for which the ship is intended. Such intermediate verification shall be endorsed on the certificate;

Intermediate verification

.4 any additional verifications as determined by the Administration.

Additional verification

19.1.2 The verifications of ships shall be carried out by officers of the

Administration. The Administration may, however, entrust the verifications to a Recognized Security Organization referred to in regulation XI-2/1.

Integrity of verification

19.1.3 In every case, the Administration concerned shall fully guarantee the completeness and efficiency of the verification and shall undertake to ensure the necessary arrangements to satisfy this obligation.

Sanction of changes

19.1.4 The security system and any associated security equipment of the ship after verification shall be maintained to conform with the provisions of regulations XI-2/4.2 and XI-2/6, this Part of the Code and the approved Ship Security Plan. After any verification under section 19.1.1 has been completed, no changes shall be made in security system and in any associated security equipment or the approved Ship Security Plan without the sanction of the Administration.

Issue or endorsement of certificate

19.2 Issue or endorsement of certificate

19.2.1 An International Ship Security Certificate shall be issued after the initial or renewal verification in accordance with the provisions of section 19.1.

19.2.2 Such certificate shall be issued or endorsed either by the Administration or by a Recognized Security Organization acting on behalf of the Administration.

19.2.3 Another Contracting Government may, at the request of the Administration, cause the ship to be verified and, if satisfied that the provisions of section 19.1.1 are complied with, shall issue or authorize the issue of an International Ship Security Certificate to the ship and, where appropriate, endorse or authorize the endorsement of that certificate on the ship, in accordance with this Code.

19.2.3.1 A copy of the certificate and a copy of the verification report shall be transmitted as soon as possible to the requesting Administration.

19.2.3.2 A certificate so issued shall contain a statement to the effect that it has been issued at the request of the Administration and it shall have the same force and receive the same recognition as the certificate issued under section 19.2.2.

19.2.4 The International Ship Security Certificate shall be drawn up in a form corresponding to the model given in the Appendix to this Code. If the language used is not English, French or Spanish, the text shall include a translation into one of these languages.

19.3 Duration and validity of certificate

Duration and validity of certificate

19.3.1 An International Ship Security Certificate shall be issued for a period specified by the Administration which shall not exceed five years.

19.3.2 When the renewal verification is completed within three months before the expiry date of the existing certificate, the new certificate shall be valid from the date of completion of the renewal verification to a date not exceeding five years from the date of expiry of the existing certificate.

19.3.2.1 When the renewal verification is completed after the expiry date of the existing certificate, the new certificate shall be valid from the date of completion of the renewal verification to a date not exceeding five years from the date of expiry of the existing certificate.

19.3.2.2 When the renewal verification is completed more than three months before the expiry date of the existing certificate, the new certificate shall be valid from the date of completion of the renewal verification to a date not exceeding five years from the date of completion of the renewal verification.

19.3.3 If a certificate is issued for a period of less than five years, the Administration may extend the validity of the certificate beyond the expiry date to the maximum period specified in section 19.3.1, provided that the verifications referred to in section 19.1.1 applicable when a certificate is issued for a period of five years are carried out as appropriate.

19.3.4 If a renewal verification has been completed and a new certificate cannot be issued or placed on board the ship before the expiry date of the existing certificate, the Administration or Recognized Security Organization acting on behalf of the Administration may endorse the existing certificate and such a certificate shall be accepted as valid for a further period which shall not exceed five months from the expiry date.

19.3.5 If a ship at the time when a certificate expires is not in a port in which it is to be verified, the Administration may extend the period of validity of the certificate but this extension shall be granted only for the purpose of allowing the ship to complete its voyage to the port in which it is to be verified, and then only in cases where it appears proper and reasonable to do so. No certificate shall be extended for a period longer than three months, and the ship to which an extension is granted shall not, on its arrival in the port in which it is to be verified, be entitled by virtue of such extension to leave that port without having a new certificate. When the renewal verification is completed, the new certificate shall be valid to a date not exceeding five years from the expiry date of the existing certificate before the extension was granted.

19.3.6 A certificate issued to a ship engaged on short voyages which has not been extended under the foregoing provisions of this section may be extended by the Administration for a period of grace of up to one month from the date of expiry stated on it. When the renewal verification is completed, the new certificate shall be valid to a date not exceeding five years from the date of expiry of the existing certificate before the extension was granted.

19.3.7 If an intermediate verification is completed before the period specified in section 19.1.1, then:

  .1 the expiry date shown on the certificate shall be amended by endorsement to a date which shall not be more than three years later than the date on which the intermediate verification was completed;

Certificate renewal and period of validity

Certificate renewal and period of validity

Cease to be valid

.2 the expiry date may remain unchanged provided one or more additional verifications are carried out so that the maximum intervals between the verifications prescribed by section 19.1.1 are not exceeded.

19.3.8 A certificate issued under section 19.2 shall cease to be valid in any of the following cases:

.1 if the relevant verifications are not completed within the periods specified under section 19.1.1;

.2 if the certificate is not endorsed in accordance with section 19.1.1.3 and 19.3.7.1, if applicable;

.3 when a Company assumes the responsibility for the operation of a ship not previously operated by that Company; and

.4 upon transfer of the ship to the flag of another State.

19.3.9 In the case of:

.1 a transfer of a ship to the flag of another Contracting Government, the Contracting Government whose flag the ship was formerly entitled to fly shall, as soon as possible, transmit to the receiving Administration copies of, or all information relating to, the International Ship Security Certificate carried by the ship before the transfer and copies of available verification reports, or

.2 a Company that assumes responsibility for the operation of a ship not previously operated by that Company, the previous Company shall as soon as possible, transmit to the receiving Company copies of any information related to the International Ship Security Certificate or to facilitate the verifications described in section 19.4.2.

Interim certification

19.4 Interim certification

19.4.1 The certificates specified in section 19.2 shall be issued only when the Administration issuing the certificate is fully satisfied that the ship complies with the requirements of section 19.1. However, after 1 July 2004, for the purposes of:

.1 a ship without a certificate, on delivery or prior to its entry or re-entry into service;

.2 transfer of a ship from the flag of a Contracting Government to the flag of another Contracting Government;

.3 transfer of a ship to the flag of a Contracting Government from a State which is not a Contracting Government; or

.4 when a Company assumes the responsibility for the operation of a ship not previously operated by that Company; until the certificate referred to in section 19.2 is issued, the Administration may cause an Interim International Ship Security Certificate to be issued, in a form corresponding to the model given in the Appendix to this Part of the Code.

19.4.2 An Interim International Ship Security Certificate shall only be issued when the Administration or Recognized Security Organization, on behalf of the Administration, has verified that:

.1 the Ship Security Assessment required by this Part of the Code has been completed,

.2 a copy of the Ship Security Plan meeting the requirements of chapter XI-2 and part A of this Code is provided on board, has been submitted for review and approval, and is being implemented on the ship;

.3 the ship is provided with a ship security alert system meeting the requirements of regulation XI-2/6, if required,

.4 the Company Security Officer:

  .1 has ensured:

    .1 the review of the Ship Security Plan for compliance with this Part of the Code,

    .2 that the plan has been submitted for approval, and

    .3 that the plan is being implemented on the ship, and

  .2 has established the necessary arrangements, including arrangements for drills, exercises and internal audits, through which the Company Security Officer is satisfied that the ship will successfully complete the required verification in accordance with section 19.1.1.1, within 6 months;

.5 arrangements have been made for carrying out the required verifications under section 19.1.1.1;

.6 the master, the ship's security officer and other ship's personnel with specific security duties are familiar with their duties and responsibilities as specified in this Part of the Code; and with the relevant provisions of the Ship Security Plan placed on board; and have been provided such information in the working language of the ship's personnel or languages understood by them; and

.7 the Ship Security Officer meets the requirements of this Part of the Code.

19.4.3 An Interim International Ship Security Certificate may be issued by the Administration or by a Recognized Security Organization authorized to act on its behalf.

19.4.4 An Interim International Ship Security Certificate shall be valid for 6 months, or until the certificate required by section 19.2 is issued, whichever comes first, and may not be extended.

19.4.5 No Contracting Government shall cause a subsequent, consecutive Interim International Ship Security Certificate to be issued to a ship if, in the judgment of the Administration or the Recognized Security Organization, one of the purposes of the ship or a Company in requesting such certificate is to avoid full compliance with chapter XI-2 and this Part of the Code beyond the period of the initial interim certificate as specified in section 19.4.4.

19.4.6 For the purposes of regulation XI-2/9, Contracting Governments may, prior to accepting an Interim International Ship Security Certificate as a valid certificate, ensure that the requirements of sections 19.4.2.4 to 19.4.2.6 have been met.

ISPS Code – Part A (Appendices)

Appendix 1

Form of the International Ship Security Certificate

Sample Certificate

INTERNATIONAL SHIP SECURITY CERTIFICATE

(official seal)
(State)

Certificate Number ....

Issued under the provisions of the
INTERNATIONAL CODE FOR THE SECURITY OF SHIPS AND OF PORT FACILITIES (ISPS CODE)

Under the authority of the Government of

....
(name of State)

by ....
(persons or organization authorized)

Name of ship: ....
Distinctive number or letters: ....
Port of registry: ....
Type of ship: ....
Gross tonnage: ....
IMO Number: ....
Name and address of the Company: ....
....
....

THIS IS TO CERTIFY:
1 that the security system and any associated security equipment of the ship has been verified in accordance with section 19.1 of part A of the ISPS Code;
2 that the verification showed that the security system and any associated security equipment of the ship is in all respects satisfactory and that the ship complies with the applicable requirements of chapter XI-2 of the Convention and part A of the ISPS Code;
3 that the ship is provided with an approved Ship Security Plan.

Date of initial / renewal verification on which this certificate is based: ....
This Certificate is valid until .... subject to verifications in accordance with section 19.1.1 of part A of the ISPS Code.
Issued at: ....
(place of issue of the Certificate)
Date of issue: ....
(signature of the duly authorized official issuing the Certificate)
(Seal or stamp of issuing authority, as appropriate)

ENDORSEMENT FOR INTERMEDIATE VERIFICATION

THIS IS TO CERTIFY that at an intermediate verification required by section 19.1.1 of part A of the ISPS Code the ship was found to comply with the relevant provisions of chapter XI-2 of the Convention and part A of the ISPS Code.

Intermediate verification   Signed ....
         (Signature of authorized official)
         Place ....
         Date ....
     (Seal or stamp of the authority, as appropriate)

ENDORSEMENT FOR ADDITIONAL VERIFICATIONS*

Additional verification   Signed ....
         (Signature of authorized official)
         Place ....
         Date ....
     (Seal or stamp of the authority, as appropriate)

Additional verification   Signed ....
         (Signature of authorized official)
         Place ....
         Date ....
     (Seal or stamp of the authority, as appropriate)

Additional verification   Signed ....
         (Signature of authorized official)
         Place ....
         Date ....
     (Seal or stamp of the authority, as appropriate)

---

* This part of the certificate shall be adapted by the Administration to indicate whether it has established additional verifications as provided for in section 19.1.1.4.

Endorsement for Intermediate Verification

Sample Certificate

Additional Verification in Accordance with Section A/19.3.7.2 of the ISPS Code

Sample Certificate

ADDITIONAL VERIFICATION IN ACCORDANCE WITH SECTION A/19.3.7.2 OF THE ISPS CODE

THIS IS TO CERTIFY that at an additional verification required by section 19.3.7.2 of part A of the ISPS Code the ship was found to comply with the relevant provisions of chapter XI-2 of the Convention and part A of the ISPS Code.

Signed ....
(Signature of authorized official)
Place ....
Date ....
(Seal or stamp of the authority, as appropriate)

Endorsement to Extend the Certificate if Valid for Less Than 5 Years where Section A/19.3.3 of the ISPS Code Applies

Sample Certificate

ENDORSEMENT TO EXTEND THE CERTIFICATE IF VALID FOR LESS THAN 5 YEARS WHERE SECTION A/19.3.3 OF THE ISPS CODE APPLIES

The ship complies with the relevant provisions of part A of the ISPS Code, and the Certificate shall, in accordance with section 19.3.3 of part A of the ISPS Code, be accepted as valid until ....

Signed ....
(Signature of authorized official)
Place ....
Date ....
(Seal or stamp of the authority, as appropriate)

Endorsement where the Renewal Verification has been Completed and Section A/19.3.4 of the ISPS Code Applies

Sample Certificate

ENDORSEMENT WHERE THE RENEWAL VERIFICATION HAS BEEN COMPLETED AND SECTION A/19.3.4 OF THE ISPS CODE APPLIES

The ship complies with the relevant provisions of part A of the ISPS Code, and the Certificate shall, in accordance with section 19.3.4 of part A of the ISPS Code, be accepted as valid until ....

Signed ....
(Signature of authorized official)
Place ....
Date ....
(Seal or stamp of the authority, as appropriate)

ENDORSEMENT TO EXTEND THE VALIDITY OF THE CERTIFICATE UNTIL REACHING THE PORT OF VERIFICATION WHERE SECTION A/19.3.5 OF THE ISPS CODE APPLIES OR FOR A PERIOD OF GRACE WHERE SECTION A/19.3.6 OF THE ISPS CODE APPLIES

This Certificate shall, in accordance with section 19.3.5 / 19.3.6* of part A of the ISPS Code, be accepted as valid until ....

Signed ....
(Signature of authorized official)
Place ....
Date ....
(Seal or stamp of the authority, as appropriate)

* Delete as appropriate

ENDORSEMENT FOR ADVANCEMENT OF EXPIRY DATE WHERE SECTION A/19.3.7.1 OF THE ISPS CODE APPLIES

In accordance with section 19.3.7.1 of part A of the ISPS Code, the new expiry date** is ....

Signed ....
(Signature of authorized official)
Place ....
Date ....
(Seal or stamp of the authority, as appropriate)

** In case of completion of this part of the certificate the expiry date shown on the front of the certificate shall also be amended accordingly.

Endorsement to Extend the Validity of the Certificate until reaching the Port of Verification where Section A/19.3.5 of the ISPS Code Applies or for a Period of Grace where Section A/19.3.6 of the ISPS Code Applies

Sample Certificate

Endorsement for Advancement of Expiry Date where Section A/19.3.7.1 of the ISPS Code Applies

Sample Certificate

Appendix 2

Form of the Interim International Ship Security Certificate

Sample Certificate

INTERIM INTERNATIONAL SHIP SECURITY CERTIFICATE

(official seal)   (State)

Certificate No: . . . .

Issued under the provisions of the
INTERNATIONAL CODE FOR THE SECURITY OF SHIPS AND OF PORT FACILITIES (ISPS CODE)
Under the authority of the Government of

. . . .
(name of State)

by   . . . .
(persons or organization authorized)

Name of ship: . . . .

Distinctive number or letters: . . . .

Port of registry: . . . .

Type of ship: . . . .

Gross tonnage: . . . .

IMO Number: . . . .

Name and address of company: . . . .
. . . .
Is this a subsequent, consecutive interim certificate? Yes/ No*
If Yes, date of issue of initial interim certificate . . . .

THIS IS TO CERTIFY THAT the requirements of section A/19.4.2 of the ISPS Code have been complied with.

This Certificate is issued pursuant to section A/19.4 of the ISPS Code.

This Certificate is valid until: . . . .

Issued at: . . . .
(place of issue of the certificate)
Date of issue: . . . .
(signature of the duly authorized official issuing the Certificate)
(Seal or stamp of issuing authority, as appropriate)
* Delete as appropriate

ISPS Code – Part B (Guidance)

1 INTRODUCTION

General

1.1 The preamble of this Code indicates that Chapter XI-2 and Part A of this Code establish the new international framework of measures to enhance maritime security and through which ships and port facilities can co-operate to detect and deter acts which threaten security in the maritime transport sector.

1.2 This introduction outlines, in a concise manner, the processes envisaged in establishing and implementing the measures and arrangements needed to achieve and maintain compliance with the provisions of Chapter XI-2 and of Part A of this Code and identifies the main elements on which guidance is offered. The guidance is provided in paragraphs 2 through to 19. It also sets down essential considerations, which should be taken into account when considering the application of the guidance relating to ships and port facilities.

1.3 If the reader's interest relates to ships alone, it is strongly recommended that this Part of the Code is still read as a whole, particularly the sections relating to port facilities. The same applies to those whose primary interest are port facilities; they should also read the sections relating to ships.

1.4 The guidance provided in the following sections relates primarily to protection of the ship when it is at a port facility. There could, however, be situations when a ship may pose a threat to the port facility, e.g. because, once within the port facility, it could be used as a base from which to launch an attack. When considering the appropriate security measures to respond to ship-based security threats, those completing the Port Facility Security Assessment or preparing the Port Facility Security Plan should consider making appropriate adaptations to the guidance offered in the following sections.

1.5 The reader is advised that nothing in this Part of the Code should be read or interpreted in conflict with any of the provisions of either Chapter XI-2 or Part A of this Code and that the aforesaid provisions always prevail and override any unintended inconsistency which may have been inadvertently expressed in this Part of the Code. The guidance provided in this Part of the Code should always be read, interpreted and applied in a manner which is consistent with the aims, objectives and principles established in Chapter XI-2 and Part A of this Code.

Responsibilities of Contracting Governments

1.6 Contracting Governments have, under the provisions of Chapter XI-2 and Part A of this Code, various responsibilities, which, amongst others, include:
- setting the applicable Security Level;
- approving the Ship Security Plan and relevant amendments to

Part B
Guidance regarding the provisions of Chapter XI-2 of the Annex to the International Convention for the Safety of Life at Sea, 1974 as amended and Part A of this Code

INTRODUCTION

"...it is strongly recommended that this Part of the Code is read as a whole..."

Guidance relates primarily to protection of a ship at a port facility

Conflicts with the provisions of either Chapter XI-2 or Part A: interpretation and application

Contracting Governments:

– responsibilities

**– verifying
compliance of ships**

**– identifying port
facilities**

**– ensuring
completions**

– approvals

– exercising controls

**–communicating
information**

**Contracting
Government
relationships with
Designated
Authorities
and
Recognised Security
Organisations**

**Duties that may not
be delegated to
Recognised Security
Organisation**

**Setting the
security level –
Contracting
Governments
responsibilities**

a previously approved plan;
- verifying the compliance of ships with the provisions of Chapter XI-2 and Part A of this Code and issuing to ships the International Ship Security Certificate;
- determining which of the port facilities located within their territory are required to designate a Port Facility Security Officer who will be responsible for the preparation of the Port Facility Security Plan;
- ensuring completion and approval of the Port Facility Security Assessment and of any subsequent amendments to a previously approved assessment;
- approving the Port Facility Security Plan and any subsequent amendments to a previously approved plan; and
- exercising control and compliance measures; testing approved plans; and
- communicating information to the International Maritime Organization and to the shipping and port industries.

1.7 Contracting Governments can designate, or establish, Designated Authorities within Government to undertake, with respect to port facilities, their security duties under Chapter XI–2 and Part A of this Code and allow Recognized Security Organizations to carry out certain work with respect to port facilities but the final decision on the acceptance and approval of this work should be given by the Contracting Government or the Designated Authority. Administrations may also delegate the undertaking of certain security duties, relating to ships, to Recognized Security Organizations. The following duties or activities cannot be delegated to a Recognized Security Organization:
- setting of the applicable security level;
- determining which of the port facilities located within the territory of a Contracting Government are required to designate a Port Facility Security Officer and to prepare a Port Facility Security Plan;
- approving a Port Facility Security Assessment or any subsequent amendments to a previously approved assessment;
- approving a Port Facility Security Plan or any subsequent amendments to a previously approved plan;
- exercising control and compliance measures; and
- establishing the requirements for a Declaration of Security.

Setting the security level

1.8 The setting of the security level applying at any particular time is the responsibility of Contracting Governments and can apply to ships and port facilities. Part A of this Code defines three security levels for international use. These are:
- Security Level 1, normal; the level at which ships and port facilities normally operate;
- Security Level 2, heightened; the level applying for as long as there is a heightened risk of a security incident; and

ISPS Code – Part B (Guidance)

– Security Level 3, exceptional, the level applying for the period of time when there is the probable or imminent risk of a security incident.

The Company and the Ship

1.9 Any Company operating ships to which Chapter XI-2 and Part A of this Code apply has to designate a Company Security Officer for the Company and a Ship Security Officer for each of its ships. The duties, responsibilities and training requirements of these officers and requirements for drills and exercises are defined in Part A of this Code.

1.10 The Company Security Officer's responsibilities include, in brief amongst others, ensuring that a Ship Security Assessment is properly carried out, that a Ship Security Plan is prepared and submitted for approval by, or on behalf of, the Administration and thereafter is placed on board each ship to which Part A of this Code applies and in respect of which that person has been appointed as the Company Security Officer.

1.11 The Ship Security Plan should indicate the operational and physical security measures the ship itself should take to ensure it always operates at Security Level 1. The plan should also indicate the additional, or intensified, security measures the ship itself can take to move to and operate at Security Level 2 when instructed to do so. Furthermore, the plan should indicate the possible preparatory actions the ship could take to allow prompt response to the instructions that may be issued to the ship by those responding at Security Level 3 to a security incident or threat thereof.

1.12 The ships to which the requirements of Chapter XI-2 and Part A of this Code apply are required to have, and operated in accordance with, a Ship Security Plan approved by, or on behalf of, the Administration. The Company and Ship Security Officer should monitor the continuing relevance and effectiveness of the plan, including the undertaking of internal audits. Amendments to any of the elements of an approved plan, for which the Administration has determined that approval is required, have to be submitted for review and approval before their incorporation in the approved plan and their implementation by the ship.

1.13 The ship has to carry an International Ship Security Certificate indicating that it complies with the requirements of Chapter XI-2 and Part A of this Code. Part A of this Code includes provisions relating to the verification and certification of the ship's compliance with the requirements on an initial, renewal and intermediate verification basis.

1.14 When a ship is at a port or is proceeding to a port of a Contracting Government, the Contracting Government has the right, under the provisions of regulation XI-2/9, to exercise various control and compliance measures with respect to that ship. The ship is subject to port State control inspections but such inspections will not normally extend to examination of the Ship Security Plan itself

The Company and the Ship:

– designation of Company Security Officer and Ship Security Officer

– Ship Security Assessment

– Ship Security Plan

– Monitoring Ship Security Plan: Internal audits, amendments and approvals

– International Ship Security Certificate

Contracting Governments: – control and compliance measures

– port State control

except in specific circumstances. The ship may, also, be subject to additional control measures if the Contracting Government exercising the control and compliance measures has reason to believe that the security of the ship has, or the port facilities it has served have been compromised.

1.15 The ship is also required to have onboard information, to be made available to Contracting Governments upon request, indicating who is responsible for deciding the employment of the ship's personnel and for deciding various aspects relating to the employment of the ship.

Onboard information: crew and ship employment

The port facility

1.16 Each Contracting Government has to ensure completion of a Port Facility Security Assessment for each of the port facilities, located within its territory, serving ships engaged on international voyages. The Contracting Government, a Designated Authority or a Recognized Security Organization may carry out this assessment. The completed Port Facility Security Assessment has to be approved by the Contracting Government or the Designated Authority concerned. This approval cannot be delegated. Port Facility Security Assessments should be periodically reviewed.

Port Facility Security Assessment

– approval and review

1.17 The Port Facility Security Assessment is fundamentally a risk analysis of all aspects of a port facility's operation in order to determine which part(s) of it are more susceptible, and/or more likely, to be the subject of attack. Security risk is a function of the threat of an attack coupled with the vulnerability of the target and the consequences of an attack.

– risk analysis

The assessment must include the following components:

- the perceived threat to port installations and infrastructure must be determined:
- the potential vulnerabilities identified; and
- the consequences of incidents calculated.

– components of the assessment

On completion of the analysis, it will be possible to produce an overall assessment of the level of risk. The Port Facility Security Assessment will help determine which port facilities are required to appoint a Port Facility Security Officer and prepare a Port Facility Security Plan.

– determine the requirement for Port Security Officer or Plan

1.18 The port facilities which have to comply with the requirements of Chapter XI-2 and Part A of this Code are required to designate a Port Facility Security Officer. The duties, responsibilities and training requirements of these officers and requirements for drills and exercises are defined in Part A of this Code.

1.19 The Port Facility Security Plan should indicate the operational and physical security measures the port facility should take to ensure that it always operates at Security Level 1. The plan should also indicate the additional, or intensified, security measures the port facility can take to move to and operate at Security Level 2 when instructed to do so. Furthermore, the plan should indicate the possible preparatory actions the port facility could take to allow

– operational and physical security measures to move to Security Level 2

prompt response to the instructions that may be issued by those responding at Security Level 3 to a security incident or threat thereof.

1.20 The port facilities which have to comply with the requirements of Chapter XI-2 and Part A of this Code are required to have, and operate in accordance with, a Port Facility Security Plan approved by the Contracting Government or by the Designated Authority concerned. The Port Facility Security Officer should implement its provisions and monitor the continuing effectiveness and relevance of the plan, including commissioning internal audits of the application of the plan. Amendments to any of the elements of an approved plan, for which the Contracting Government or the Designated Authority concerned has determined that approval is required, have to be submitted for review and approval before their incorporation in the approved plan and their implementation at the port facility. The Contracting Government or the Designated Authority concerned may test the effectiveness of the plan. The Port Facility Security Assessment covering the port facility or on which the development of the plan has been based should be regularly reviewed. All these activities may lead to amendment of the approved plan. Any amendments to specified elements of an approved plan will have to be submitted for approval by the Contracting Government or by the Designated Authority concerned.

1.21 Ships using port facilities may be subject to the port State control inspections and additional control measures outlined in regulation XI-2/9. The relevant authorities may request the provision of information regarding the ship, its cargo, passengers and ship's personnel prior to the ship's entry into port. There may be circumstances in which entry into port could be denied.

Information and communication

1.22 Chapter XI-2 and Part A of this Code require Contracting Governments to provide certain information to the International Maritime Organization and for information to be made available to allow effective communication between Contracting Governments and between Company/Ship Security Officers and the Port Facility Security Officers.

2 DEFINITIONS

2.1 No guidance is provided with respect to the definitions set out in Chapter XI-2 or Part A of this Code.

2.2 For the purpose of this Part of the Code:

.1 *section* means a section of Part A of the Code and is indicated as 'section A/<*followed by the number of the section*>';

.2 *paragraph* means a paragraph of this Part of the Code and is indicated as 'paragraph <*followed by the number of the paragraph*>'; and

.3 *Contracting Government*, when used in paragraphs 14 to 18,

Port Facility Security Plan – duties of Port Facility Security Officer:

– testing effectiveness

– regular review

– approvals

Port state control

Denial of ship's entry into port

Provision of information to IMO

Definitions

'section'

'paragraph'

'Contracting Government'

means the Contracting Government within whose territory the port facility is located. and includes a reference to the Designated Authority.

3 APPLICATION

General
3.1 The guidance given in this Part of the Code should be taken into account when implementing the requirements of Chapter XI-2 and Part A of this Code.

3.2 However, it should be recognized that the extent to which the guidance on ships applies will depend on the type of ship, its cargoes and/or passengers, its trading pattern and the characteristics of the port facilities visited by the ship.

3.3 Similarly, in relation to the guidance on port facilities, the extent to which this guidance applies will depend on the port facilities, the types of ships using the port facility, the types of cargo and/or passengers and the trading patterns of visiting ships.

3.4 The provisions of Chapter XI-2 and Part A of this Code are not intended to apply to port facilities designed and used primarily for military purposes.

4 RESPONSIBILITIES OF CONTRACTING GOVERNMENTS

Security of assessments and plans
4.1 Contracting Governments should ensure that appropriate measures are in place to avoid unauthorized disclosure of, or access to, security sensitive material relating to Ship Security Assessments, Ship Security Plans, Port Facility Security Assessments and Port Facility Security Plans, and to individual assessments or plans.

Designated authorities
4.2 Contracting Governments may identify a Designated Authority within Government to undertake their security duties relating to port facilities as set out in Chapter XI-2 or Part A of this Code.

Recognized Security Organizations
4.3 Contracting Governments may authorize a Recognized Security Organization (RSO) to undertake certain security related activities, including:

.1 approval of Ship Security Plans, or amendments thereto, on behalf of the Administrations

.2 verification and certification of compliance of ships with the requirements of Chapter XI-2 and Part A of this Code on behalf of the Administration; and

.3 conducting Port Facility Security Assessments required by the Contracting Government.

4.4 An RSO may also advise or provide assistance to Companies or

ISPS Code – Part B (Guidance)

port facilities on security matters, including Ship Security Assessments, Ship Security Plans, Port Facility Security Assessments and Port Facility Security Plans. This can include completion of a Ship Security Assessment or Plan or Port Facility Security Assessment or Plan. If an RSO has done so in respect of a ship security assessment or plan, that RSO should not be authorized to approve that ship security plan.

4.5 When authorizing an RSO, Contracting Governments should give consideration to the competency of such an organization. An RSO should be able to demonstrate:

.1 expertise in relevant aspects of security;

.2 appropriate knowledge of ship and port operations, including knowledge of ship design and construction if providing services in respect of ships and port design and construction if providing services in respect of port facilities;

.3 their capability to assess the likely security risks that could occur during ship and port facility operations including the ship/port interface and how to minimise such risks;

.4 their ability to maintain and improve the expertise of their personnel;

.5 their ability to monitor the continuing trustworthiness of their personnel;

.6 their ability to maintain appropriate measures to avoid unauthorized disclosure of, or access to, security sensitive material;

.7 their knowledge of the requirements Chapter XI-2 and Part A of this Code and relevant national and international legislation and security requirements;

.8 their knowledge of current security threats and patterns;

.9 their knowledge on recognition and detection of weapons, dangerous substances and devices;

.10 their knowledge on recognition, on a non-discriminatory basis, of characteristics and behavioural patterns of persons who are likely to threaten security;

.11 their knowledge on techniques used to circumvent security measures;

.12 their knowledge of security and surveillance equipment and systems and their operational limitations.

When delegating specific duties to a RSO, Contracting Governments, including Administrations, should ensure that the RSO has the competencies needed to undertake the task.

4.6 A Recognized Organization, as defined in regulation I/6 and fulfiling the requirements of regulation XI-1/1, may be appointed as a RSO provided it has the appropriate security related expertise listed in paragraph 4.5.

4.7 A Port or Harbour Authority or Port Facility operator may be appointed as a RSO provided it has the appropriate security related expertise listed in paragraph 4.5.

Setting the security level

4.8 In setting the security level Contracting Governments should take account of general and specific threat information. Contracting Governments should set the security level applying to ships or port facilities at one of three levels:

- **Security level 1**: normal, the level at which the ship or port facility normally operates;
- **Security level 2**: heightened, the level applying for as long as there is a heightened risk of a security incident; and
- **Security level 3**: exceptional, the level applying for the period of time when there is the probable or imminent risk of a security incident.

4.9 Setting Security Level 3 should be an exceptional measure applying only when there is credible information that a security incident is probable or imminent. Security level 3 should only be set for the duration of the identified security threat or actual security incident. While the security levels may change from Security Level 1, through Security Level 2 to Security Level 3, it is also possible that the security levels will change directly from Security Level 1 to Security Level 3.

4.10 At all times the Master of a ship has the ultimate responsibility for the safety and security of the ship. Even at Security Level 3 a Master may seek clarification or amendment of instructions issued by those responding to a security incident, or threat thereof, if there are reasons to believe that compliance with any instruction may imperil the safety of the ship.

4.11 The Company Security Officer (CSO) or the Ship Security Officer (SSO) should liaise at the earliest opportunity with the Port Facility Security Officer (PFSO) of the port facility the ship is intended to visit to establish the security level applying for that ship at the port facility. Having established contact with a ship, the PFSO should advise the ship of any subsequent change in the port facility's security level and should provide the ship with any relevant security information.

4.12 While there may be circumstances when an individual ship may be operating at a higher security level than the port facility it is visiting, there will be no circumstances when a ship can have a lower security level than the port facility it is visiting. If a ship has a higher security level than the port facility it intends to use, the CSO or SSO should advise the PFSO without delay. The PFSO should undertake an assessment of the particular situation in consultation with the CSO or SSO and agree on appropriate security measures with the ship, which may include completion and signing of a Declaration of Security.

4.13 Contracting Governments should consider how information on changes in security levels should be promulgated rapidly. Administrations may wish to use NAVTEX messages or Notices to Mariners as the method for notifying such changes in security levels to ship and CSO and SSO. Or, they may wish to consider other methods of communication that provide equivalent or better speed and coverage. Contracting Governments should establish means of notifying PFSOs of changes in security levels. Contracting Governments should compile and maintain the contact details for a list of those who need to be informed of changes in security levels. Whereas the security level need not be regarded as being particularly sensitive, the underlying threat information may be highly sensitive. Contracting Governments should give careful consideration to the type and detail of the information conveyed and the method by which it is conveyed, to SSOs, CSOs and PFSOs.

Contact points and information on Port Facility Security Plans

4.14 Where a port facility has a PFSP, that fact has to be communicated to the Organization and that information must also be made available to CSO and SSOs. No further details of the PFSP have to be published other than that it is in place. Contracting Governments should consider establishing either central or regional points of contact, or other means of providing up to date information on the locations where PFSPs are in place, together with contact details for the relevant PFSO. The existence of such contact points should be publicised. They could also provide information on the Recognized Security Organizations appointed to act on behalf of the Contracting Government, together with details of the specific responsibility and conditions of authority delegated to such Recognized Security Organizations.

4.15 In the case of a port that does not have a PFSP (and therefore does not have a PFSO) the central or regional point of contact should be able to identify a suitably qualified person ashore who can arrange for appropriate security measures to be in place, if needed, for the duration of the ship's visit.

4.16 Contracting Governments should also provide the contact details of Government officers to whom an SSO, a CSO and a PFSO can report security concerns. These Government officers should assess such reports before taking appropriate action. Such reported concerns may have a bearing on the security measures falling under the jurisdiction of another Contracting Government. In that case, the Contracting Governments should consider contacting their counterpart in the other Contracting Government to discuss whether remedial action is appropriate. For this purpose, the contact details of the Government officers should be communicated to the International Maritime Organization.

4.17 Contracting Governments should also make the information indicated in paragraphs 4.14 to 4.16, available to other Contracting Governments on request.

Identification documents

4.18 Contracting Governments are encouraged to issue appropriate identification documents to Government officials entitled to board ships or enter port facilities when performing their official duties and

Contracting Governments:

contact lists:
– for security level changes
– maintaining sensitive contact information and distribution

Port Facility Security Plans:

– contact points and information to be made public

Contact for port's without a PFSP

Contact details of Government Officers for security reports

Inter-Contracting Government transfer of information

I.D. for Government Officials

to establish procedures whereby the authenticity of such documents might be verified.

Appropriate security for platforms and rigs

Fixed and floating platforms and mobile offshore drilling units on location
4.19 Contracting Governments should consider establishing appropriate security measures for fixed and floating platforms and mobile offshore drilling units on location to allow interaction with ships which are required to comply with the provisions of Chapter XI-2 and Part A of this Code*.

Measures for non-Part A ships

Ships which are not required to comply with Part A of this Code
4.20 Contracting Governments should consider establishing appropriate security measures to enhance the security of ships to which this Chapter XI-2 and Part A of this Code does not apply and to ensure that any security provisions applying to such ships allow interaction with ships to which Part A of this Code applies.

Ships at sea: – threats and security incidents

Threats to ships and other incidents at sea
4.21 Contracting Governments should provide general guidance on the measures considered appropriate to reduce the security risk to ships flying their flag when at sea. They should provide specific advice on the action to be taken in accordance with Security Levels 1 to 3, if:

– guidance from Contracting Governments

  .1 there is a change in the security level applying to the ship while it is at sea, e.g. because of the geographical area in which it is operating or relating to the ship itself; and

  .2 there is a security incident or threat thereof involving the ship while at sea.

– direct communication with Flag state

Contracting Governments should establish the best methods and procedures for these purposes. In the case of an imminent attack the ship should seek to establish direct communication with those responsible in the flag State for responding to security incidents.

Point of advice:

4.22 Contracting Governments should also establish a point of contact for advice on security for any ship:

– to Flag state ships

  .1 entitled to fly their flag; or

  .2 operating in their territorial sea or having communicated an intention to enter their territorial sea.

– ships on transit in territorial waters

4.23 Contracting Governments should offer advice to ships operating in their territorial sea or having communicated an intention to enter their territorial sea, which could include advice:

  .1 to alter or delay their intended passage;

---

* Refer to: "Establishment of appropriate measures to enhance the security of ships, port facilities, mobile offshore drilling units on location and fixed and floating platforms not covered by Chapter XI-2 of 1974 SOLAS Convention", adopted by the Conference on Maritime Security by Resolution 7. (see Page 119)

.2 to navigate on a particular course or proceed to a specific location;

.3 on the availability of any personnel or equipment that could be placed on the ship;

.4 to co-ordinate the passage, arrival into port or departure from port, to allow escort by patrol craft or aircraft (fixed-wing or helicopter).

Contracting Governments should remind ships operating in their territorial sea, or having communicated an intention to enter their territorial sea, of any temporary restricted areas that they have published.

4.24 Contracting Governments should recommend that ships operating in their territorial sea, or having communicated an intention to enter their territorial sea, implement expeditiously, for the ship's protection and for the protection of other ships in the vicinity, any security measure the Contracting Government may have advised.

4.25 The plans prepared by the Contracting Governments for the purposes given in paragraph 4.22 should include information on an appropriate point of contact, available on a 24-hour basis, within the Contracting Government including the Administration. These plans should also include information on the circumstances in which the Administration considers assistance should be sought from nearby coastal States, and a procedure for liaison between Port Facility Security Officers (PFSOs) and Ship Security Officers (SSOs).

Alternative security agreements

4.26 Contracting Governments, in considering how to implement Chapter XI-2 and Part A of this Code, may conclude one or more agreements with one or more Contracting Governments. The scope of an agreement is limited to short international voyages on fixed routes between port facilities in the territory of the parties to the agreement. When concluding an agreement, and thereafter, the Contracting Governments should consult other Contracting Governments and Administrations with an interest in the effects of the agreement. Ships flying the flag of a State that is not party to the agreement should only be allowed to operate on the fixed routes covered by the agreement if their Administration agrees that the ship should comply with the provisions of the agreement and requires the ship to do so. In no case can such an agreement compromise the level of security of other ships and port facilities not covered by it, and specifically, all ships covered by such an agreement may not conduct ship-to-ship activities with ships not so covered. Any operational interface undertaken by ships covered by the agreement should be covered by it. The operation of each agreement must be continually monitored and amended when the need arises and in any event should be reviewed every 5 years.

Equivalent arrangements for port facilities

4.27 For certain specific port facilities with limited or special operations but with more than occasional traffic, it may be appropriate

Contracting Governments:

– advice and instruction to ships transiting territorial waters

– check on implementation of advice

– details of 24/7 point of contact

– assistance from nearby coastal states

Alternative security arrangements:

– short international voyages

– fixed routes

– continual monitoring

– 5-year review

Port facilities with limited operations

to ensure compliance by security measures equivalent to those prescribed in Chapter XI-2 and in Part A of this Code. This can, in particular, be the case for terminals such as those attached to factories, or quaysides with no frequent operations.

Manning level
4.28 In establishing the minimum safe manning of a ship the Administration should take into account* that the minimum safe manning provisions established by regulation V/14** only address the safe navigation of the ship. The Administration should also take into account any additional workload which may result from the implementation of the ship's security plan and ensure that the ship is sufficiently and effectively manned. In doing so the Administration should verify that ships are able to implement the hours of rest and other measures to address fatigue which have been promulgated by national law, in the context of all shipboard duties assigned to the various shipboard personnel.

Control and compliance measures***

General
4.29 Regulation XI-2/9 describes the control and compliance measures applicable to ships under Chapter XI-2. It is divided into three distinct sections; control of ships already in a port, control of ships intending to enter a port of another Contracting Government, and additional provisions applicable to both situations.
4.30 Regulation XI-2/9.1, control of ships in port, implements a system for the control of ships while in the port of a foreign country where duly authorized officers of the Contracting Government (duly authorized officers) have the right to go on board the ship to verify that the required certificates are in proper order. Then if there are clear grounds to believe the ship does not comply, control measures such as additional inspections or detention may be taken. This reflects current control systems[†]. Regulation XI-2/9.1 builds on such

---

* *Refer to: "Further work by IMO pertaining to enhancement of maritime security", adopted by Resolution 3 of the 2002 SOLAS Conference, inviting, amongst others, the IMO to review Assembly Resolution A.890(21) on Principles of Safe Manning. This review may also lead to amendments of regulation V/14. (see Page 112)*
** *As was in force on the date of adoption of this Code.*
****Refer to: "Further work by IMO pertaining to Enhancement of Maritime Security", adopted by Res. 3 of the 2002 SOLAS Conference (see Page 112), inviting, amongst others, the IMO to review Assembly Resolutions A.787(19) & A.882(21) on Procedures for port State control*
† *See regulation I/19 and regulation IX/6.2 of SOLAS 74 as amended, article 21 of Load Line 66 as modified by the 1988 Load Line Protocol, articles 5 and 6, regulation 8A of Annex I, regulation 15 of Annex II of MARPOL 73/78 as amended, article X of STCW 78 as amended and IMO Assembly Resolutions A.787(19) and A.882(21).*

systems and allows for additional measures (including expulsion of a ship from a port to be taken as a control measure) when duly authorized officers have clear grounds for believing that a ship is in non-compliance with the requirements of Chapter XI-2 or Part A of this Code. Regulation XI-2/9.3 describes the safeguards that promote fair and proportionate implementation of these additional measures.

4.31 Regulation XI-2/9.2 applies control measures to ensure compliance to ships intending to enter a port of another Contracting Government and introduces an entirely different concept of control within Chapter XI-2, applying to security only. Under this regulation measures may be implemented prior to the ship entering port, to better ensure security. Just as in regulation XI-2/9.1, this additional control system is based on the concept of clear grounds for believing the ship does not comply with Chapter XI-2 or Part A of this Code, and includes significant safeguards in regulations XI-2/9.2.2 and XI-2/9.2.5 as well as in regulation XI-2/9.3.

4.32 Clear grounds that the ship is not in compliance means evidence or reliable information that the ship does not correspond with the requirements of Chapter XI-2 or Part A of this Code, taking into account the guidance given in this Part of the Code. Such evidence or reliable information may arise from the duly authorized officer's professional judgement or observations gained while verifying the ship's International Ship Security Certificate or Interim International Ship Security Certificate issued in accordance with Part A of this Code ('Certificate') or from other sources. Even if a valid certificate is on board the ship, the duly authorized officers may still have clear grounds for believing that the ship is not in compliance based on their professional judgment.

4.33 Examples of possible clear grounds under regulations XI-2/9.1 and XI-2/9.2 may include, when relevant:

.1 evidence from a review of the certificate that it is not valid or it has expired;

.2 evidence or reliable information that serious deficiencies exist in the security equipment, documentation or arrangements required by Chapter XI-2 and Part A of this Code;

.3 receipt of a report or complaint which, in the professional judgment of the duly authorized officer, contains reliable information clearly indicating that the ship does not comply with the requirements of Chapter XI-2 or Part A of this Code;

.4 evidence or observation gained by a duly authorized officer using professional judgment that the master or ship's personnel is not familiar with essential shipboard security procedures or cannot carry out drills related to the security of the ship or that such procedures or drills have not been carried out;

.5 evidence or observation gained by a duly authorized officer using professional judgment that key members of the ship's personnel are not able to establish proper communication with any other key members of ship's personnel with security responsibilities on board the ship;

Control and compliance of:

– ships intending to enter a port

– ships clearly not in compliance

– examples of non-compliance

.6 evidence or reliable information that the ship has embarked persons, or loaded stores or goods at a port facility or from another ship where either the port facility or the other ship is in violation of Chapter XI-2 or Part A of this Code, and the ship in question has not completed a Declaration of Security, nor taken appropriate, special or additional security measures or has not maintained appropriate ship security procedures;

.7 evidence or reliable information that the ship has embarked persons, or loaded stores or goods at a port facility or from another source (e.g., another ship or helicopter transfer) where either the port facility or the other source is not required to comply with Chapter XI-2 or Part A of this Code, and the ship has not taken appropriate, special or additional security measures or has not maintained appropriate security procedures;

.8 and if the ship holds a subsequent, consecutively issued Interim International Ship Security Certificate as described in section A/19.4, and if, in the professional judgment of an officer duly authorized, one of the purposes of the ship or a Company in requesting such a certificate is to avoid full compliance with Chapter XI-2 and Part A of this Code beyond the period of the initial interim certificate as described in section A/19.4.4

4.34 The international law implications of regulation XI-2/9 are particularly relevant, and the regulation should be implemented with regulation XI-2/2.4 in mind, as the potential exists for situations where either measures will be taken which fall outside the scope of Chapter XI-2, or where rights of affected ships, outside Chapter XI-2, should be considered. Thus, regulation XI-2/9 does not prejudice the Contracting Government from taking measures having a basis in, and consistent with, international law, to ensure the safety or security of persons, ships, port facilities and other property in cases where the ship, although in compliance with Chapter XI-2 and Part A of this Code, is still considered to present a security risk.

4.35 When a Contracting Government imposes control measures on a ship, the Administration should, without delay, be contacted with sufficient information to enable the Administration to fully liaise with the Contracting Government.

Control of ships in port

4.36 Where the non-compliance is either a defective item of equipment or faulty documentation leading to the ship's detention and the non-compliance cannot be remedied in the port of inspection, the Contracting Government may allow the ship to sail to another port provided that any conditions agreed between the port States and the Administration or master are met.

Ships intending to enter the port of another Contracting Government

4.37 Regulation XI-2/9.2.1 lists the information Contracting

ISPS Code – Part B (Guidance)

Governments may require from a ship as a condition of entry into port. One item of information listed is confirmation of any special or additional measures taken by the ship during its last ten calls at a port facility. Examples could include:

.1 records of the measures taken while visiting a port facility located in the territory of a State which is not a Contracting Government especially those measures that would normally have been provided by port facilities located in the territories of Contracting Governments; and

.2 any Declarations of Security that were entered into with port facilities or other ships.

4.38 Another item of information listed, that may be required as a condition of entry into port, is confirmation that appropriate ship security procedures were maintained during ship-to-ship activity conducted within the period of the last 10 calls at a port facility. It would not normally be required to include records of transfers of pilots, customs, immigration, security officials nor bunkering, lightering, loading of supplies and unloading of waste by ship within port facilities as these would normally fall within the auspices of the Port Facility Security Plan.

Examples of information that might be given include:

.1 records of the measures taken while engaged in a ship to ship activity with a ship flying the flag of a State which is not a Contracting Government especially those measures that would normally have been provided by ships flying the flag of Contracting Governments;

.2 records of the measures taken while engaged in a ship to ship activity with a ship that is flying the flag of a Contracting Government but is not required to comply with the provisions of Chapter XI-2 and Part A of this Code such as a copy of any security certificate issued to that ship under other provisions; and

.3 in the event that persons or goods rescued at sea are on board, all known information about such persons or goods, including their identities when known and the results of any checks run on behalf of the ship to establish the security status of those rescued. It is not the intention of Chapter XI-2 or Part A of this Code to delay or prevent the delivery of those in distress at sea to a place of safety. It is the sole intention of Chapter XI-2 and Part A of this Code to provide States with enough appropriate information to maintain their security integrity.

4.39 Examples of other practical security related information that may be required as a condition of entry into port in order to assist with ensuring the safety and security of persons, port facilities, ships and other property include:

.1 information contained in the Continuous Synopsis Record;

.2 location of the ship at the time the report is made;

.3 expected time of arrival of the ship in port;

Information required as condition of port entry:

– records of measures taken in non-Contracting Government ports

– any Declarations of Security

– records of appropriate ship-to-ship measures taken in last 10 port facility calls

– examples of appropriate measures

– rescued persons

– examples of other practical security related information

.4 crew list;

.5 general description of cargo aboard the ship;

.6 passenger list; and

.7 information required to be carried under regulation XI-2/5.

Right of Master to withdraw intention to enter port

4.40 Regulation XI-2/9.2.5 allows the Master of a ship, upon being informed that the coastal or port State will implement control measures under regulation XI-2/9.2, to withdraw the intention for the ship to enter port. If the Master withdraws that intention, regulation XI-2/9 no longer applies, and any other steps that are taken must be based on, and consistent with, international law.

Additional provisions

Ships denied entry or expelled from port: – promulgation of relevant information to other 'relevant States' (see below)

4.41 In all cases where a ship is denied entry or expelled from a port, all known facts should be communicated to the authorities of relevant States. This communication should consist of the following when known:

.1 name of ship, its flag, the ship's identification number, call sign, ship type and cargo;

.2 reason for denying entry or expulsion from port or port areas;

.3 if relevant, the nature of any security non-compliance;

.4 if relevant, details of any attempts made to rectify any non-compliance, including any conditions imposed on the ship for the voyage;

.5 past port(s) of call and next declared port of call;

.6 time of departure and likely estimated time of arrival at those ports;

.7 any instructions given to ship, e.g., reporting on route;

.8 available information on the security level at which the ship is currently operating;

.9 information regarding any communications the port State has had with the Administration;

.10 contact point within the port State making the report for the purpose of obtaining further information;

.11 crew list; and

.12 any other relevant information.

'Relevant States'

4.42 Relevant States to contact should include those along the ship's intended passage to its next port, particularly if the ship intends to enter the territorial sea of that coastal State. Other relevant States could include previous ports of call, so that further information might be obtained and security issues relating to the previous ports resolved.

Measures taken are proportional and reasonable

4.43 In exercising control and compliance measures, the duly authorized officers should ensure that any measures or steps imposed are proportionate. Such measures or steps should be reasonable and of the minimum severity and duration necessary to rectify or mitigate the non-compliance.

'delay'

4.44 The word "delay" in regulation XI-2/9.3.5.1 also refers to situations where, pursuant to actions taken under this regulation, the ship is unduly denied entry into port or the ship is unduly expelled from port.

Non-party ships and ships below convention size

4.45 With respect to ships flying the flag of a State which is not a Contracting Government to the Convention and not a Party to the 1988 SOLAS Protocol*, Contracting Governments should not give more favourable treatment to such ships. Accordingly, the requirements of regulation XI-2/9 and the guidance provided in this Part of the Code should be applied to those ships.

4.46 Ships below Convention size are subject to measures by which States maintain security. Such measures should be taken with due regard to the requirements in Chapter XI-2 and the guidance provided in this Part of the Code.

5   DECLARATION OF SECURITY

General

5.1 A Declaration of Security (DoS) should be completed when the Contracting Government of the port facility deems it to be necessary or when a ship deems it necessary.

5.1.1 The need for a DoS may be indicated by the results of the Port Facility Security Assessment (PFSA) and the reasons and circumstances in which a DoS is required should be set out in the Port Facility Security Plan (PFSP).

5.1.2 The need for a DoS may be indicated by an Administration for ships entitled to fly its flag or as a result of a Ship Security Assessment and should be set out in the Ship Security Plan.

5.2 It is likely that a DoS will be requested at higher security levels, when a ship has a higher security level than the port facility, or another ship with which it interfaces, and for ship/port interface or ship to ship activities that pose a higher risk to persons, property or the environment for reasons specific to that ship, including its cargo or passengers or the circumstances at the port facility or a combination of these factors.

5.2.1 In the case that a ship or an Administration, on behalf of ships entitled to fly its flag, requests completion of a DoS, the Port Facility Security Officer (PFSO) or Ship Security Officer (SSO) should acknowledge the request and discuss appropriate security measures.

5.3 A PFSO may also initiate a DoS prior to ship/port interfaces that are identified in the approved PFSA as being of particular concern. Examples may include the embarking or disembarking passengers, and the transfer, loading or unloading of dangerous goods or hazardous substances. The PFSA may also identify facilities at or near highly populated areas or economically significant operations that warrant a DoS.

5.4 The main purpose of a DoS is to ensure agreement is reached

Non-party ships:

– treatment by Contracting Governments

– ships below convention size

DECLARATION OF SECURITY (DoS)

– need for DoS

– request for DoS

– acknowledgement of request for DoS

– situations that may initiate a DoS

---

* *Protocol of 1988 relating to the International Convention for the Safety of Life at Sea, 1974.*

ISPS Code – Part B (Guidance)

between the ship and the port facility or with other ships with which it interfaces as to the respective security measures each will undertake in accordance with the provisions of their respective approved security plans.

5.4.1 The agreed DoS should be signed and dated by both the port facility and the ship(s), as applicable, to indicate compliance with Chapter XI-2 and Part A of this Code and should include its duration, the relevant security level, or levels and the relevant contact details.

5.4.2 A change in the security level may require that a new or revised DoS be completed.

5.5 The DoS should be completed in English, French or Spanish or in a language common to both the port facility and the ship or the ships, as applicable.

5.6 A model DoS is included in Appendix 1 to this Part of the Code. This model is for a DoS between a ship and a port facility. If the DoS is to cover two ships this model should be appropriately adjusted.

6   OBLIGATIONS OF THE COMPANY

General

6.1 Regulation XI-2/5 requires the company to provide the Master of the ship with information to meet the requirements of the Company under the provisions of this regulation. This information should include items such as:

.1   parties responsible for appointing shipboard personnel, such as ship management companies, manning agents, contractors, concessionaires (for example, retail sales outlets, casinos, etc.);

.2   parties responsible for deciding the employment of the ship including, time or bareboat charterer(s) or any other entity acting in such capacity; and

.3   in cases when the ship is employed under the terms of a charter party, the contact details of those parties including time or voyage charterers.

6.2 In accordance with regulation XI-2/5 the Company is obliged to update and keep this information current as and when changes occur.

6.3 This information should be in English, French or Spanish language.

6.4 With respect to ships constructed before 1 July 2004, this information should reflect the actual condition on that date.

6.5 With respect to ships constructed on or after 1 July 2004 and for ships constructed before 1 July 2004 which were out of service on 1 July 2004, the information should be provided as from the date of entry of the ship into service and should reflect the actual condition on that date.

6.6 After 1 July 2004 when a ship is withdrawn from service the information should be provided as from the date of re-entry of the ship into service and should reflect the actual condition on that date.

6.7 Previously provided information that does not relate to the actual condition on that date need not be retained on board.

6.8 When the responsibility for the operation of the ship is assumed by another Company, the information relating to the Company, which operated the ship, is not required to be left on board.

In addition other relevant guidance is provided under sections 8, 9 and 13.

7   SHIP SECURITY

Relevant guidance is provided under sections 8, 9 and 13.

8   SHIP SECURITY ASSESSMENT

Security assessment

8.1 The Company Security Officer (CSO) is responsible for ensuring that a Ship Security Assessment (SSA) is carried out for each of the ships in the Company's fleet which is required to comply with the provisions of Chapter XI-2 and Part A of this Code for which the CSO is responsible. While the CSO need not necessarily personally undertake all the duties associated with the post, the ultimate responsibility for ensuring that they are properly performed remains with the individual CSO.

8.2 Prior to commencing the SSA, the CSO should ensure that advantage is taken of information available on the assessment of threat for the ports at which the ship will call or at which passengers embark or disembark and about the port facilities and their protective measures. The CSO should study previous reports on similar security needs. Where feasible, the CSO should meet with appropriate persons on the ship and in the port facilities to discuss the purpose and methodology of the assessment. The CSO should follow any specific guidance offered by the Contracting Governments.

8.3 A SSA should address the following elements on board or within the ship:

.1 physical security;

.2 structural integrity;

.3 personnel protection systems;

.4 procedural policies;

.5 radio and telecommunication systems, including computer systems and networks; and

.6 other areas that may, if damaged or used for illicit observation, pose a risk to persons, property, or operations on board the ship or within a port facility.

8.4 Those involved in a SSA should be able to draw upon expert assistance in relation to:

.1 knowledge of current security threats and patterns;

.2 recognition and detection of weapons, dangerous substances and devices;

.3 recognition, on a non-discriminatory basis, of characteristics and behavioural patterns of persons who are likely to threaten security;

– change of Company

SHIP SECURITY

SHIP SECURITY ASSESSMENT

Extent of Ship Security Assessments and responsibility for ensuring performance

Compiling and assessment of early and available port information

Components of the Ship Security Assessment

Provision of expert assistance

.4 techniques used to circumvent security measures;

.5 methods used to cause a security incident;

.6 effects of explosives on ship's structures and equipment;

.7 ship security;

.8 ship/port interface business practices;

.9 contingency planning, emergency preparedness and response;

.10 physical security;

.11 radio and telecommunications systems, including computer systems and networks;

.12 marine engineering; and

.13 ship and port operations.

8.5 The CSO should obtain and record the information required to conduct an assessment, including:

.1 the general layout of the ship;

.2 the location of areas which should have restricted access, such as navigation bridge, machinery spaces of category A and other control stations as defined in chapter II-2, etc.;

.3 the location and function of each actual or potential access point to the ship;

.4 changes in the tide which may have an impact on the vulnerability or security of the ship;

.5 the cargo spaces and stowage arrangements;

.6 the locations where the ship's stores and essential maintenance equipment is stored;

.7 the locations where unaccompanied baggage is stored;

.8 the emergency and stand-by equipment available to maintain essential services

.9 the number of ship's personnel, any existing security duties and any existing training requirement practices of the Company;

.10 existing security and safety equipment for the protection of passengers and ship's personnel;

.11 escape and evacuation routes and assembly stations which have to be maintained to ensure the orderly and safe emergency evacuation of the ship;

.12 existing agreements with private security companies providing ship/waterside security services; and

.13 existing security measures and procedures in effect, including inspection and, control procedures, identification systems, surveillance and monitoring equipment, personnel identification documents and communication, alarms, lighting, access control and other appropriate systems.

8.6 The SSA should examine each identified point of access, including open weather decks, and evaluate its potential for use by individuals who might seek to breach security. This includes points of access available to individuals having legitimate access as well as those who seek to obtain unauthorized entry.

8.7 The SSA should consider the continuing relevance of the existing security measures and guidance, procedures and operations, under

ISPS Code – Part B (Guidance)

both routine and emergency conditions and should determine security guidance including:

.1 the restricted areas;

.2 the response procedures to fire or other emergency conditions;

.3 the level of supervision of the ship's personnel, passengers, visitors, vendors, repair technicians, dock workers, etc.;

.4 the frequency and effectiveness of security patrols;

.5 the access control systems, including identification systems;

.6 the security communications systems and procedures;

.7 the security doors, barriers and lighting; and

.8 the security and surveillance equipment and systems, if any.

8.8 The SSA should consider the persons, activities, services and operations that it is important to protect. This includes:

.1 the ship's personnel;

.2 passengers, visitors, vendors, repair technicians, port facility personnel, etc;

.3 the capacity to maintain safe navigation and emergency response;

.4 the cargo, particularly dangerous goods or hazardous substances;

.5 the ship's stores;

.6 the ship security communication equipment and systems, if any; and

.7 the ship's security surveillance equipment and systems, if any.

8.9 The SSA should consider all possible threats, which may include the following types of security incidents:

.1 damage to, or destruction of, the ship or of a port facility, e.g. by explosive devices, arson, sabotage or vandalism;

.2 hijacking or seizure of the ship or of persons on board;

.3 tampering with cargo, essential ship equipment or systems or ship's stores;

.4 unauthorized access or use, including presence of stowaways;

.5 smuggling weapons or equipment, including weapons of mass destruction;

.6 use of the ship to carry those intending to cause a security incident and/or their equipment;

.7 use of the ship itself as a weapon or as a means to cause damage or destruction;

.8 attacks from seaward whilst at berth or at anchor; and

.9 attacks whilst at sea.

8.10 The SSA should take into account all possible vulnerabilities, which may include:

.1 conflicts between safety and security measures;

.2 conflicts between shipboard duties and security assignments;

.3 watch-keeping duties, number of ship's personnel, particularly with implications on crew fatigue, alertness and performance;

.4 any identified security training deficiencies; and

.5 any security equipment and systems, including communication systems.

Review relevance of existing security measures (contd)

Identification of persons and services to protect

Consideration of possible threats:

– examples

Consideration of vulnerabilities

8.11 The CSO and SSO should always have regard to the effect that security measures may have on ship's personnel who will remain on the ship for long periods. When developing security measures, particular consideration should be given to the convenience, comfort and personal privacy of the ship's personnel and their ability to maintain their effectiveness over long periods.

8.12 Upon completion of the SSA, a report shall be prepared, consisting of a summary of how the assessment was conducted, a description of each vulnerability found during the assessment and a description of counter measures that could be used to address each vulnerability. The report shall be protected from unauthorized access or disclosure.

8.13 If the SSA has not been carried out by the Company, the report of the SSA should be reviewed and accepted by the CSO.

On-scene security survey

8.14 The on-scene security survey is an integral part of any SSA. The on-scene security survey should examine and evaluate existing shipboard protective measures, procedures and operations for:

.1 ensuring the performance of all ship security duties;

.2 monitoring restricted areas to ensure that only authorized persons have access;

.3 controlling access to the ship, including any identification systems;

.4 monitoring of deck areas and areas surrounding the ship;

.5 controlling the embarkation of persons and their effects (accompanied and unaccompanied baggage and ship's personnel personal effects);

.6 supervising the handling of cargo and the delivery of ship's stores; and

.7 ensuring that ship security communication, information, and equipment are readily available.

9   SHIP SECURITY PLAN

General

9.1 The Company Security Officer (CSO) has the responsibility of ensuring that a Ship Security Plan (SSP) is prepared and submitted for approval. The content of each individual SSP should vary depending on the particular ship it covers. The Ship Security Assessment (SSA) will have identified the particular features of the ship and the potential threats and vulnerabilities. The preparation of the SSP will require these features to be addressed in detail. Administrations may prepare advice on the preparation and content of a SSP.

9.2 All SSPs should:

.1 detail the organizational structure of security for the ship;

.2 detail the ship's relationships with the Company, port facilities, other ships and relevant authorities with security responsibility;

.3 detail the communication systems to allow effective continuous communication within the ship and between the ship and others, including port facilities;

.4 detail the basic security measures for Security Level 1, both operational and physical, that will always be in place;

.5 detail the additional security measures that will allow the ship to progress without delay to Security Level 2 and, when necessary, to Security Level 3;

.6 provide for regular review, or audit, of the SSP and for its amendment in response to experience or changing circumstances; and

.7 reporting procedures to the appropriate Contracting Governments contact points.

9.3 Preparation of an effective SSP should rest on a thorough assessment of all issues that relate to the security of the ship, including, in particular, a thorough appreciation of the physical and operational characteristics, including the voyage pattern, of the individual ship.

9.4 All SSPs should be approved by, or on behalf of, the Administration. If an Administration uses a Recognized Security Organization (RSO) to review or approve the SSP the RSO should not be associated with any other RSO that prepared, or assisted in the preparation of, the plan.

9.5 CSOs and Ship Security Officers (SSOs) should develop procedures to:

.1 assess the continuing effectiveness of the SSP; and

.2 prepare amendments of the plan subsequent to its approval.

9.6 The security measures included in the SSP should be in place when the initial verification for compliance with the requirements of Chapter XI-2 and Part A of this Code will be carried out. Otherwise the process of issue to the ship of the required International Ship Security Certificate cannot be carried out. If there is any subsequent failure of security equipment or systems, or suspension of a security measure for whatever reason, equivalent temporary security measures should be adopted, notified to, and agreed by, the Administration.

Organization and performance of ship security duties

9.7 In addition to the guidance given in section 9.2, the SSP should establish the following which relate to all security levels:

.1 the duties and responsibilities of all shipboard personnel with a security role;

.2 the procedures or safeguards necessary to allow such continuous communications to be maintained at all times;

.3 the procedures needed to assess the continuing effectiveness of security procedures and any security and surveillance equipment and systems, including procedures for identifying and responding to equipment or systems failure or malfunction;

Ship Security Plan:

– requirements (contd)

Consideration of ship characteristics and voyage pattern

Approvals and approval by an RSO

Procedures for continuing effectiveness

Application of SSP measures in relation to the International Ship Security Certificate

Ship security duties:

– shipboard personnel

– communications

– assessing continuing effectiveness of measures

– security sensitive
information

– maintenance of
security equipment

– reporting

– dangerous goods

Shipboard Security
Measures at each
Security Level

Access to the ship
(general):

– application of
access restrictions

– ship's personnel
and visitors
ID system

– persons to be
denied access

.4 the procedures and practices to protect security sensitive information held in paper or electronic format;

.5 the type and maintenance requirements, of security and surveillance equipment and systems, if any;

.6 the procedures to ensure the timely submission, and assessment, of reports relating to possible breaches of security or security concerns; and

.7 procedures to establish, maintain and up-date an inventory of any dangerous goods or hazardous substances carried on board, including their location.

9.8 The remainder of this section addresses specifically the security measures that could be taken at each security level covering:

.1 access to the ship by ship's personnel, passengers, visitors, etc;

.2 restricted areas on the ship;

.3 handling of cargo;

.4 delivery of ship's stores;

.5 handling unaccompanied baggage; and

.6 monitoring the security of the ship.

Access to the ship

9.9 The SSP should establish the security measures covering all means of access to the ship identified in the SSA. This should include any:

.1 access ladders;

.2 access gangways;

.3 access ramps;

.4 access doors, side scuttles, windows and ports;

.5 mooring lines and anchor chains; and

.6 cranes and hoisting gear.

9.10 For each of these the SSP should identify the appropriate locations where access restrictions or prohibitions should be applied for each of the security levels. For each security level the SSP should establish the type of restriction or prohibition to be applied and the means of enforcing them.

9.11 The SSP should establish for each security level the means of identification required to allow access to the ship and for individuals to remain on the ship without challenge, this may involve developing an appropriate identification system allowing for permanent and temporary identifications, for ship's personnel and visitors respectively. Any ship identification system should, when it is practicable to do so, be co-ordinated with that applying to the port facility. Passengers should be able to prove their identity by boarding passes, tickets, etc., but should not be permitted access to restricted areas unless supervised. The SSP should establish provisions to ensure that the identification systems are regularly updated, and that abuse of procedures should be subject to disciplinary action.

9.12 Those unwilling or unable to establish their identity and/or to confirm the purpose of their visit when requested to do so should be denied access to the ship and their attempt to obtain access should be reported, as appropriate, to the SSOs, the CSOs, the Port Facility

Security Officer (PFSO) and to the national or local authorities with security responsibilities.

9.13 The SSP should establish the frequency of application of any access controls particularly if they are to be applied on a random, or occasional, basis.

Security Level 1

9.14 At Security Level 1, the SSP should establish the security measures to control access to the ship, where the following may be applied:

.1 checking the identity of all persons seeking to board the ship and confirming their reasons for doing so by checking, for example, joining instructions, passenger tickets, boarding passes, work orders etc;

.2 in liaison with the port facility the ship should ensure that designated secure areas are established in which inspections and searching of persons, baggage (including carry on items), personal effects, vehicles and their contents can take place;

.3 in liaison with the port facility the ship should ensure that vehicles destined to be loaded on board car carriers, RoRo and other passenger ships are subjected to search prior to loading, in accordance with the frequency required in the SSP;

.4 segregating checked persons and their personal effects from unchecked persons and their personal effects;

.5 segregating embarking from disembarking passengers;

.6 identification of access points that should be secured or attended to prevent unauthorized access;

.7 securing, by locking or other means, access to unattended spaces adjoining areas to which passengers and visitors have access; and

.8 providing security briefings to all ship personnel on possible threats, the procedures for reporting suspicious persons, objects or activities and the need for vigilance.

9.15 At Security Level 1, all those seeking to board a ship should be liable to search. The frequency of such searches, including random searches, should be specified in the approved SSP and should be specifically approved by the Administration. Such searches may best be undertaken by the port facility in close co-operation with the ship and in close proximity to it. Unless there are clear security grounds for doing so, members of the ship's personnel should not be required to search their colleagues or their personal effects. Any such search shall be undertaken in a manner which fully takes into account the human rights of the individual and preserves their basic human dignity.

Security Level 2

9.16 At Security Level 2, the SSP should establish the security measures to be applied to protect against a heightened risk of a security incident to ensure higher vigilance and tighter control, which may include:

Margin notes:

- frequency of access controls

Access to ship at Security Level 1:

- ID check

- ship/port inspection areas

- vehicle checking on RoRo and passenger vessels

- segregation of checked/unchecked; boarding/leaving

- attended access

- unattended space

- crew security briefings

- searching of persons boarding

- crew searches

- human rights

Access to ship at Security Level 2:

- enhanced measures

Access to ship at Security Level 2 (contd):

– measures

.1 assigning additional personnel to patrol deck areas during silent hours to deter unauthorized access;

.2 limiting the number of access points to the ship, identifying those to be closed and the means of adequately securing them;

.3 deterring waterside access to the ship, including, for example, in liaison with the port facility, provision of boat patrols;

.4 establishing a restricted area on the shore-side of the ship, in close co-operation with the port facility;

.5 increasing the frequency and detail of searches of persons, personal effects, and vehicles being embarked or loaded onto the ship;

.6 escorting visitors on the ship;

.7 providing additional specific security briefings to all ship personnel on any identified threats, re-emphasising the procedures for reporting suspicious persons, objects, or activities and the stressing the need for increased vigilance; and

.8 carrying out a full or partial search of the ship.

Access to ship at Security Level 3:

Security Level 3

9.17 At Security Level 3, the ship should comply with the instructions issued by those responding to the security incident or threat thereof. The SSP should detail the security measures which could be taken by the ship, in close co-operation with those responding and the port facility, which may include:

– measures

.1 limiting access to a single, controlled, access point;

.2 granting access only to those responding to the security incident or threat thereof;

.3 directions of persons on board;

.4 suspension of embarkation or disembarkation;

.5 suspension of cargo handling operations, deliveries etc;

.6 evacuation of the ship;

.7 movement of the ship; and

.8 preparing for a full or partial search of the ship.

Restricted areas on the ship:

Restricted areas on the ship

9.18 The SSP should identify the restricted areas to be established on the ship, specify their extent, times of application, the security measures to be taken to control access to them and those to be taken to control activities within them. The purpose of restricted areas are to:

– purpose

.1 prevent unauthorized access;

.2 protect passengers, ship's personnel, and personnel from port facilities or other agencies authorized to be on board the ship;

.3 protect sensitive security areas within the ship; and

.4 protect cargo and ship's stores from tampering.

– policies and practices

9.19 The SSP should ensure that there are clearly established policies and practices to control access to all restricted areas them.

ISPS Code – Part B (Guidance)

9.20 The SSP should provide that all restricted areas should be clearly marked indicating that access to the area is restricted and that unauthorized presence within the area constitutes a breach of security.

– marking of restricted access areas

9.21 Restricted areas may include:

- .1 navigation bridge, machinery spaces of category A and other control stations as defined in Chapter II-2;
- .2 spaces containing security and surveillance equipment and systems and their controls and lighting system controls;
- .3 ventilation and air-conditioning systems and other similar spaces;
- .4 spaces with access to potable water tanks, pumps, or manifolds;
- .5 spaces containing dangerous goods or hazardous substances;
- .6 spaces containing cargo pumps and their controls;
- .7 cargo spaces and spaces containing ship's stores;
- .8 crew accommodation; and
- .9 any other areas as determined by the CSO, through the SSA to which access must be restricted to maintain the security of the ship.

– scope and examples of restricted areas

Security Level 1

9.22 At Security Level 1, the SSP should establish the security measures to be applied to restricted areas, which may include:

- .1 locking or securing access points;
- .2 using surveillance equipment to monitor the areas;
- .3 using guards or patrols; and
- .4 using automatic intrusion detection devices to alert the ship's personnel of unauthorized access.

Restricted areas on the ship at Security Level 1:

– security measures

Security Level 2

9.23 At Security Level 2, the frequency and intensity of the monitoring of, and control of access to restricted areas should be increased to ensure that only authorized persons have access. The SSP should establish the additional security measures to be applied, which may include:

- .1 establishing restricted areas adjacent to access points;
- .2 continuously monitoring surveillance equipment; and
- .3 dedicating additional personnel to guard and patrol restricted areas.

Restricted areas on the ship at Security Level 2:

– additional security measures

Security Level 3

9.24 At Security Level 3, the ship should comply with the instructions issued by those responding to the security incident or threat thereof. The SSP should detail the security measures which could be taken by the ship, in close co-operations with those responding and the port facility, which may include:

- .1 setting up of additional restricted areas on the ship in proximity to the security incident, or the believed location of

Restricted areas on the ship at Security Level 3:

– enhanced security measures

the security threat, to which access is denied; and

.2 searching of restricted areas as part of a search of the ship.

Handling of Cargo:
– general

– inventory control

– tampering with
cargo

Handling of Cargo
at Security Level 1:

– measures to
check cargo

– procedures to
check cargo

– frequent cargo
movements and
off-site checking
and sealing

Handling of Cargo
at Security Level 2:

– additional
security measures

Handling of cargo

9.25 The security measures relating to cargo handling should:

.1 prevent tampering; and

.2 prevent cargo that is not meant for carriage from being accepted and stored on board the ship.

9.26 The security measures, some of which may have to be applied in liaison with the port facility, should include inventory control procedures at access points to the ship. Once on board the ship, cargo should be capable of being identified as having been approved for loading onto the ship. In addition, security measures should be developed to ensure that cargo, once on board, is not tampered with.

Security Level 1

9.27 At Security Level 1, the SSP should establish the security measures to be applied during cargo handling, which may include:

.1 routine checking of cargo, cargo transport units and cargo spaces prior to, and during, cargo handling operations;

.2 checks to ensure that cargo being loaded matches the cargo documentation;

.3 ensuring, in liaison with the port facility, that vehicles to be loaded on board car-carriers, RoRo and passenger ships are subjected to search prior to loading, in accordance with the frequency required in the SSP; and

.4 checking of seals or other methods used to prevent tampering.

9.28 Checking of cargo may be accomplished by the following means:

.1 visual and physical examination; and

.2 using scanning/detection equipment, mechanical devices, or dogs.

9.29 When there are regular, or repeated, cargo movement the CSO or SSO may, in consultation with the port facility, agree arrangements with shippers or others responsible for such cargo covering off-site checking, sealing, scheduling, supporting documentation, etc. Such arrangements should be communicated to and agreed with the PFSO concerned.

Security Level 2

9.30 At Security Level 2, the SSP should establish the additional security measures to be applied during cargo handling, which may include:

.1 detailed checking of cargo, cargo transport units and cargo spaces;

.2 intensified checks to ensure that only the intended cargo is loaded;

.3 intensified searching of vehicles to be loaded on car-carriers, RoRo and passenger ships; and

.4 increased frequency and detail in checking of seals or other methods used to prevent tampering.

9.31 Detailed checking of cargo may be accomplished by the following means:

.1 increasing the frequency and detail of visual and physical examination;

.2 increasing the frequency of the use of scanning/detection equipment, mechanical devices, or dogs; and

.3 co-ordinating enhanced security measures with the shipper or other responsible party in accordance with an established agreement and procedures.

Security Level 3

9.32 At Security Level 3, the ship should comply with the instructions issued by those responding to the security incident or threat thereof. The SSP should detail the security measures which could be taken by the ship, in close co-operation with those responding and the port facility, which may include:

.1 suspension of the loading or unloading of cargo; and

.2 verify the inventory of dangerous goods and hazardous substances carried on board, if any, and their location.

Delivery of ship's stores

9.33 The security measures relating to the delivery of ship's stores should:

.1 ensure checking of ship's stores and package integrity;

.2 prevent ship's stores from being accepted without inspection;

.3 prevent tampering; and

.4 prevent ship's stores from being accepted unless ordered.

9.34 For ships regularly using the port facility it may be appropriate to establish procedures involving the ship, its suppliers and the port facility covering notification and timing of deliveries checking to ensure stores match the order prior to being loaded on board; and their documentation. There should always be some way of confirming that stores presented for delivery are accompanied by evidence that they have been ordered by the ship.

Security Level 1

9.35 At Security Level 1, the SSP should establish the security measures to be applied during delivery of ship's stores, which may include:

.1 checking to ensure stores match the order prior to being loaded on board; and

.2 ensuring immediate secure stowage of ship's stores.

Security Level 2

9.36 At Security Level 2, the SSP should establish the additional security measures to be applied during delivery of ship's stores by exercising checks prior to receiving stores on board and intensifying inspections.

Handling of Cargo at Security Level 2 (contd):

– detailed checking of cargo

Handling of Cargo at Security Level 3:

– suspension of cargo operations

– verification of inventory

Delivery of Ship's Stores:

– general measures

– for ships regularly visiting same port

Delivery of Ship's Stores at Security Level 1:

– security measures

Delivery of Ship's Stores at Security Level 2:

– additional security measures

ISPS Code – Part B (Guidance)

Security Level 3

9.37 At Security Level 3, the ship should comply with the instructions issued by those responding to the security incident or threat thereof. The SSP should detail the security measures which could be taken by the ship, in close co-operation with those responding and the port

facility, which may include:

   .1 subjecting ship's stores to more extensive checking;

   .2 preparation for restriction or suspension of handling of ship's stores; and

   .3 refusal to accept ship's stores on board the ship.

Handling unaccompanied baggage

9.38 The SSP should establish the security measures to be applied to ensure that unaccompanied baggage (i.e. any baggage, including personal effects, which is not with the passenger or member of ship's personnel at the point of inspection or search) is identified and subjected to appropriate screening, including searching, before it is accepted on board the ship. It is not envisaged that such baggage will be subjected to screening by both the ship and the port facility, and in cases where both are suitably equipped, the responsibility for screening should rest with the port facility. Close co-operation with the port facility is essential and steps should be taken to ensure that unaccompanied baggage is handled securely after screening.

Security Level 1

9.39 At Security Level 1, the SSP should establish the security measures to be applied when handling unaccompanied baggage to ensure that unaccompanied baggage is screened or searched up to and including 100 percent, which may include use of x-ray screening.

Security Level 2

9.40 At Security Level 2, the SSP should establish the additional security measures to be applied when handling unaccompanied baggage which should include 100 percent x-ray screening of all unaccompanied baggage.

Security Level 3

9.41 At Security Level 3, the ship should comply with the instructions issued by those responding to the security incident or threat thereof. The SSP should detail the security measures which could be taken by the ship, in close co-operation with those responding and the port facility, which may include:

   .1 subjecting such baggage to more extensive screening, for example x-raying it from at least two different angles;

   .2 preparation for restriction or suspension of handling of unaccompanied baggage; and

   .3 refusal to accept unaccompanied baggage on board the ship.

ISPS Code – Part B (Guidance)

Monitoring the Security of the Ship

9.42 The ship should have the capability to monitor the ship, the restricted areas on board and areas surrounding the ship. Such monitoring capabilities may include use of:

.1 lighting;

.2 watch-keepers, security guards and deck watches including patrols; and

.3 automatic intrusion detection devices and surveillance equipment.

9.43 When used, automatic intrusion detection devices should activate an audible and/or visual alarm at a location that is continuously attended or monitored.

9.44 The SSP should establish the procedures and equipment needed at each security level and the means of ensuring that monitoring equipment will be able to perform continually, including consideration of the possible effects of weather conditions or of power disruptions.

Security Level 1

9.45 At Security Level 1, the SSP should establish the security measures to be applied which may be a combination of lighting, watch keepers, security guards or use of security and surveillance equipment to allow ship's security personnel to observe the ship in general, and barriers and restricted areas in particular.

9.46 The ship's deck and access points to the ship should be illuminated during hours of darkness and periods of low visibility while conducting ship/port interface activities or at a port facility or anchorage when necessary. While underway, when necessary, ships should use the maximum lighting available consistent with safe navigation, having regard to the provisions of the International Regulations for the Prevention of Collisions at Sea in force. The following should be considered when establishing the appropriate level and location of lighting:

.1 the ship's personnel should be able to detect activities beyond the ship, on both the shore side and the waterside;

.2 coverage should include the area on and around the ship;

.3 coverage should facilitate personnel identification at access points; and

.4 coverage may be provided through coordination with the port facility.

Security Level 2

9.47 At Security Level 2, the SSP should establish the additional security measures to be applied to enhance the monitoring and surveillance capabilities, which may include:

.1 increasing the frequency and detail of security patrols;

.2 increasing the coverage and intensity of lighting or the use of security and surveillance and equipment;

.3 assigning additional personnel as security lookouts; and

Monitoring the Security of the Ship:

– restricted areas and ship environs

– automatic intrusion devices

– performance of security monitoring equipment

Monitoring the Security of the Ship at Security Level 1:

– general measures

– illumination of deck areas in port and underway

Monitoring the Security of the Ship at Security Level 2:

– additional security measures

Monitoring the Security of the Ship at Security Level 2 (contd):

– additional lighting

Monitoring the Security of the Ship at Security Level 3:

– ship and port measures

Differing Security Levels:

– measures to adopt

Activities not covered by the Code:

– criteria for ship's procedures and security measures

.4 ensuring coordination with waterside boat patrols, and foot or vehicle patrols on the shore-side, when provided.

9.48 Additional lighting may be necessary to protect against a heightened risk of a security incidents. When necessary, the additional lighting requirements may be accomplished by coordinating with the port facility to provide additional shore side lighting.

Security Level 3
9.49 At Security Level 3, the ship should comply with the instructions issued by those responding to the security incident or threat thereof. The SSP should detail the security measures which could be taken by the ship, in close co-operation with those responding and the port facility, which may include:

.1 switching on of all lighting on, or illuminating the vicinity of, the ship;

.2 switching on of all on board surveillance equipment capable of recording activities on, or in the vicinity of, the ship;

.3 maximising the length of time such surveillance equipment can continue to record;

.4 preparation for underwater inspection of the hull of the ship; and

.5 initiation of measures, including the slow revolution of the ship's propellers, if practicable, to deter underwater access to the hull of the ship.

Differing security levels
9.50 The SSP should establish details of the procedures and security measures the ship could adopt if the ship is at a higher security level than that applying to a port facility.

Activities not covered by the Code
9.51 The SSP should establish details of the procedures and security measures the ship should apply when:

.1 it is at a port of a State which is not a Contracting Government;

.2 it is interfacing with a ship to which this Code does not apply*;

.3 it is interfacing with fixed or floating platforms or a mobile drilling unit on location; or

.4 it is interfacing with a port or port facility which is not required to comply with Chapter XI-2 and Part A of this Code.

---

* Refer to: "Further work by the International Maritime Organization pertaining to Enhancement of maritime security and to Establishment of appropriate measures to enhance the security of ships, port facilities, mobile offshore drilling units on location and fixed and floating platforms not covered by Chapter XI–2 of the 1974 SOLAS Convention", adopted by the Conference on Maritime Security by Resolutions 3 and 7 respectively. (see Pages 112 & 119)

ISPS Code – Part B (Guidance)

Declarations of Security

9.52 The SSP should detail how requests for DoS from a port facility will be handled and the circumstances under which the ship itself should request a DoS.

Audit and review

9.53 The SSP should establish how the CSO and the SSO intend to audit the continued effectiveness of the SSP and the procedure to be followed to review, update or amend the SSP.

10   RECORDS

General

10.1 Records should be available to duly authorized officers of Contracting Governments to verify that the provisions of ship security plans are being implemented.

10.2 Records may be kept in any format but should be protected from unauthorized access or disclosure.

11   COMPANY SECURITY OFFICER

Relevant guidance is provided under sections 8, 9 and 13.

12   SHIP SECURITY OFFICER

Relevant guidance is provided under sections 8, 9 and 13.

13   TRAINING, DRILLS AND EXERCISES ON SHIP SECURITY

Training

13.1 The Company Security Officer (CSO) and appropriate shore based Company personnel, and the Ship Security Officer (SSO), should have knowledge of, and receive training, in some or all of the following, as appropriate:

- .1 security administration;
- .2 relevant international conventions, codes and recommendations;
- .3 relevant Government legislation and regulations;
- .4 responsibilities and functions of other security organizations;
- .5 methodology of ship security assessment;
- .6 methods of ship security surveys and inspections;
- .7 ship and port operations and conditions;
- .8 ship and port facility security measures;
- .9 emergency preparedness and response and contingency planning;
- .10 instruction techniques for security training and education, including security measures and procedures;
- .11 handling sensitive security related information and security related communications;

.12 knowledge of current security threats and patterns;

.13 recognition and detection of weapons, dangerous substances and devices;

.14 recognition, on a non discriminatory basis, of characteristics and behavioural patterns of persons who are likely to threaten security;

.15 techniques used to circumvent security measures;

.16 security equipment and systems and their operational limitations;

.17 methods of conducting audits, inspection, control and monitoring;

.18 methods of physical searches and non-intrusive inspections;

.19 security drills and exercises, including drills and exercises with port facilities; and

.20 assessment of security drills and exercises.

Additional training for SSO

13.2 In addition the SSO should have adequate knowledge of, and receive training, in some or all of the following, as appropriate:

.1 the layout of the ship;

.2 the ship security plan and related procedures (including scenario-based training on how to respond);

.3 crowd management and control techniques;

.4 operations of security equipment and systems; and

.5 testing, calibration and whilst at sea maintenance of security equipment and systems.

Shipboard personnel:

– knowledge and ability to undertake security duties

13.3 Shipboard personnel having specific security duties should have sufficient knowledge and ability to perform their assigned duties, including, as appropriate:

.1 knowledge of current security threats and patterns;

.2 recognition and detection of weapons, dangerous substances and devices;

.3 recognition of characteristics and behavioural patterns of persons who are likely to threaten security;

.4 techniques used to circumvent security measures;

.5 crowd management and control techniques;

.6 security related communications;

.7 knowledge of the emergency procedures and contingency plans;

.8 operations of security equipment and systems;

.9 testing, calibration and whilst at sea maintenance of security equipment and systems;

.10 inspection, control, and monitoring techniques; and

.11 methods of physical searches of persons, personal effects, baggage, cargo, and ship's stores.

– knowledge of and familiarity with SSP

13.4 All other shipboard personnel should have sufficient knowledge of and be familiar with relevant provisions of the SSP, including:

.1 the meaning and the consequential requirements of the different security levels;

.2 knowledge of the emergency procedures and contingency plans;

.3 recognition and detection of weapons, dangerous substances and devices;

.4 recognition, on a non discriminatory basis, of characteristics and behavioural patterns of persons who are likely to threaten security; and

.5 techniques used to circumvent security measures.

Drills and exercises

13.5 The objective of drills and exercises is to ensure that shipboard personnel are proficient in all assigned security duties at all security levels and the identification of any security related deficiencies, which need to be addressed.

13.6 To ensure the effective implementation of the provisions of the ship security plan, drills should be conducted at least once every three months. In addition, in cases where more than 25 percent of the ship's personnel has been changed, at any one time, with personnel that has not previously participated in any drill on that ship, within the last 3 months, a drill should be conducted within one week of the change. These drills should test individual elements of the plan such as those security threats listed in paragraph 8.9.

13.7 Various types of exercises which may include participation of company security officers, port facility security officers, relevant authorities of Contracting Governments as well as ship security officers, if available, should be carried out at least once each calendar year with no more than 18 months between the exercises. These exercises should test communications, coordination, resource availability, and response. These exercises may be:

.1 full scale or live;

.2 tabletop simulation or seminar; or

.3 combined with other exercises held such as search and rescue or emergency response exercises.

13.8 Company participation in an exercise with another Contracting Government should be recognized by the Administration.

14   PORT FACILITY SECURITY

Relevant guidance is provided under section 15, 16 and 18.

15   PORT FACILITY SECURITY ASSESSMENT

General

15.1 The Port Facility Security Assessment (PFSA) may be conducted by a Recognized Security Organization (RSO). However, approval of a completed PFSA should only be given by the relevant Contracting Government.

15.2 If a Contracting Government uses a RSO to review or verify compliance of the PFSA, the RSO should not be associated with any other RSO that prepared or assisted in the preparation of that assessment.

15.3 A PFSA should address the following elements within a port facility:

Marginal notes

Drills and exercises

– objective

– drills at least every 3 months or within 1 week of major personnel changes

– exercises each calendar year

– content of exercises

– inter-country participation approvals

PORT FACILITY SECURITY

PORT FACILITY SECURITY ASSESSMENT

– undertakings and approvals

– RSO independence

.1 physical security;
.2 structural integrity;
.3 personnel protection systems;
.4 procedural policies;
.5 radio and telecommunication systems, including computer systems and networks;
.6 relevant transportation infrastructure;
.7 utilities; and
.8 other areas that may, if damaged or used for illicit observation, pose a risk to persons, property, or operations within the port facility.

15.4 Those involved in a PFSA should be able to draw upon expert assistance in relation to:

.1 knowledge of current security threats and patterns;
.2 recognition and detection of weapons, dangerous substances and devices;
.3 recognition, on a non-discriminatory basis, of characteristics and behavioural patterns of persons who are likely to threaten security;
.4 techniques used to circumvent security measures;
.5 methods used to cause a security incident;
.6 effects of explosives on structures and port facility services;
.7 port facility security;
.8 port business practices;
.9 contingency planning, emergency preparedness and response;
.10 physical security measures e.g. fences;
.11 radio and telecommunications systems, including computer systems and networks;
.12 transport and civil engineering; and
.13 ship and port operations.

Identification and evaluation of important assets and infrastructure it is important to protect

15.5 The identification and evaluation of important assets and infrastructure is a process through which the relative importance of structures and installations to the functioning of the port facility can be established. This identification and evaluation process is important because it provides a basis for focusing mitigation strategies on those assets and structures which it is more important to protect from a security incident. This process should take into account potential loss of life, the economic significance of the port, symbolic value, and the presence of Government installations.

15.6 Identification and evaluation of assets and infrastructure should be used to prioritise their relative importance for protection. The primary concern should be avoidance of death or injury. It is also important to consider whether the port facility, structure or installation can continue to function without the asset, and the extent to which rapid re-establishment of normal functioning is possible.

15.7 Assets and infrastructure that should be considered important to protect may include:

.1 accesses, entrances, approaches, and anchorages, manoeuvring and berthing areas;

.2 cargo facilities, terminals, storage areas, and cargo handling equipment;

.3 systems such as electrical distribution systems, radio and telecommunication systems and computer systems and networks;

.4 port vessel traffic management systems and aids to navigation;

.5 power plants, cargo transfer piping, and water supplies;

.6 bridges, railways, roads;

.7 port service vessels, including pilot boats, tugs, lighters etc;

.8 security and surveillance equipment and systems; and

.9 the waters adjacent to the port facility.

15.8 The clear identification of assets and infrastructure is essential to the evaluation of the port facility's security requirements, the prioritisation of protective measures, and decisions concerning the allocation of resources to better protect the port facility. The process may involve consultation with the relevant authorities relating to structures adjacent to the port facility which could cause damage within the facility or be used for the purpose of causing damage to the facility or for illicit observation of the facility or for diverting attention.

Identification of the possible threats to the assets and infrastructure and the likelihood of their occurrence, in order to establish and prioritise security measures

15.9 Possible acts that could threaten the security of assets and infrastructure, and the methods of carrying out those acts, should be identified to evaluate the vulnerability of a given asset or location to a security incident, and to establish and prioritise security requirements to enable planning and resource allocations. Identification and evaluation of each potential act and its method should be based on various factors, including threat assessments by Government agencies. By identifying and assessing threats, those conducting the assessment do not have to rely on worst-case scenarios to guide planning and resource allocations.

15.10 The PFSA should include an assessment undertaken in consultation with the relevant national security organizations to determine:

.1 any particular aspects of the port facility, including the vessel traffic using the facility, which make it likely to be the target of an attack;

.2 the likely consequences in terms of loss of life, damage to property, economic disruption, including disruption to transport systems, of an attack on, or at, the port facility;

.3 the capability and intent of those likely to mount such an attack; and

.4 the possible type, or types, of attack, producing an overall

---

Assets and infrastructure deemed important to protect

– consultation with relevant authorities relating to structures adjacent to port facility

Possible threats, their likelihood and prioritising security measures

– general

– national security organisation input into PFSA

---

assessment of the level of risk against which security measures have to be developed.

15.11 The PFSA should consider all possible threats, which may include the following types of security incidents:

.1 damage to, or destruction of, the port facility or of the ship, e.g. by explosive devices, arson, sabotage or vandalism;

.2 hijacking or seizure of the ship or of persons on board;

.3 tampering with cargo, essential ship equipment or systems or ship's stores;

.4 unauthorized access or use including presence of stowaways;

.5 smuggling weapons or equipment, including weapons of mass destruction;

.6 use of the ship to carry those intending to cause a security incident and their equipment;

.7 use of the ship itself as a weapon or as a means to cause damage or destruction;

.8 blockage; of port entrances, locks, approaches etc; and

.9 nuclear, biological and chemical attack.

15.12 The process should involve consultation with the relevant authorities relating to structures adjacent to the port facility which could cause damage within the facility or be used for the purpose of causing damage to the facility or for illicit observation of the facility or for diverting attention.

Identification, selection, and prioritisation of countermeasures and procedural changes and their level of effectiveness in reducing vulnerability

15.13 The identification and prioritisation of countermeasures is designed to ensure that the most effective security measures are employed to reduce the vulnerability of a port facility or ship/port interface to the possible threats.

15.14 Security measures should be selected on the basis of factors such as whether they reduce the probability of an attack and should be evaluated using information that includes:

.1 security surveys, inspections and audits;

.2 consultation with port facility owners and operators, and owners/operators of adjacent structures if appropriate;

.3 historical information on security incidents; and

.4 operations within the port facility.

Identification of vulnerabilities

15.15 Identification of vulnerabilities in physical structures, personnel protection systems, processes, or other areas that may lead to a security incident can be used to establish options to eliminate or mitigate those vulnerabilities. For example, an analysis might reveal vulnerabilities in a port facility's security systems or unprotected infrastructure such as water supplies, bridges etc that could be resolved through physical measures, e.g. permanent barriers, alarms, surveillance equipment etc.

15.16 Identification of vulnerabilities should include consideration of:

.1 waterside and shore-side access to the port facility and ships berthing at the facility;

.2 structural integrity of the piers, facilities, and associated structures;

.3 existing security measures and procedures, including identification systems;

.4 existing security measures and procedures relating to port services and utilities;

.5 measures to protect radio and telecommunication equipment, port services and utilities, including computer systems and networks;

.6 adjacent areas that may be exploited during, or for, an attack;

.7 existing agreements with private security companies providing waterside/shore-side security services;

.8 any conflicting policies between safety and security measures and procedures;

.9 any conflicting port facility and security duty assignments;

.10 any enforcement and personnel constraints;

.11 any deficiencies identified during training and drills; and

.12 any deficiencies identified during daily operation, following incidents or alerts, the report of security concerns, the exercise of control measures, audits etc.

16 PORT FACILITY SECURITY PLAN

General

16.1 Preparation of the Port Facility Security Plan (PFSP) is the responsibility of the Port Facility Security Officer (PFSO). While the PFSO need not necessarily personally undertake all the duties associated with the post the ultimate responsibility for ensuring that they are properly performed remains with the individual PFSO.

16.2 The content of each individual PFSP should vary depending on the particular circumstances of the port facility, or facilities, it covers. The Port Facility Security (PFSA) will have identified the particular features of the port facility, and of the potential security risks, that have led to the need to appoint a PFSO and to prepare a PFSP. The preparation of the PFSP will require these features, and other local or national security considerations, to be addressed in the PFSP and for appropriate security measures to be established so as to minimise the likelihood of a breach of security and the consequences of potential risks. Contracting Governments may prepare advice on the preparation and content of a PFSP.

16.3 All PFSPs should:

.1 detail the security organization of the port facility,

.2 the organization's links with other relevant authorities and the necessary communication systems to allow the effective continuous operation of the organization and its links with

Identification of vulnerabilities

– considerations

PORT FACILITY SECURITY PLAN

Preparation – responsibilities and duties

Content – identifying features and risks

Contracting Government input

All PFSPs:

– content

others, including ships in port;

.3 detail the basic Security Level 1 measures, both operational and physical, that will be in place;

.4 detail the additional security measures that will allow the port facility to progress without delay to Security Level 2 and, when necessary, to Security Level 3;

.5 provide for regular review, or audit, of the PFSP and for its amendments in response to experience or changing circumstances; and

.6 detail reporting procedures to the appropriate Contracting Governments contact points.

16.4 Preparation of an effective PFSP will rest on a thorough assessment of all issues that relate to the security of the port facility, including, in particular, a thorough appreciation of the physical and operational characteristics of the individual port facility.

16.5 Contracting Government should approve the PFSPs of the port facilities under their jurisdiction. Contracting Governments should develop procedures to assess the continuing effectiveness of each PFSP and may require amendment of the PFSP prior to its initial approval or subsequent to its approval. The PFSP should make provision for the retention of records of security incidents and threats, reviews, audits, training, drills and exercises as evidence of compliance with those requirements.

16.6 The security measures included in the PFSP should be in place within a reasonable period of the PFSP's approval and the PFSP should establish when each measure will be in place. If there is likely to be any delay in their provision this should be discussed with the Contracting Government responsible for approval of the PFSP and satisfactory alternative temporary security measures that provide an equivalent level of security should be agreed to cover any interim period.

16.7 The use of firearms on or near ships and in port facilities may pose particular and significant safety risks, in particular in connection with certain dangerous or hazardous substances and should be considered very carefully. In the event that a Contracting Government decides that it is necessary to use armed personnel in these areas, that Contracting Government should ensure that these personnel are duly authorized and trained in the use of their weapons and that they are aware of the specific risks to safety that are present in these areas. If a Contracting Government authorizes the use of firearms they should issue specific safety guidelines on their use. The PFSP should contain specific guidance on this matter in particular with regard its application to ships carrying dangerous goods or hazardous substances.

Organization and performance of port facility security duties

16.8 In addition to the guidance given under section 16.3, the PFSP should establish the following which relate to all security levels:

.1 the role and structure of the port facility security organization;

.2 the duties, responsibilities and training requirements of all port facility personnel with a security role and the performance measures needed to allow their individual effectiveness to be assessed;

.3 the port facility security organization's links with other national or local authorities with security responsibilities;

.4 the communication systems provided to allow effective and continuous communication between port facility security personnel, ships in port and, when appropriate, with national or local authorities with security responsibilities;

.5 the procedures or safeguards necessary to allow such continuous communications to be maintained at all times;

.6 the procedures and practices to protect security sensitive information held in paper or electronic format;

.7 the procedures to assess the continuing effectiveness of security measures, procedures and equipment, including identification of, and response to, equipment failure or malfunction;

.8 the procedures to allow the submission, and assessment, of reports relating to possible breaches of security or security concerns;

.9 procedures relating to cargo handling;

.10 procedures covering the delivery of ship's stores;

.11 the procedures to maintain, and update, records of dangerous goods and hazardous substances and their location within the port facility;

.12 the means of alerting and obtaining the services of waterside patrols and specialist search teams, including bomb searches and underwater searches;

.13 the procedures for assisting ship security officers in confirming the identity of those seeking to board the ship when requested; and

.14 the procedures for facilitating shore leave for ship's personnel or personnel changes, as well as access of visitors to the ship including representatives of seafarers. welfare and labour organizations.

16.9 The remainder of this section addresses specifically the security measures that could be taken at each security level covering:

.1 access to the port facility;

.2 restricted areas within the port facility;

.3 handling of cargo;

.4 delivery of ship's stores;

.5 handling unaccompanied baggage; and

.6 monitoring the security of the port facility.

Access to the port facility

16.10 The PFSP should establish the security measures covering all means of access to the port facility identified in the PFSA.

16.11 For each of these the PFSP should identify the appropriate locations where access restrictions or prohibitions should be applied

Port facility security duties: organisation and performance (contd)

Specific measures at each Security Level

Access to the port facility

– access restrictions

Access to the port facility (contd):

– port facility personnel and visitors ID system

– persons to be denied access

– location of personnel and vehicle searches

– segregation of checked/unchecked personnel and boarding/leaving passengers

– frequency of access controls

Access to the port facility at Security Level 1:

– control points

for each of the security levels. For each security level the PFSP should specify the type of restriction or prohibition to be applied and the means of enforcing them.

16.12 The PFSP should establish for each security level the means of identification required to allow access to the port facility and for individuals to remain within the port facility without challenge, this may involve developing an appropriate identification system allowing for permanent and temporary identifications, for port facility personnel and for visitors respectively. Any port facility identification system should, when it is practicable to do so, be co-ordinated with that applying to ships that regularly use the port facility. Passengers should be able to prove their identity by boarding passes, tickets, etc., but should not be permitted access to restricted areas unless supervised. The PFSP should establish provisions to ensure that the identification systems are regularly updated, and that abuse of procedures should be subject to disciplinary action.

16.13 Those unwilling or unable to establish their identity and/or to confirm the purpose of their visit when requested to do so should be denied access to the port facility and their attempt to obtain access should be reported to the PFSO and to the national or local authorities with security responsibilities.

16.14 The PFSP should identify the locations where persons, personal effects, and vehicle searches are to be undertaken. Such locations should be covered to facilitate continuous operation regardless of prevailing weather conditions, in accordance with the frequency laid down in the PFSP. Once subjected to search persons, personal effects and vehicles should proceed directly to the restricted holding, embarkation or car loading areas.

16.15 The PFSP should establish separate locations for checked and unchecked persons and their effects and if possible separate areas for embarking/disembarking passengers, ship's personnel and their effects to ensure that unchecked persons are not able to come in contact with checked persons.

16.16 The PFSP should establish the frequency of application of any access controls particularly if they are to be applied on a random, or occasional, basis.

Security Level 1

16.17 At Security Level 1, the PFSP should establish the control points where the following security measures may be applied:

   .1   restricted areas which should be bound by fencing or other barriers to a standard which should be approved by the Contracting Government;

   .2   checking identity of all persons seeking entry to the port facility in connection with a ship, including passengers, ship's personnel and visitors and confirming their reasons for doing so by checking, for example, joining instructions, passenger tickets, boarding passes, work orders, etc;

   .3   checking vehicles used by those seeking entry to the port facility in connection with a ship;

.4 verification of the identity of port facility personnel and those employed within the port facility and their vehicles;

.5 restricting access to exclude those not employed by the port facility or working within it, if they are unable to establish their identity;

.6 undertaking searches of persons, personal effects, vehicles and their contents; and

.7 identification of any access points not in regular use which should be permanently closed and locked.

16.18 At Security Level 1, all those seeking access to the port facility should be liable to search. The frequency of such searches, including random searches, should be specified in the approved PFSP and should be specifically approved by the Contracting Government. Unless there are clear security grounds for doing so, members of the ship's personnel should not be required to search their colleagues or their personal effects. Any such search shall be undertaken in a manner which fully takes into account the human rights of the individual and preserves their basic human dignity.

Security Level 2

16.19 At Security Level 2, the PFSP should establish the additional security measures to be applied, which may include:

.1 assigning additional personnel to guard access points and patrol perimeter barriers;

.2 limiting the number of access points to the port facility, and identify those to be closed and the means of adequately securing them;

.3 providing for means of impeding movement through the remaining access points, e.g. security barriers;

.4 increasing the frequency of searches of persons, personal effects, and vehicles;

.5 deny access to visitors who are unable to provide a verifiable justification for seeking access to the port facility; and

.6 using of patrol vessels to enhance waterside security.

Security Level 3

16.20 At Security Level 3, the port facility should comply with instructions issued by those responding to the security incident or threat thereof. The PFSP should detail the security measures which could be taken by the port facility, in close co-operation with those responding and the ships at the port facility, which may include:

.1 suspension of access to all, or part of, the port facility;

.2 granting access only to those responding to the security incident or threat thereof;

.3 suspension of pedestrian or vehicular movement within all, or part, of the port facility;

.4 increased security patrols within the port facility, if appropriate;

Access to the port facility at Security Level 1 (contd):

– random searches

– respect of human rights

Access to the port facility at Security Level 2:

– additional security measures

Access to the port facility at Security Level 3:

– responding to incident or threat

Access to the port facility at Security Level 3 (contd):

.5 suspension of port operations within all, or part, of the port facility;

.6 direction of vessel movements relating to all, or part, of the port facility; and

.7 evacuation of all, or part of, the port facility.

Restricted areas within the port facility

Port facility restricted areas:

16.21 The PFSP should identify the restricted areas to be established within the port facility, specify their extent, times of application, the security measures to be taken to control access to them and those to be taken to control activities within them. This should also include, in appropriate circumstances, measures to ensure that temporary restricted areas are security swept both before and after that area is established. The purpose of restricted areas is to:

– temporary areas

– purpose of restricted areas

.1 protect passengers, ship's personnel, port facility personnel and visitors, including those visiting in connection with a ship;

.2 protect the port facility;

.3 protect ships using, and serving, the port facility;

.4 protect sensitive security locations and areas within the port facility;

.5 to protect security and surveillance equipment and systems; and

.6 protect cargo and ship's stores from tampering.

– control measures

16.22 The PFSP should ensure that all restricted areas have clearly established security measures to control:

.1 access by individuals;

.2 the entry, parking, loading and unloading of vehicles;

.3 movement and storage of cargo and ship's stores; and

.4 unaccompanied baggage or personal effects.

– marking of restricted areas

16.23 The PFSP should provide that all restricted areas should be clearly marked indicating that access to the area is restricted and that unauthorized presence within the area constitutes a breach of security.

– automatic intrusion devices

16.24 When automatic intrusion detection devices are installed they should alert a control centre which can respond to the triggering of an alarm.

– scope and examples of restricted areas

16.25 Restricted areas may include:

.1 shore and waterside areas immediately adjacent to the ship;

.2 embarkation and disembarkation areas, passenger and ship's personnel holding and processing areas including search points;

.3 areas where loading, unloading or storage of cargo and stores is undertaken;

.4 locations where security sensitive information, including cargo documentation, is held;

.5 areas where dangerous goods and hazardous substances are held;

.6 vessel traffic management system control rooms, aids to navigation and port control buildings, including security and surveillance control rooms;

.7 areas where security and surveillance equipment are stored or located;

.8 essential electrical, radio and telecommunication, water and other utility installations; and

.9 other locations in the port facility where access by vessels, vehicles and individuals should be restricted.

16.26 The security measures may extend, with the agreement of the relevant authorities, to restrictions on unauthorized access to structures from which the port facility can be observed.

– extension of restricted areas to off-site structures

Security Level 1

16.27 At Security Level 1, the PFSP should establish the security measures to be applied to restricted areas, which may include:

Port facility restricted areas at Security Level 1:

.1 provision of permanent or temporary barriers to surround the restricted area whose standard should be accepted by the Contracting Government;

– PFSP general security measures

.2 provision of access points where access can be controlled by security guards when in operation and which can be effectively locked or barred when not in use;

.3 providing passes which must be displayed to identify individuals entitlement to be within the restricted area;

.4 clearly marking vehicles allowed access to restricted areas;

.5 providing guards and patrols;

.6 providing automatic intrusion detection devices, or surveillance equipment or systems to detect unauthorized access into, or movement within restricted areas; and

.7 control of the movement of vessels in the vicinity of ships using the port facility.

Security Level 2

16.28 At Security Level 2, the PFSP should establish the enhancement of the frequency and intensity of the monitoring of, and control of access to, restricted areas. The PFSP should establish the additional security measures, which may include:

Port facility restricted areas at Security Level 2:

– PFSP additional measures

.1 enhancing the effectiveness of the barriers or fencing surrounding restricted areas, including the use of patrols or automatic intrusion detection devices;

.2 reducing the number of access points to restricted areas and enhancing the controls applied at the remaining accesses;

.3 restrictions on parking adjacent to berthed ships;

.4 further restricting access to the restricted areas and movements and storage within them;

.5 use of continuously monitored and recording surveillance equipment;

.6 enhancing the number and frequency of patrols including waterside patrols undertaken on the boundaries of the restricted areas and within the areas;

.7 establishing and restricting access to areas adjacent to the restricted areas; and

.8 enforcing restrictions on access by unauthorized craft to the waters adjacent to ships using the port facility.

Security Level 3

16.29 At Security Level 3, the port facility should comply with the instructions issued by those responding to the security incident or threat thereof. The PFSP should detail the security measures which could be taken by the port facility, in close co-operation with those responding and the ships at the port facility, which may include:

.1 setting up of additional restricted areas within the port facility in proximity to the security incident, or the believed location of the security threat, to which access is denied; and

.2 preparing for the searching of restricted areas as part of a search of all, or part, of the port facility.

Handling of cargo

16.30 The security measures relating to cargo handling should:

.1 prevent tampering; and

.2 prevent cargo that is not meant for carriage from being accepted and stored within the port facility.

16.31 The security measures should include inventory control procedures at access points to the port facility. Once within the port facility cargo should be capable of being identified as having been checked and accepted for loading onto a ship or for temporary storage in a restricted area while awaiting loading. It may be appropriate to restrict the entry of cargo to the port facility that does not have a confirmed date for loading.

Security Level 1

16.32 At Security Level 1, the PFSP should establish the security measures to be applied during cargo handling, which may include:

.1 routine checking of cargo, cargo transport units and cargo storage areas within the port facility prior to, and during, cargo handling operations;

.2 checks to ensure that cargo entering the port facility matches the delivery note or equivalent cargo documentation;

.3 searches of vehicles; and

.4 checking of seals and other methods used to prevent tampering upon entering the port facility and upon storage within the port facility.

16.33 Checking of cargo may be accomplished by some or all of the following means:

.1 visual and physical examination; and

.2 using scanning/detection equipment, mechanical devices, or dogs.

16.34 When there are regular, or repeated, cargo movement the Company Security Officer (CSO) or the Ship Security Officer (SSO) may, in consultation with the port facility, agree arrangements with shippers or others responsible for such cargo covering off-site checking, sealing, scheduling, supporting documentation, etc. Such arrangements should be communicated to and agreed with the PFSO concerned.

Security Level 2

16.35 At Security Level 2, the PFSP should establish the additional security measures to be applied during cargo handling to enhance control, which may include:

.1 detailed checking of cargo, cargo transport units and cargo storage areas within the port facility;

.2 intensified checks, as appropriate, to ensure that only the documented cargo enters the port facility, is temporarily stored there and then loaded onto the ship;

.3 intensified searches of vehicles; and

.4 increased frequency and detail in checking of seals and other methods used to prevent tampering.

16.36 Detailed checking of cargo may be accomplished by some or all of the following means:

.1 increasing the frequency and detail of checking of cargo, cargo transport units and cargo storage areas within the port facility (visual and physical examination);

.2 increasing the frequency of the use of scanning/detection equipment, mechanical devices, or dogs; and

.3 co-ordinating enhanced security measures with the shipper or other responsible party in addition to an established agreement and procedures.

Security Level 3

16.37 At Security Level 3, the port facility should comply with the instructions issued by those responding to the security incident or threat thereof. The PFSP should detail the security measures which could be taken by the port facility, in close co-operation with those responding and the ships at the port facility, which may include:

.1 restriction or suspension of cargo movements or operations within all, or part, of the port facility or specific ships; and

.2 verifying the inventory of dangerous goods and hazardous substances held within the port facility and their location.

Delivery of ship's stores

16.38 The security measures relating to the delivery of ship's stores should:

.1 ensure checking of ship's stores and package integrity;

.2 prevent ship's stores from being accepted without inspection;

.3 prevent tampering;

.4 prevent ship's stores from being accepted unless ordered;

.5 ensure searching the delivery vehicle; and

.6 ensure escorting delivery vehicles within the port facility.

16.39 For ships regularly using the port facility it may be appropriate to establish procedures involving the ship, its suppliers and the port

Handling of Cargo at Security Level 2:

– PFSP additional measures

– detailed checking of cargo

Handling of Cargo at Security Level 3:

– enhanced PFSP security measures

Delivery of Ship's Stores

– general measures

– for ships regularly visiting same port

facility covering notification and timing of deliveries and their documentation. There should always be some way of confirming that stores presented for delivery are accompanied by evidence that they have been ordered by the ship.

Delivery of Ship's Stores at Security Level 1:

– security measures

Security Level 1

16.40 At Security Level 1, the PFSP should establish the security measures to be applied to control the delivery of ship's stores, which may include:

.1 checking of ship's stores;

.2 advance notification as to composition of load, driver details and vehicle registration; and

.3 searching the delivery vehicle.

– means of checking ship's stores

16.41 Checking of ship's stores may be accomplished by some or all of the following means:

.1 visual and physical examination; and

.2 using scanning/detection equipment, mechanical devices or dogs.

Delivery of Ship's Stores at Security Level 2:

– additional security measures

Security Level 2

16.42 At Security Level 2, the PFSP should establish the additional security measures to be applied to enhance the control of the delivery of ship's stores, which may include:

.1 detailed checking of ship's stores;

.2 detailed searches of the delivery vehicles;

.3 co-ordination with ship personnel to check the order against the delivery note prior to entry to the port facility; and

.4 escorting the delivery vehicle within the port facility.

– detailed means of checking ship's stores

16.43 Detailed checking of ship's stores may be accomplished by some or all of the following means:

.1 increasing the frequency and detail of searches of delivery vehicles;

.2 increasing the use of scanning/detection equipment, mechanical devices, or dogs; and

.3 restricting, or prohibiting, entry of stores that will not leave the port facility within a specified period.

Delivery of Ship's Stores at Security Level 3:

– enhanced security measures

Security Level 3

16.44 At Security Level 3, the port facility should comply with the instructions issued by those responding to the security incident or threat thereof. The PFSP should detail the security measures which could be taken by the port facility, in close co-operation with those responding and the ships at the port facility which may include preparation for restriction, or suspension, of the delivery of ship's stores within all, or part, of the port facility.

Handling Unaccompanied Baggage

Handling unaccompanied baggage

16.45 The PFSP should establish the security measures to be applied to ensure that unaccompanied baggage (i.e. any baggage, including

ISPS Code – Part B (Guidance)

personal effects, which is not with the passenger or member of ship's personnel at the point of inspection or search) is identified and subjected to appropriate screening, including searching, before is allowed in the port facility and, depending on the storage arrangements, before it is transferred between the port facility and the ship. It is not envisaged that such baggage will be subjected to screening by both the port facility and the ship, and in cases where both are suitably equipped, the responsibility for screening should rest with the port facility. Close co-operation with the ship is essential and steps should be taken to ensure that unaccompanied baggage is handled securely after screening.

Security Level 1
16.46 At Security Level 1, the PFSP should establish the security measures to be applied when handling unaccompanied baggage to ensure that unaccompanied baggage is screened or searched up to and including 100 percent, which may include use of x-ray screening.

Security Level 2
16.47 At Security Level 2, the PFSP should establish the additional security measures to be applied when handling unaccompanied baggage which should include 100 percent x-ray screening of all unaccompanied baggage.

Security Level 3
16.48 At Security Level 3, the port facility should comply with the instructions issued by those responding to the security incident or threat thereof. The PFSP should detail the security measures which could be taken by the port facility, in close co-operation with those responding and the ships at the port facility, which may include:
  .1 subjecting such baggage to more extensive screening, for example x-raying it from at least two different angles;
  .2 preparations for restriction or suspension of handling or unaccompanied baggage; and
  .3 refusal to accept unaccompanied baggage into the port facility.

Monitoring the security of the port facility
16.49 The port facility security organization should have the capability to monitor the port facility and its nearby approaches, on land and water, at all times, including the night hours and periods of limited visibility, the restricted areas within the port facility, the ships at the port facility and areas surrounding ships. Such monitoring can include use of:
  .1 lighting;
  .2 security guards, including foot, vehicle and waterborne patrols; and
  .3 automatic intrusion detection devices and surveillance equipment.

Handling of unaccompanied baggage

Handling of unaccompanied baggage at Security Level 1:

Handling of unaccompanied baggage at Security Level 2:

Handling of unaccompanied baggage at Security Level 3:

Monitoring the Security of the Port Facility

– on land and water in all visibility conditions

Monitoring the
Security of the Port
Facility (contd):
– automatic intrusion
devices

– performance of
security monitoring
equipment

Monitoring the
Security of the
Port Facility at
Security Level 1:

– general measures

Monitoring the
Security of the
Port Facility at
Security Level 2:

– additional security
measures

Monitoring the
Security of the
Port Facility at
Security Level 3:

– additional
response measures

PFSP at Differing
Security Levels:
– measures to adopt

16.50 When used, automatic intrusion detection devices should activate an audible and/or visual alarm at a location that is continuously attended or monitored.

16.51 The PFSP should establish the procedures and equipment needed at each security level and the means of ensuring that monitoring equipment will be able to perform continually, including consideration of the possible effects of weather or of power disruptions.

Security Level 1

16.52 At Security Level 1, the PFSP should establish the security measures to be applied which may be a combination of lighting, security guards or use of security and surveillance equipment to allow port facility security personnel to:

.1 observe the general port facility area, including shore and water-side accesses to it;

.2 observe access points, barriers and restricted areas; and

.3 allow port facility security personnel to monitor areas and movements adjacent to ships using the port facility, including augmentation of lighting provided by the ship itself.

Security Level 2

16.53 At Security Level 2, the PFSP should establish the additional security measures to be applied to enhance the monitoring and surveillance capability, which may include:

.1 increasing the coverage and intensity of lighting and surveillance equipment, including the provision of additional lighting and surveillance coverage;

.2 increasing the frequency of foot, vehicle or waterborne patrols; and

.3 assigning additional security personnel to monitor and patrol.

Security Level 3

16.54 At Security Level 3, the port facility should comply with the instructions issued by those responding to the security incident or threat thereof. The PFSP should detail the security measures which could be taken by the port facility, in close co-operation with those responding and the ships at the port facility, which may include:

.1 switching on all lighting within, or illuminating the vicinity of, the port facility;

.2 switching on all surveillance equipment capable of recording activities within, or adjacent to, the port facility; and

.3 maximising the length of time such surveillance equipment can continue to record.

Differing security levels

16.55 The PFSP should establish details of the procedures and security measures the port facility could adopt if the port facility is at a lower security level than that applying to a ship.

Activities not covered by the Code

16.56 The PFSP should establish details of the procedures and security measures the port facility should apply when:

.1 it is interfacing with a ship which has been at a port of a State which not a Contracting Government;

.2 it is interfacing with a ship to which this Code does not apply; and

.3 it is interfacing with fixed or floating platforms or mobile offshore drilling units on location.

Declarations of security

16.57 The PFSP should establish the procedures to be followed when on the instructions of the Contracting Government the PFSO requests a Declaration of Security or when a DoS is requested by a ship.

Audit, review and amendment

16.58 The PFSP should establish how the PFSO intends to audit the continued effectiveness of the PFSP and the procedure to be followed to review, update or amend the PFSP.

16.59 The PFSP should be reviewed at the discretion of the PFSO. In addition it should be reviewed:

.1 if the PFSA relating to the port facility is altered;

.2 if an independent audit of the PFSP or the Contracting Government's testing of the port facility security organization identifies failings in the organization or questions the continuing relevance of significant element of the approved PFSP;

.3 following security incidents or threats thereof involving the port facility; and

.4 following changes in ownership or operational control of the port facility.

16.60 The PFSO can recommend appropriate amendments to the approved plan following any review of the plan. Amendments to the PFSP relating to:

.1 proposed changes which could fundamentally alter the approach adopted to maintaining the security of the port facility; and

.2 the removal, alteration or replacement of permanent barriers, security and surveillance equipment and systems etc., previously considered essential in maintaining the security of the port facility;

should be submitted to the Contracting Government that approved the original PFSP for their consideration and approval. Such approval can be given by, or on behalf of, the Contracting Government with, or without, amendments to the proposed changes. On approval of the PFSP the Contracting Government should indicate which procedural or physical alterations have to be submitted to it for approval.

PFSP: Activities not covered by the Code

PFSP: Declarations of Security

Audit and review of the PFSP

Amendments to the PFSP

ISPS Code – Part B (Guidance)

Approval of Port Facility Security Plans

16.61 PFSPs have to be approved by the relevant Contracting Government which should establish appropriate procedures to provide for:

.1 the submission of PFSPs to them;

.2 the consideration of PFSPs;

.3 the approval of PFSPs, with or without amendments;

.4 consideration of amendments submitted after approval; and

.5 procedures for inspecting or auditing the continuing relevance of the approved PFSP.

At all stages steps should be taken to ensure that the contents of the PFSP remains confidential.

Statement of Compliance of a Port Facility

16.62 The Contracting Government within whose territory a port facility is located may issue an appropriate Statement of Compliance of a Port Facility (SoCPF) indicating:

.1 the port facility;

.2 that the port facility complies with the provisions of chapter XI-2 and Part A of the Code;

.3 the period of validity of the SoCPF which should be specified by the Contracting Governments but should not exceed five years; and

.4 the subsequent verification arrangements established by the Contracting Government and a confirmation when these are carried out.

16.63 The Statement of Compliance of a Port Facility should be in the form set out in the appendix to this Part of the Code. If the language used is not Spanish, French or English, the Contracting Government, if it considers it appropriate, may also include a translation into one of these languages.

17 PORT FACILITY SECURITY OFFICER

General

17.1 In those exceptional instances where the Ship Security Officer has questions about the validity of identification documents of those seeking to board the ship for official purposes, the Port Facility Security Officer should assist.

17.2 The Port Facility Security Officer should not be responsible for routine confirmation of the identity of those seeking to board the ship.

In addition other relevant guidance is provided under sections 15, 16 and 18.

ISPS Code – Part B (Guidance)

18 TRAINING, DRILLS AND EXERCISES ON PORT FACILITY SECURITY

Training

18.1 The Port Facility Security Officer should have knowledge and receive training, in some or all of the following, as appropriate:

.1 security administration;

.2 relevant international conventions, codes and recommendations;

.3 relevant Government legislation and regulations;

.4 responsibilities and functions of other security organizations;

.5 methodology of port facility security assessment;

.6 methods of ship and port facility security surveys and inspections;

.7 ship and port operations and conditions;

.8 ship and port facility security measures;

.9 emergency preparedness and response and contingency planning;

.10 instruction techniques for security training and education, including security measures and procedures;

.11 handling sensitive security related information and security related communications;

.12 knowledge of current security threats and patterns;

.13 recognition and detection of weapons, dangerous substances and devices;

.14 recognition, on a non discriminatory basis, of characteristics and behavioural patterns of persons who are likely to threaten the security;

.15 techniques used to circumvent security measures;

.16 security equipment and systems, and their operational limitations;

.17 methods of conducting audits, inspection, control and monitoring;

.18 methods of physical searches and non-intrusive inspections;

.19 security drills and exercises, including drills and exercises with ships; and

.20 assessment of security drills and exercises.

18.2 Port facility personnel having specific security duties should have knowledge and receive training, in some or all of the following, as appropriate:

.1 knowledge of current security threats and patterns;

.2 recognition and detection of weapons, dangerous substances and devices;

.3 recognition of characteristics and behavioural patterns of persons who are likely to threaten security;

.4 techniques used to circumvent security measures;

.5 crowd management and control techniques;

.6 security related communications;

.7 operations of security equipment and systems;

Training of PFSO (contd)

Training of Port Facility personnel

Drills and exercises – port facilities

– drills at least every 3 months

– exercises each calendar year

Verification and Certification of Ships

.8 testing, calibration and maintenance of security equipment and systems;

.9 inspection, control, and monitoring techniques; and

.10 methods of physical searches of persons, personal effects, baggage, cargo, and ship's stores.

18.3 All other port facility personnel should have knowledge of and be familiar with relevant provisions of the PFSP, in some or all of the following, as appropriate:

.1 the meaning and the consequential requirements of the different security levels;

.2 recognition and detection of weapons, dangerous substances and devices;

.3 recognition of characteristics and behavioural patterns of persons who are likely to threaten the security; and

.4 techniques used to circumvent security measures.

Drills and exercises

18.4 The objective of drills and exercises is to ensure that port facility personnel are proficient in all assigned security duties, at all security levels, and to identify any security related deficiencies, which need to be addressed.

18.5 To ensure the effective implementation of the provisions of the port facility security plan, drills should be conducted at least every three months unless the specific circumstances dictate otherwise. These drills should test individual elements of the plan such as those security threats listed in paragraph 15.11.

18.6 Various types of exercises which may include participation of port facility security officers, in conjunction with relevant authorities of Contracting Governments, company security officers, or ship security officers, if available, should be carried out at least once each calendar year with no more than 18 months between the exercises. Requests for the participation of company security officers or ships security officers in joint exercises should be made bearing in mind the security and work implications for the ship. These exercises should test communication, coordination, resource availability and response. These exercises may be:

.1 full scale or live;

.2 tabletop simulation or seminar; or

.3 combined with other exercises held such as emergency response or other port State authority exercises.

19   VERIFICATION AND CERTIFICATION OF SHIPS

No additional guidance.

DECLARATION OF SECURITY

Appendix 1

Form of a
Declaration of
Security between a
Ship and a Port
Facility (DoS)

Sample layout
Page 1

Name of Ship: _____
Port of Registry: _____
IMO Number: _____
Name of Port Facility: _____

This Declaration of Security is valid from .... until ...., for the following activities: ....
.... (list the activities with relevant details) under the following security levels:

Security level(s) for the ship: _____

Security level(s) for the port facility: _____

The port facility and ship agree to the following security measures and responsibilities to ensure compliance with the requirements of Part A of the International Code for the Security of Ships and of Port Facilities.

Activity	The affixing of the initials of the SSO or PFSO under these columns indicates that the activity will be done, in accordance with relevant approved plan, by	
	The ship:	The port facility:
Ensuring the performance of all security duties		
Monitoring restricted areas to ensure that only authorized personnel have access		
Controlling access to the port facility		
Controlling access to the ship		
Monitoring of the port facility, including berthing areas and areas surrounding the ship		
Monitoring of the ship, including berthing areas and areas surrounding the ship		
Handling of cargo		
Delivery of ship's stores		

* This form of Declaration of Security is for use between a ship and a port facility. If the Declaration of Security is to cover two ships this model should be appropriately modified. (Official Text)

Appendices to Part B

Activity	The ship:	The port facility:
Handling unaccompanied baggage		
Controlling the embarkation of persons and their effects		
Ensuring that security communication is readily available between the ship and port facility		

The signatories to this agreement certify that security measures and arrangements for both the port facility and the ship during the specified activities meet the provisions of Chapter XI-2 and Part A of Code that will be implemented in accordance with the provisions already stipulated in their approved plan or the specific arrangements agreed to and set out in the attached annex

Dated at ....on the ....

Signed for and on behalf of	
the ship:	the port facility:

(Signature of Master or Ship Security Officer)   *(Signature of Port Facility Security Officer)*

Name and title of person who signed	
Name: Title:	Name: Title :

Contact Details *(to be completed as appropriate)* *(indicate the telephone numbers or the radio channels or frequencies to be used)*	
for the ship:	for the port facility:

Master: Port Facility:

Ship Security Officer: Port Facility Security Officer:

Company:

Company Security Officer:

Appendices to Part B

Appendix 2

Form of a Statement
of Compliance of a
Port Facility (SoCPF)

Sample layout

STATEMENT OF COMPLIANCE
OF A PORT FACILITY

(Official seal)   *(State)*

Statement Number: . . . .

Issued under the provisions of Part B of the
INTERNATIONAL CODE FOR THE SECURITY OF
SHIPS AND OF PORT FACILITIES (ISPS CODE)

The Government of . . . .
(name of the State)

Name of the Port Facility :   . . . .
Address of the Port Facility :   . . . .

THIS IS TO CERTIFY that the compliance of this port facility with
the provisions of Chapter XI-2 and Part A of the International Code
for the Security of Ships and of Port Facilities (ISPS Code) has been
verified and that this port facility operates in accordance with the
approved Port Facility Security Plan. This plan has been approved
for the following *<specify the types of operations, types of ship or
activities or other relevant information>* (delete as appropriate):

> Passenger ship
> Passenger high speed craft
> Cargo high speed craft
> Bulk carrier
> Oil tanker
> Chemical tanker
> Gas carrier
> Mobile offshore Drilling Units
> Cargo ships other than those referred to above

This Statement of Compliance is valid until . . . ., subject to
verifications (as indicated overleaf)

Issued at: . . . .
(place of issue of the statement)

Date of issue: . . . .
(Signature of the duly authorized official issuing the document)

(Seal or stamp of issuing authority, as appropriate)

ENDORSEMENT FOR VERIFICATIONS

The Government of *<insert name of the State>* has established that the validity of this Statement of Compliance is subject to *<insert relevant details of the verifications (e.g. mandatory annual or unscheduled)>*.

THIS IS TO CERTIFY that, during a verification carried out in accordance with paragraph B/16.62.4 of the ISPS Code, the port facility was found to comply with the relevant provisions of Chapter XI-2 of the Convention and Part A of the ISPS Code.

1st VERIFICATION

    Signed: . . . .
    (Signature of authorized official)

    Place: . . . .

    Date: . . . .

2nd VERIFICATION

    Signed: . . . .
    (Signature of authorized official)

    Place: . . . .

    Date: . . . .

3rd VERIFICATION

    Signed: . . . .
    (Signature of authorized official)

    Place: . . . .

    Date: . . . .

4th VERIFICATION

    Signed: . . . .
    (Signature of authorized official)

    Place: . . . .

    Date: . . . .

****

Amendments to SOLAS 1974

The Conference of
Contracting
Governments to the
International
Convention for the
Safety of Life at Sea,
1974, as Adopted on
12 December 2002

Resolution 1

Amendments to
existing SOLAS
Chapter V and
Chapter XI,

and new
Chapter XI-2

ADOPTION OF AMENDMENTS TO THE ANNEX TO THE INTERNATIONAL CONVENTION FOR THE SAFETY OF LIFE AT SEA, 1974

The Conference

Bearing in Mind the purposes and principles of the Charter of the United Nations concerning the maintenance of international peace and security and the promotion of friendly relations and co-operation among States,

Deeply Concerned about the world-wide escalation of acts of terrorism in all its forms, which endanger or take innocent human lives, jeopardize fundamental freedoms and seriously impair the dignity of human beings,

Being Aware of the importance and significance of shipping to the world trade and economy and, therefore, being determined to safeguard the worldwide supply chain against any breach resulting from terrorist attacks against ships, ports, offshore terminals or other facilities,

Considering that unlawful acts against shipping jeopardize the safety and security of persons and property, seriously affect the operation of maritime services and undermine the confidence of the peoples of the world in the safety of maritime navigation,

Considering that the occurrence of such acts is a matter of grave concern to the international community as a whole, while also recognizing the importance of the efficient and economic movement of world trade,

Being Convinced of the urgent need to develop international co-operation between States in devising and adopting effective and practical measures, additional to those already adopted by the International Maritime Organization (hereinafter referred to as "the Organization"), to prevent and suppress unlawful acts directed against shipping in its broad sense,

Recalling the United Nations Security Council resolution 1373(2001), adopted on 28 September 2001, requiring States to take measures to prevent and suppress terrorist acts, including calling on States to implement fully anti-terrorist conventions,

Having Noted the Co-operative G8 Action on Transport Security (in particular, the Maritime Security section thereof), endorsed by the G8 Leaders during their Summit in Kananaskis, Alberta (Canada) in June 2002,

Amendments to SOLAS 1974

Recalling article VIII(c) of the International Convention for the Safety of Life at Sea, 1974, as amended (hereinafter referred to as "the Convention"), concerning the procedure for amending the Convention by a Conference of Contracting Governments,

Noting resolution A.924(22) entitled "Review of measures and procedures to prevent acts of terrorism which threaten the security of passengers and crew and the safety of ships", adopted by the Assembly of the Organization on 20 November 2001, which, *inter alia*:

(a) recognizes the need for the Organization to review, with the intent to revise, existing international legal and technical measures, and to consider appropriate new measures, to prevent and suppress terrorism against ships and to improve security aboard and ashore in order to reduce the risk to passengers, crew and post personnel on board ships and in port areas and to the vessels and their cargoes; and

(b) requests the Organization's Maritime Safety Committee, the Legal Committee and the Facilitation Committee under the direction of the Council to undertake, on a high priority basis, a review to ascertain whether there is a need to update the instruments referred to in the preambular paragraphs of the aforesaid resolution and any other relevant IMO instrument under their scope and/or to adopt other security measures and, in the light of such a review, to take action as appropriate;

Having Identified resolution A.584(14) entitled "Measures to prevent unlawful acts which threaten the safety of ships and the security of their passengers and crew", MSC/Circ.443 on "Measures to prevent unlawful acts against passengers and crew on board ships" and MSC/Circ.754 on "Passenger ferry security" among the IMO instruments relevant to the scope of resolution A.924(22),

Recalling resolution 5 entitled "Future amendments to chapter XI of the 1974 SOLAS Convention on special measures to enhance maritime safety", adopted by the 1994 Conference of Contracting Government to the International Convention for the Safety of Life at Sea, 1974,

Having Considered amendments to the Annex of the Convention proposed and circulated to all Members of the Organization and to all Contracting Governments to the Convention,

1. **ADOPTS**, in accordance with article VIII(c)(ii) of the Convention, amendments to the Annex of the Convention, the text of which is given in the Annex to the present resolution;

2. **DETERMINES**, in accordance with article VIII(b)(vi)(2)(bb) of

Resolution 1:

Amendments to existing SOLAS Chapter V and Chapter XI,

and new Chapter XI-2

the Convention, that the aforementioned amendments shall be deemed to have been accepted on 1 January 2004, unless, prior to that date, more than one third of the Contracting Governments to the Convention or Contracting Governments the combined merchant fleets of which constitute not less than 50% of the gross tonnage of the world's merchant fleet, have notified their objections to the amendments;

3. **INVITES** Contracting Governments to the Convention to note that, in accordance with article VIII(b)(vii)(2) of the Convention, the said amendments shall enter into force on 1 July 2004 upon their acceptance in accordance with paragraph 2 above;

4. **REQUESTS** the Secretary-General of the Organization, in conformity with article VIII(b)(v) of the Convention, to transmit certified copies of the present resolution and the text of the amendments contained in the Annex to all Contracting Governments to the Convention;

5. **FURTHER REQUESTS** the Secretary-General to transmit copies of this resolution and its Annex to all Members of the Organization, which are not Contracting Governments to the Convention.

Amendments to SOLAS 1974

AMENDMENTS TO THE ANNEX TO THE INTERNATIONAL CONVENTION FOR THE SAFETY OF LIFE AT SEA, 1974 AS AMENDED

CHAPTER V

SAFETY OF NAVIGATION

Regulation 19
Carriage requirements for shipborne navigational systems and equipment

1   *The existing subparagraphs .4, .5 and .6 of paragraph 2.4.2 are replaced by the following:*

" **.4** in the case of ships, other than passenger ships and tankers, of 300 gross tonnage and upwards but less than 50,000 gross tonnage, not later than the first safety equipment survey* after 1 July 2004 or by 31 December 2004, whichever occurs earlier; and"

2   *The following new sentence is added at the end of the existing subparagraph .7 of paragraph 2.4:*

" Ships fitted with AIS shall maintain AIS in operation at all times except where international agreements, rules or standards provide for the protection of navigational information.

CHAPTER XI

SPECIAL MEASURES TO ENHANCE MARITIME SAFETY

3   *The existing chapter XI is renumbered as chapter XI-1.*

Regulation 3
Ship identification number

4   *The following text is inserted after the title of the regulation:*

" (Paragraphs 4 and 5 apply to all ships to which this regulation applies. For ships constructed before 1 July 2004, the requirements of paragraphs 4 and 5 shall be complied with not later than the first scheduled dry-docking of the ship after 1 July 2004)"

Resolution 1:
Amendments to existing SOLAS Chapter V
Shipborne navigational instruments
– date of application
– operation of AIS at all times
Amendments to existing SOLAS Chapter XI
Re-number Ch XI as Chapter XI-1
– date of application

Amendments to SOLAS 1974

Resolution 1:
Amendments to
Chapter XI

SHIP'S
IDENTIFICATION
NUMBER:

– location on hull

– location in
machinery spaces

– position and
visibility

– size

– method of
permanent marking

– other approved
methods

CONTINUOUS
SYNOPSIS RECORD

– all ships

– on-board record of
ship's history

5   *The existing paragraph 4 is deleted and the following new text is inserted:*

" **4** The ship's identification number shall be permanently marked:

.1 in a visible place either on the stern of the ship or on either side of the hull, amidships port and starboard, above the deepest assigned load line or either side of the superstructure, port and starboard or on the front of the superstructure or, in the case of passenger ships, on a horizontal surface visible from the air; and

.2 in an easily accessible place either on one of the end transverse bulkheads of the machinery spaces, as defined in regulation II-2/3.30, or on one of the hatchways or, in the case of tankers, in the pump-room or, in the case of ships with RoRo spaces, as defined in regulation II-2/3.41, on one of the end transverse bulkheads of the RoRo spaces.

5.1   The permanent marking shall be plainly visible, clear of any other markings on the hull and shall be painted in a contrasting colour.

5.2   The permanent marking referred to in paragraph 4.1 shall be not less than 200 mm in height. The permanent marking referred to in paragraph 4.2 shall not be less than 100 mm in height. The width of the marks shall be proportionate to the height.

5.3   The permanent marking may be made by raised lettering or by cutting it in or by centre punching it or by any other equivalent method of marking the ship identification number which ensures that the marking is not easily expunged.

5.4   On ships constructed of material other than steel or metal, the Administration shall approve the method of marking the ship identification number."

6   *The following new regulation 5 is added after the existing regulation 4:*

" **Regulation 5**
Continuous Synopsis Record

1   Every ship to which chapter I applies shall be issued with a Continuous Synopsis Record.

2.1   The Continuous Synopsis Record is intended to provide an on-board record of the history of the ship with respect to the information recorded therein.

Amendments to SOLAS 1974

2.2 For ships constructed before 1 July 2004, the Continuous Synopsis Record shall, at least, provide the history of the ship as from 1 July 2004.

3 The Continuous Synopsis Record shall be issued by the Administration to each ship that is entitled to fly its flag and it shall contain at least, the following information:

.1 the name of the State whose flag the ship is entitled to fly;

.2 the date on which the ship was registered with that State;

.3 the ship's identification number in accordance with regulation 3;

.4 the name of the ship;

.5 the port at which the ship is registered;

.6 the name of the registered owner(s) and their registered address(es);

.7 the name of the registered bareboat charterer(s) and their registered address(es), if applicable;

.8 the name of the Company, as defined in regulation IX/1, its registered address and the address(es) from where it carries out the safety management activities;

.9 the name of all classification society(ies) with which the ship is classed;

.10 the name of the Administration or of the Contracting Government or of the Recognized Security Organization which has issued the Document of Compliance (or the Interim Document of Compliance), specified in the ISM Code as defined in regulation IX/1, to the Company operating the ship and the name of the body which has carried out the audit on the basis of which the document was issued, if other than that issuing the document;

.11 the name of the Administration or of the Contracting Government or of the recognized organization that has issued the Safety Management Certificate (or the Interim Safety Management Certificate), specified in the ISM Code as defined in regulation IX/1, to the ship and the name of the body which has carried out the audit on the basis of which the certificate was issued, if other than that issuing the certificate;

.12 the name of the Administration or of the Contracting

**Resolution 1:
Continuous Synopsis
Record (contd)**

– older ships

– content:
 – flag

 – registration date

 – ship's ID no.

 – ship's name

 – registered port

 – owners

 – charterers

 – company details

 – class

 – Administration
issued Document
of Compliance
(DoC)

 – Administration
issued ISM
Certificate

**Resolution 1:
Continuous Synopsis
Record (contd)**

**– Administration
issued Ship Security
Certificate**

**– cessation of
registration**

– updating entries

**– issuing of revised
versions or
amendments by
Administration**

**– interim updating
by Master or
Company**

– languages

**– format and
preservation of
earlier entries**

**– transfer of ship to
new owner**

Government or of the Recognized Security Organization that has issued the International Ship Security Certificate (or an Interim International Ship Security Certificate), specified in part A of the ISPS Code as defined in regulation XI-2/1, to the ship and the name of the body which has carried out the verification on the basis of which the certificate was issued, if other than that issuing the certificate; and

.13 the date on which the ship ceased to be registered with that State.

4.1   Any changes relating to the entries referred to in paragraphs 3.4 to 3.12 shall be recorded in the Continuous Synopsis Record so as to provide updated and current information together with the history of the changes.

4.2   In case of any changes relating to the entries referred to in paragraph 4.1, the Administration shall issue, as soon as is practically possible but not later than three months from the date of the change, to the ships entitled to fly its flag either a revised and updated version of the Continuous Synopsis Record or appropriate amendments thereto.

4.3   In case of any changes relating to the entries referred to in paragraph 4.1, the Administration, pending the issue of a revised and updated version of the Continuous Synopsis Record, shall authorise and require either the Company as defined in regulation IX/1 or the master of the ship to amend the Continuous Synopsis Record to reflect the changes. In such cases, after the Continuous Synopsis Record has been amended the Company shall, without delay, inform the Administration accordingly.

5.1   The Continuous Synopsis Record shall be in English, French or Spanish language. Additionally, a translation of the Continuous Synopsis Record into the official language or languages of the Administration may be provided.

5.2   The Continuous Synopsis Record shall be in the format developed by the Organization and shall be maintained in accordance with guidelines developed by the Organization. Any previous entries in the Continuous Synopsis Record shall not be modified, deleted or, in any way, erased or defaced.

6   Whenever a ship is transferred to the flag of another State or the ship is sold to another owner (or is taken over by another bareboat charterer) or another Company assumes the responsibility for the operation of the ship, the Continuous Synopsis Record shall be left on board.

7   When a ship is to be transferred to the flag of another State, the Company shall notify the Administration of the name of the State under whose flag the ship is to be transferred so as to enable the Administration to forward to that State a copy of the Continuous Synopsis Record covering the period during which the ship was under their jurisdiction.

Resolution 1:
Continuous Synopsis Record (contd)

– transfer of ship to new flag

8   When a ship is transferred to the flag of another State the Government of which is a Contracting Government, the Contracting Government of the State whose flag the ship was flying hitherto shall transmit to the Administration as soon as possible after the transfer takes place a copy of the relevant Continuous Synopsis Record covering the period during which the ship was under their jurisdiction together with any Continuous Synopsis Records previous issued to the ship by other States.

9   When a ship is transferred to the flag of another State, the Administration shall append the previous Continuous Synopsis Records to the Continuous Synopsis Record the Administration will issue to the ship so to provide the continuous history record intended by this regulation.

– inter-flag continuity of record

10   The Continuous Synopsis Record shall be kept on board the ship and shall be available for inspection at all times."

– kept on board for inspection

7   *The following new chapter XI-2 is inserted after the renumbered chapter XI-1:*

"CHAPTER XI-2
SPECIAL MEASURES TO ENHANCE MARITIME SECURITY

Regulation 1
Definitions

NEW CHAPTER XI-2
Special Measures to Enhance Maritime Security

1   For the purpose of this chapter, unless expressly provided otherwise:

DEFINITIONS

.1   **Bulk carrier** means a bulk carrier as defined in regulation IX/1.6.

Ship types

.2   **Chemical tanker** means a chemical tanker as defined in regulation VII/8.2.

.3   **Gas carrier** means a gas carrier as defined in regulation VII/11.2.

.4   **High-speed craft** means a craft as defined in regulation X/1.2.

Resolution 1:
New SOLAS
Chapter XI-2 (contd)

Definitions (contd):

– ship/port interface

– port facility

– ship-to-ship
activity

– Designated
Authority

International Code
for the Security of
Ships and of Port
Facilities

– Part A: mandatory
– Part B:
recommendatory

Condition of
adoption:
Part A

Part B

.5 **Mobile offshore drilling unit** means a mechanically propelled mobile offshore drilling unit, as defined in regulation IX/1, not on location.

.6 **Oil tanker** means an oil tanker as defined in regulation II-1/2.12.

.7 **Company** means a Company as defined in regulation IX/1.

.8 **Ship/port interface** means the interactions that occur when a ship is directly and immediately affected by actions involving the movement of persons, goods or the provisions of port services to or from the ship.

.9 **Port Facility** is a location, as determined by the Contracting Government or by the Designated Authority, where the ship/port interface takes place. This includes areas such as anchorages, waiting berths and approaches from seaward, as appropriate.

.10 **Ship to ship activity** means any activity not related to a port facility that involves the transfer of goods or persons from one ship to another.

.11 **Designated Authority** means the organization(s) or the administration(s) identified, within the Contracting Government, as responsible for ensuring the implementation of the provisions of this chapter pertaining to port facility security and ship/port interface, from the point of view of the port facility.

.12 **International Ship and Port Facility Security (ISPS) Code** means the International Code for the Security of Ships and of Port Facilities consisting of Part A (the provisions of which shall be treated as mandatory) and part B (the provisions of which shall be treated as recommendatory), as adopted, on 12 December 2002, by resolution 2 of the Conference of Contracting Governments to the International Convention for the Safety of Life at Sea, 1974 as may be amended by the Organization, provided that:

.1 amendments to part A of the Code are adopted, brought into force and take effect in accordance with article VIII of the present Convention concerning the amendment procedures applicable to the Annex other than chapter I; and

.2 amendments to part B of the Code are adopted by the Maritime Safety Committee in accordance with its Rules of Procedure.

Amendments to SOLAS 1974

.13 Security incident means any suspicious act or circumstance threatening the security of a ship, including a mobile offshore drilling unit and a high speed craft, or of a port facility or of any ship/port interface or any ship to ship activity.

.14 Security level means the qualification of the degree of risk that a security incident will be attempted or will occur.

.15 Declaration of Security means an agreement reached between a ship and either a port facility or another ship with which it interfaces specifying the security measures each will implement.

.16 Recognized Security Organization means an organization with appropriate expertise in security matters and with appropriate knowledge of ship and port operations authorized to carry out an assessment, or a verification, or an approval or a certification activity, required by this chapter or by part A of the ISPS Code.

2 The term "ship", when used in regulations 3 to 13, includes mobile offshore drilling units and high-speed craft.

3 The term **"all ships"**, when used in this chapter, means any ship to which this chapter applies.

4 The term **"Contracting Government"**, when used in regulations 3, 4, 7, 10, 11, 12 and 13 includes a reference to the Designated Authority.

Regulation 2
Application

1 This chapter applies to:

.1 the following types of ships engaged on international voyages:

.1.1 passenger ships, including high-speed passenger craft;

.1.2 cargo ships, including high-speed craft, of 500 gross tonnage and upwards; and

.1.3 mobile offshore drilling units; and

.2 port facilities serving such ships engaged on international voyages.

2 Notwithstanding the provisions of paragraph 1.2,

Resolution 1:
New SOLAS
Chapter XI-2

– security incident

– Security level

– Declaration of Security

Recognised Security Organisation

"Ship" includes rigs and high-speed craft

"all ships"

"Contracting Government"

APPLICATION OF CHAPTER XI-2

Applies to:

– ship types

– port facilities

**Resolution 1:
New SOLAS
Chapter XI-2 (contd)**

**– extent of
application for port
facilities with
occasional
international service**

**– exception for
warships and
non-commercial
Government vessels**

**– compliance with
international law**

**SECURITY –
CONTRACTING
GOVERNMENT'S
OBLIGATIONS:**

**– setting/updating
ship security levels**

**– setting/updating
port security levels
and advising ships**

**REQUIREMENTS
FOR COMPANIES
AND SHIPS**

**– company
compliance**

– ship compliance

Contracting Governments shall decide the extent of application of this chapter and of the relevant sections of part A of the ISPS Code to those port facilities within their territory which, although used primarily by ships not engaged on international voyages, are required, occasionally, to serve ships arriving or departing on an international voyage.

2.1   Contracting Governments shall base their decisions, under paragraph 2, on a port facility security assessment carried out in accordance with the provisions of part A of the ISPS Code.

2.2   Any decision which a Contracting Government makes, under paragraph 2, shall not compromise the level of security intended to be achieved by this chapter or by part A of the ISPS Code.

3   This chapter does not apply to warships, naval auxiliaries or other ships owned or operated by a Contracting Government and used only on Government non-commercial service.

4   Nothing in this chapter shall prejudice the rights or obligations of States under international law.

Regulation 3
Obligations of Contracting Governments with respect to security

1   Administrations shall set security levels and ensure the provision of security level information to ships entitled to fly their flag. When changes in security level occur, security level information shall be updated as the circumstance dictates.

2   Contracting Governments shall set security levels and ensure the provision of security level information to port facilities within their territory, and to ships prior to entering a port or whilst in a port within their territory. When changes in security level occur, security level information shall be updated as the circumstance dictates.

Regulation 4
Requirements for Companies and Ships

1   Companies shall comply with the relevant requirements of this chapter and of part A of the ISPS Code, taking into account the guidance given in part B of the ISPS Code.

2   Ships shall comply with the relevant requirements of this chapter and of part A of the ISPS Code, taking into account the guidance given in part B of the ISPS Code, and such compliance shall be verified and certified as provided for in part A of the ISPS Code.

3   Prior to entering a port or whilst in a port within the territory of a Contracting Government, a ship shall comply with the requirements for the security level set by that Contracting Government, if such security level is higher than the security level set by the Administration for that ship.

4   Ships shall respond without undue delay to any change to a higher security level.

5   Where a ship is not in compliance with the requirements of this chapter or of part A of the ISPS Code, or cannot comply with the requirements of the security level set by the Administration or by another Contracting Government and applicable to that ship, then the ship shall notify the appropriate competent authority prior to conducting any ship/port interface or prior to entry into port, whichever occurs earlier.

Regulation 5
Specific responsibility of Companies

The Company shall ensure that the master has available on board, at all times, information through which officers duly authorised by a Contracting Government can establish:

.1 who is responsible for appointing the members of the crew or other persons currently employed or engaged on board the ship in any capacity on the business of that ship;

.2 who is responsible for deciding the employment of the ship; and

.3 in cases where the ship is employed under the terms of charter party(ies), who are the parties to such charter party(ies).

Regulation 6
Ship security alert system

1   All ships shall be provided with a ship security alert system, as follows:

.1 ships constructed on or after 1 July 2004;

.2 passenger ships, including high-speed passenger craft, constructed before 1 July 2004, not later than the first survey of the radio installation after 1 July 2004;

.3 oil tankers, chemical tankers, gas carriers, bulk carriers and cargo high speed craft, of 500 gross tonnage and upwards constructed before 1 July 2004, not later than the first survey of the radio installation after 1 July 2004; and

---

Resolution 1: New SOLAS Chapter XI-2

– ship's security level prior to port entry

– ship response to raising security level

– ships unable to comply with Part A or set security level

RESPONSIBILITIES OF COMPANIES:

– provision of Master's onboard information

– crew employers

– ship employers

– charterers

SHIP SECURITY ALERT SCHEME

– provision to ship types

.4 other cargo ships of 500 gross tonnage and upward and mobile offshore drilling units constructed before 1 July 2004, not later than the first survey of the radio installation after 1 July 2006.

2   The ship security alert system, when activated, shall:

.1 initiate and transmit a ship-to-shore security alert to a competent authority designated by the Administration, which in these circumstances may include the Company, identifying the ship, its location and indicating that the security of the ship is under threat or it has been compromised;

.2 not send the ship security alert to any other ships;

.3 not raise any alarm on-board the ship; and

.4 continue the ship security alert until deactivated and/or reset.

3   The ship security alert system shall:

.1 be capable of being activated from the navigation bridge and in at least one other location; and

.2 conform to performance standards not inferior to those adopted by the Organization.

4   The ship security alert system activation points shall be designed so as to prevent the inadvertent initiation of the ship security alert.

5   The requirement for a ship security alert system may be complied with by using the radio installation fitted for compliance with the requirements of chapter IV, provided all requirements of this regulation are complied with.

6   When an Administration receives notification of a ship security alert, that Administration shall immediately notify the State(s) in the vicinity of which the ship is presently operating.

7   When a Contracting Government receives notification of a ship security alert from a ship which is not entitled to fly its flag, that Contracting Government shall immediately notify the relevant Administration and, if appropriate, the State(s) in the vicinity of which the ship is presently operating.

Regulation 7
Threats to ships

1   Contracting Governments shall set security levels and

Amendments to SOLAS 1974

ensure the provision of security level information to ships operating in their territorial sea or having communicated an intention to enter their territorial sea.

2   Contracting Governments shall provide a point of contact through which such ships can request advice or assistance and to which such ships can report any security concerns about other ships, movements or communications.

3   Where a risk of attack has been identified, the Contracting Government concerned shall advise the ships concerned and their Administrations of:

.1 the current security level;

.2 any security measures that should be put in place by the ships concerned to protect themselves from attack, in accordance with the provisions of part A of the ISPS Code; and

.3 security measures that the coastal State has decided to put in place, as appropriate.

Regulation 8
Master's discretion for ship safety and security

1   The master shall not be constrained by the Company, the charterer or any other person from taking or executing any decision which, in the professional judgement of the master, is necessary to maintain the safety and security of the ship. This includes denial of access to persons (except those identified as duly authorized by a Contracting Government) or their effects and refusal to load cargo, including containers or other closed cargo transport units.

2   If, in the professional judgement of the master, a conflict between any safety and security requirements applicable to the ship arises during its operations, the master shall give effect to those requirements necessary to maintain the safety of the ship. In such cases, the master may implement temporary security measures and shall forthwith inform the Administration and, if appropriate, the Contracting Government in whose port the ship is operating or intends to enter. Any such temporary security measures under this regulation shall, to the highest possible degree, be commensurate with the prevailing security level. When such cases are identified, the Administration shall ensure that such conflicts are resolved and that the possibility of recurrence is minimised.

Resolution 1: New SOLAS Chapter XI-2

Threats to Ships:

– point of contact for ship advice

Risk of Attack:
– advice to ships and Administrations of:

– security level

– ship security measures

– coastal State security measures

MASTER'S DISCRETION

Freedom to use professional judgement

– denial of access, refusal of cargo

– conflict between safety and security requirements

Regulation 9
Control and compliance measures

1 Control of ships in port

1.1 For the purpose of this chapter, every ship to which this chapter applies is subject to control when in a port of another Contracting Government by officers duly authorised by that Government, who may be the same as those carrying out the functions of regulation I/19. Such control shall be limited to verifying that there is onboard a valid International Ship Security Certificate or a valid Interim International Ships Security Certificate issued under the provisions of part A of the ISPS Code (Certificate), which if valid shall be accepted, unless there are clear grounds for believing that the ship is not in compliance with the requirements of this chapter or part A of the ISPS Code.

1.2 When there are such clear grounds, or where no valid Certificate is produced when required, the officers duly authorized by the Contracting Government shall impose any one or more control measures in relation to that ship as provided in paragraph 1.3. Any such measures imposed must be proportionate, taking into account the guidance given in part B of the ISPS Code.

1.3 Such control measures are as follows: inspection of the ship, delaying the ship, detention of the ship, restriction of operations including movement within the port, or expulsion of the ship from port. Such control measures may additionally or alternatively include other lesser administrative or corrective measures.

2 Ships intending to enter a port of another Contracting Government

2.1 For the purpose of this chapter, a Contracting Government may require that ships intending to enter its ports provide the following information to officers duly authorized by that Government to ensure compliance with this chapter prior to entry into port with the aim of avoiding the need to impose control measures or steps:

.1 that the ship possesses a valid Certificate and the name of its issuing authority;

.2 the security level at which the ship is currently operating;

.3 the security level at which the ship operated in any previous port where it has conducted a ship/port interface within the timeframe specified in paragraph 2.3;

.4 any special or additional security measures that were taken by the ship in any previous port where it has conducted a ship/port

Amendments to SOLAS 1974

interface within the timeframe specified in paragraph 2.3;

.5 that the appropriate ship security procedures were maintained during any ship to ship activity within the timeframe specified in paragraph 2.3; or

.6 other practical security related information (but not details of the ship security plan), taking into account the guidance given in part B of the ISPS Code.

If requested by the Contracting Government, the ship or the Company shall provide confirmation, acceptable to that Contracting Government, of the information required above.

2.2   Every ship to which this chapter applies intending to enter the port of another Contracting Government shall provide the information described in paragraph 2.1 on the request of the officers duly authorized by that Government. The master may decline to provide such information on the understanding that failure to do so may result in denial of entry into port.

2.3   The ship shall keep records of the information referred to in paragraph 2.1 for the last 10 calls at port facilities.

2.4   If, after receipt of the information described in paragraph 2.1, officers duly authorised by the Contracting Government of the port in which the ship intends to enter have clear grounds for believing that the ship is in non-compliance with the requirements of this chapter or part A of the ISPS Code, such officers shall attempt to establish communication with and between the ship and the Administration in order to rectify the non-compliance. If such communication does not result in rectification, or if such officers have clear grounds otherwise for believing that the ship is in non-compliance with the requirements of this chapter or part A of the ISPS Code, such officers may take steps in relation to that ship as provided in paragraph 2.5. Any such steps taken must be proportionate, taking into account the guidance given in part B of the ISPS Code.

2.5   Such steps are as follows:

.1 a requirement for the rectification of the non-compliance;

.2 a requirement that the ship proceed to a location specified in the territorial sea or internal waters of that Contracting Government;

.3 inspection of the ship, if the ship is in the territorial sea of the Contracting Government the port of which the ship intends to enter; or

**Resolution 1:
New SOLAS
Chapter XI-2
Control of ships
entering a foreign
port (contd)
– maintenance of
security measures**

**– other security-
related information**

**– confirmation by all
parties**

**– revision of
information on
request and Master's
right of denial**

**– records for last 10
port visits**

**– establishing
communication with
vessels in non-
compliance**

**– 'proportionate'
action by Contracting
Government officers
for ships in non-
compliance**

**– Step-by-step
action/requirement
for rectification of
non-compliance**

– isolation of ship

– inspection of ship

Resolution 1:
New SOLAS
Chapter XI-2
Control of ships
entering a
foreign port (contd)

– denial of entry

.4 denial of entry into port.

Prior to initiating any such steps, the ship shall be informed by the Contracting Government of its intentions. Upon this information the master may withdraw the intention to enter that port. In such cases, this regulation shall not apply.

3 Additional provisions

Action to be taken by
officers of Contracting
Governments on:

– imposing control
measures

3.1 In the event:

.1 of the imposition of a control measure, other than a lesser administrative or corrective measure, referred to in paragraph 1.3; or

.2 any of the steps referred to in paragraph 2.5 are taken,

an officer duly authorized by the Contracting Government shall forthwith inform in writing the Administration specifying which control measures have been imposed or steps taken and the reasons thereof. The Contracting Government imposing the control measures or steps shall also notify the recognized security organization, which issued the Certificate relating to the ship concerned and the Organization when any such control measures have been imposed or steps taken.

– denying port entry
or expulsion of
the ship

3.2 When entry into port is denied or the ship is expelled from port, the authorities of the port State should communicate the appropriate facts to the authorities of the State of the next appropriate ports of call, when known, and any other appropriate coastal States, taking into account guidelines to be developed by the Organization. Confidentiality and security of such notification shall be ensured.

3.3 Denial of entry into port, pursuant to paragraphs 2.4 and 2.5, or expulsion from port, pursuant to paragraphs 1.1 to 1.3, shall only be imposed where the officers duly authorized by the Contracting Government have clear grounds to believe that the ship poses an immediate threat to the security or safety of persons, or of ships or other property and there are no other appropriate means for removing that threat.

3.4 The control measures referred to in paragraph 1.3 and the steps referred to in paragraph 2.5 shall only be imposed, pursuant to this regulation, until the non-compliance giving rise to the control measures or steps has been corrected to the satisfaction of the Contracting Government, taking into account actions proposed by the ship or the Administration, if any.

3.5 When Contracting Governments exercise control under

Amendments to SOLAS 1974

paragraph 1 or take steps under paragraph 2:

.1 all possible efforts shall be made to avoid a ship being unduly detained or delayed. If a ship is thereby unduly detained, or delayed, it shall be entitled to compensation for any loss or damage suffered; and

.2 necessary access to the ship shall not be prevented for emergency or humanitarian reasons and for security purposes.

Regulation 10
Requirements for port facilities

1   Port facilities shall comply with the relevant requirements of this chapter and part A of the ISPS Code, taking into account the guidance given in part B of the ISPS Code.

2   Contracting Governments with a port facility or port facilities within their territory, to which this regulation applies, shall ensure that:

.1 port facility security assessments are carried out, reviewed and approved in accordance with the provisions of part A of the ISPS Code; and

.2 port facility security plans are developed, reviewed, approved and implemented in accordance with the provisions of part A of the ISPS Code.

3   Contracting Governments shall designate and communicate the measures required to be addressed in a port facility security plan for the various security levels, including when the submission of a Declaration of Security will be required.

Regulation 11
Alternative security agreements

1   Contracting Governments may, when implementing this chapter and part A of the ISPS Code, conclude in writing bilateral or multilateral agreements with other Contracting Governments on alternative security arrangements covering short international voyages on fixed routes between port facilities located within their territories.

2   Any such agreement shall not compromise the level of security of other ships or of port facilities not covered by the agreement.

3   No ship covered by such an agreement shall conduct any

Resolution 1: New SOLAS Chapter XI-2 Control of ships (contd)
– avoiding undue delay to ship
– compensation for delay
– maintaining emergency access

PORT FACILITY REQUIREMENTS

– compliance

– requirements of Contracting Governments

– Port Security Assessments

– Port Security Plans

– designation of measures required at security levels

ALTERNATIVE SECURITY AGREEMENTS

– bilateral or multilateral agreements to cover fixed routes/short international voyages

– ship-to-ship limitations

Amendments to SOLAS 1974

Resolution 1: New
SOLAS Chapter XI-2

Review of alternative
security
arrangements

EQUIVALENT
SECURITY
ARRANGEMENTS

– approval for a ship
or group of ships

– approval for a port
facility or group of
port facilities

COMMUNICATION
OF INFORMATION

Contracting
Governments to
provide:

– national authority
contact details

– locations of
approved port
facilities

– response personnel
for ship-to-shore
alerts and inter-
Government
communications

ship-to-ship activities with any ship not covered by the agreement.

4   Such agreements shall be reviewed periodically, taking into account the experience gained as well as any changes in the particular circumstances or the assessed threats to the security of the ships, the port facilities or the routes covered by the agreement.

Regulation 12
Equivalent security arrangements

1   An Administration may allow a particular ship or a group of ships entitled to fly its flag to implement other security measures equivalent to those prescribed in this chapter or in part A of the ISPS Code, provided such security measures are at least as effective as those prescribed in this chapter or part A of the ISPS Code. The Administration, which allows such security measures, shall communicate to the Organization particulars thereof.

2   When implementing this chapter and part A of the ISPS Code, a Contracting Government may allow a particular port facility or a group of port facilities located within it territory, other than those covered by an agreement concluded under regulation 11, to implement security measures equivalent to those prescribed in this chapter or in Part A of the ISPS Code, provided such security measures are at least as effective as those prescribed in this chapter or part A of the ISPS Code. The Contracting Government, which allows such security measures, shall communicate to the Organization particulars thereof.

Regulation 13
Communication of information

1   Contracting Governments shall, not later than 1 July 2004, communicate to the Organization and shall make available for the information of Companies and Ships:

.1 the names and contact details of their national authority or authorities responsible for ship and port facility security;

.2 the locations within their territory covered by the approved port facility security plans.

.3 the names and contact details of those who have been designated to be available at all times to receive and act upon the ship-to-shore security alerts, referred to in regulation 6.2.1;

.4 the names and contact details of those who have been designated to be available at all times to receive and act upon any communications from Contracting Governments exercising control

Amendments to SOLAS 1974

and compliance measures, referred to in regulation 9.3.1; and

.5 the names and contact details of those who have been designated to be available at all times to provide advice or assistance to ships and to whom ships can report any security concerns, referred to in regulation 7.2;

and thereafter update such information as and when changes relating thereto occur. The Organization shall circulate such particulars to other Contracting Governments for the information of their officers.

2   Contracting Governments shall, not later than 1 July 2004, communicate to the Organization the names and contact details of any recognized security organizations authorized to act on their behalf together with details of the specific responsibility and conditions of authority delegated to such organizations. Such information shall be updated as and when changes relating thereto occur. The Organization shall circulate such particulars to other Contracting Governments for the information of their officers.

3   Contracting Governments shall, not later than 1 July 2004 communicate to the Organization a list showing the approved port facility security plans for the port facilities located within their territory together with the location or locations covered by each approved port facility security plan and the corresponding date of approval and thereafter shall further communicate when any of the following changes take place:

.1 changes in the location or locations covered by an approved port facility security plan are to be introduced or have been introduced. In such cases the information to be communicated shall indicate the changes in the location or locations covered by the plan and the date as of which such changes are to be introduced or were implemented;

.2 an approved port facility security plan, previously included in the list submitted to the Organization, is to be withdrawn or has been withdrawn. In such cases, the information to be communicated shall indicate the date on which the withdrawal will take effect or was implemented. In these cases, the communication shall be made to the Organization as soon as is practically possible; and

.3 additions are to be made to the list of approved port facility security plans. In such cases, the information to be communicated shall indicate the location or locations covered by the plan and the date of approval.

4   Contracting Governments shall, at five year intervals after

Resolution 1: New SOLAS Chapter XI-2

– contact details for ship security concerns

– security organisations authorised to act on behalf of Contracting Governments

– provision of list of approved Port Facility Security Plans

– provision of updates to Port facility Security Plans

– notice of withdrawal of a previously approved Port Facility Security Plans

– notice of additions to Port Facility Security Plans

**Resolution 1: New
SOLAS Chapter XI-2**

**– 5-yearly update of
list of approved Port
facility Security Plans**

**– notice of
agreement to
alternative security
agreements**

1 July 2004, communicate to the Organization a revised and updated list showing all the approved port facility security plans for the port facilities located within their territory together with the location or locations covered by each approved port facility security plan and the corresponding date of approval (and the date of approval of any amendments thereto) which will supersede and replace all information communicated to the Organization, pursuant to paragraph 3, during the preceding five years.

5   Contracting Governments shall communicate to the Organization information that an agreement under regulation 11 has been concluded. The information communicated shall include:

.1 the names of the Contracting Governments which have concluded the agreement;

.2 the port facilities and the fixed routes covered by the agreement;

.3 the periodicity of review of the agreement;

.4 the date of entry into force of the agreement; and

.5 information on any consultations which have taken place with other Contracting Governments;

and thereafter shall communicate, as soon as practically possible, to the Organization information when the agreement has been amended or has ended.

6   Any Contracting Government which allows, under the provisions of regulation 12, any equivalent security arrangements with respect to a ship entitled to fly its flag or with respect to a port facility located within its territory, shall communicate to the Organization particulars thereof.

7   The Organization shall make available the information communicated under paragraph 3 to other Contracting Governments upon request."

Conference Resolutions

FURTHER WORK BY THE INTERNATIONAL MARITIME
ORGANIZATION PERTAINING TO THE ENHANCEMENT OF
MARITIME SECURITY

Conference
Resolution 3
Adopted on
12 December 2002

Further work by the
IMO pertaining to
the enhancement of
maritime security

THE CONFERENCE,

Having Adopted amendments to the International Convention for
the Safety of Life at Sea, 1974, as amended (hereinafter referred to
as "the Convention"), concerning special measures to enhance
maritime safety and security,

Recognising the need for further work in the area of enhancement of
maritime security and in order to ensure the global and uniform
application and implementation of the special measures to enhance
maritime security adopted by the Conference,

1. Invites the International Maritime Organization (hereinafter
referred to as "the Organization"), bearing in mind the provisions of
Chapter XI-2 of the Convention and the International Ship and Port
Facility Security (ISPS) Code (hereinafter referred to as "the ISPS
Code"), to:

(a) develop training guidance such as model courses for ship
security officers, company security officers, port facility
security officers and company, ship and port security
personnel;

*– to develop training
(i.e. model courses)
for SSO, CSO, PFSO
and security
personnel*

(b) review the Organization's Assembly resolution A.787(19) as
amended by resolution A.882(21) on Procedures for port State
control and, if found necessary, develop appropriate
amendments thereto;

*– to review
procedures for port
State control*

(c) consider the need and, if necessary, develop further guidance
on control and compliance measures on aspects other than
those already addressed in part B of the ISPS Code;

*– to develop further
guidance on control
and compliance
measures*

(d) consider the need and, if necessary, develop guidelines on
recognized security organizations;

*– to develop
guidance on RSOs*

(e) review the Organisation's Assembly resolution A.890(21) on
Principles of safe manning and, if found necessary, develop
appropriate amendments thereto;

*– to review 'safe
manning'*

(f) review the aspect of security of ships to which Chapter XI-2 of
the Convention applies when interfacing with floating
production storage units and floating storage units and take
action as appropriate;

*– to review ship's
interface with
FPSO/FSO units*

Conference Resolutions

**Conference
Resolution 3**

**– facilitation of
maritime traffic
(arrivals/departures),
standard forms, EDI**

**– review guidelines
on Smuggling**

**– consider any other
guidance**

**– to adopt changes
before 1 July 2004**

**Impact assessment on
the long-range
ship identification
and tracking**

(g) consider, in the context of security, relevant aspects of facilitation of maritime traffic such as, for example, port arrivals and departures, standardized forms of reporting and electronic data interchange and take action as appropriate;

(h) review the Organization's Assembly resolution A.872(20) on Guidelines for the Prevention and Suppression of the Smuggling of Drugs, Psychotropic Substances and Precursor Chemicals on Ships Engaged in International Maritime Traffic and, if necessary, develop appropriate amendments thereto; and

(i) consider the need and, if necessary, develop any other guidance or guidelines to ensure the global, uniform and consistent implementation of the provisions of chapter XI-2 of the Convention or part A of the ISPS Code;

and to adopt them in time before the entry into force of the amendments to the Convention adopted by the Conference or as and when the Organization considers appropriate;

2. **Invites Also** the Organization to carry out, as a matter of urgency, an impact assessment of the proposals to implement the long-range identification and tracking of ships and, if found necessary, develop and adopt appropriate performance standards and guidelines for long-range ship identification and tracking systems.

Conference Resolutions

FUTURE AMENDMENTS TO CHAPTERS XI-1 AND XI-2 OF THE
1974 SOLAS CONVENTION ON SPECIAL MEASURES TO
ENHANCE MARITIME SAFETY AND SECURITY

THE CONFERENCE,

Having Adopted amendments to the International Convention for
the Safety of Life at Sea (SOLAS), 1974, as amended (hereinafter
referred to as "the Convention"), concerning special measures to
enhance maritime safety and security,

Noting the special nature of the measures now included in the new
chapter XI-2 of the Convention aimed at enhancing maritime
security,

Recognising the need for urgent and special measures to enhance
maritime security and the desire of Contracting Governments to
bring these measures into force as soon as possible,

Noting Also that it may be necessary, due to the special nature of the
issues involved, to frequently amend, in the future, the provisions of
chapter XI-2 of the Convention in order to respond, in a proactive
manner, to new or emerging security risks and threats,

Recalling Resolution 5 entitled "Future amendments to Chapter XI
of the 1974 SOLAS Convention on special measures to enhance
maritime safety", adopted by the 1994 Conference of Contracting
Government to the International Convention for the Safety of Life at
Sea, 1974,

Desiring that future amendments to chapters XI-1 and XI-2 of the
Convention are adopted, brought into force and given effect in the
shortest possible time,

Recommends that future amendments to the provisions of chapters
XI-1 and XI-2 of the Convention should be adopted by either the
Maritime Safety Committee of the International Maritime
Organization in accordance with article VIII(b) of the Convention or
by a Conference of Contracting Governments to the Convention in
accordance with article VIII(c) thereof.

Conference
Resolution 4
(adopted on
12 December 2002)

Future Amendments
to Chapters XI-1 and
XI-2 of the 1974
SOLAS Convention
on Special Measures
to Enhance Maritime
Safety and Security

– no delay for future
amendments

– role of Maritime
Safety Committee or
Conference of
Contracting
Governments

Conference Resolutions

Conference
Resolution 5
(adopted on
12 December 2002)

Promotion of
Technical
Co-operation and
Assistance

PROMOTION OF TECHNICAL CO-OPERATION AND ASSISTANCE

THE CONFERENCE,

Having Adopted amendments to the International Convention for the Safety of Life at Sea, 1974, as amended (hereinafter referred to as "the Convention"), concerning special measures to enhance maritime safety and security,

Recalling operative paragraph 5 of resolution A.924(22) on "Review of measures and procedures to prevent acts of terrorism which threaten the security of passengers and crews and the safety of ships", adopted on 20 November 2001 by the Assembly of the International Maritime Organization (hereinafter referred to as "the Organization"), whereby the Secretary-General of the Organization is requested to take appropriate measures within the Integrated Technical Co-operation Programme to assist Governments to assess, put in place or enhance, as the case may be, appropriate infrastructure and measures to strengthen port safety and security so as to prevent and suppress terrorist acts directed against ports and port personnel as well as ships in port areas, passengers and crew,

Being Appreciative of the steps already taken by the Secretary-General of the Organization, in response to request of the Assembly of the Organization, to provide assistance to States in strengthening their maritime and port security infrastructure and measures,

Recognizing the need for the development of appropriate legislation and the putting in place of appropriate infrastructure for ship and port facility security and relevant training facilities in order to ensure the global and uniform application and implementation of the special measures adopted to enhance maritime security,

Recognizing Also the importance of adequate education and training for seafarers and port facility personnel to contribute to the overall efforts to enhance maritime security,

Recognizing Further that, in some cases, there may be limited infrastructure, facilities and training programmes for obtaining the experience required for the purpose of preventing acts which threaten the security of ships and of port facilities, particularly in developing countries,

Believing that the promotion of technical co-operation at the international level will assist those States not yet having adequate expertise or facilities for providing training and experience to assess, put in place or enhance appropriate infrastructure and, in general, implement the measures required by the adopted amendments necessary to strengthen maritime security on board ships and ashore,

Integrated Technical
Co-operation
Programme

– to provide
assistance to States

– to develop
appropriate global
legislation and
training

– to develop training
for seafarers an
port personnel

– limited resources
for gaining security
experience

– promotion of
technical co-
operation at an
international level

Conference Resolutions

Emphasising, in this regard, the vital role that safe and secure shipping and port operations play in sustainable socio-economic development,

1. **Strongly Urges** Contracting Governments to the Convention and Member States of the Organization to:

(a) provide, in co-operation with the Organization, assistance to those States which have difficulty in implementing or meeting the requirements of the adopted amendments or the ISPS Code; and

(b) use the Integrated Technical Co-operation Programme of the Organization as one of the main instruments to obtain assistance in advancing effective implementation of, and compliance with, the adopted amendments and the ISPS Code;

2. **Requests** the Secretary-General of the Organization to make adequate provision, within the Integrated Technical Co-operation Programme, to strengthen further the assistance that is already being provided and to promote, in co-operation, as appropriate, with relevant international organizations, the enhancement of the Organization's capacity to address the future needs of developing countries for continued education and training and the improvement of their maritime and port security infrastructure and measures;

3. **Invites** donors, international organizations and the shipping and port industry to contribute financial, human and/or in-kind resources to the Integrated Technical Co-operation Programme of the Organization for its maritime and port security activities;

4. **Invites Also** the Secretary General to give early consideration to establishing a Maritime Security Trust Fund for the purpose of providing a dedicated source of financial support for maritime security technical-co-operation activities and, in particular, for providing support for national initiatives in developing countries to strengthen their maritime security infrastructure and measures.

Conference Resolutions

**Conference
Resolution 6
(adopted on
12 December 2002)**

**Early Implementation
of the Special
Measures to Enhance
Maritime Security**

**EARLY IMPLEMENTATION OF THE SPECIAL MEASURES TO
ENHANCE MARITIME SECURITY**

THE CONFERENCE,

Having Adopted amendments to the International Convention for
the Safety of Life at Sea, 1974, as amended (hereinafter referred to
as 2the Convention"), concerning special measures to enhance
maritime safety and security,

Recognising the important contribution that the implementation of
the special measures adopted will make towards the safe and secure
operation of ships, for pollution prevention and for the safety and
security of those on board and ashore,

Recognising Also that the task of implementing the requirements of
chapter XI-2 of the Convention and of the International Ship and Port
Facility Security (ISPS) Code (hereinafter referred to as "the Code")
will place a significant burden on Contracting Governments,
Administrations, Recognized Security Organizations,

**– recalling the need
for ships to have a
SSP and ISSC by
1 July 2004**

Recalling that the Code from 1 July 2004, requires each ship to
which the provisions of chapter XI-2 of the Convention and part A of
the Code apply, to be provided with an appropriate Ship Security
Plan,

Recalling Also that each such ship is required to be provided with an
International Ship Security Certificate not later than 1 July 2004,

**– recognising the
delay of late
approval of a SSP**

Recognising Further that the process of verifying the compliance of
a ship, to which the provisions of chapter XI-2 of the Convention and
part A of the Code apply, with the requirements of the chapter XI-2
and of the Code cannot be undertaken until the Ship Security Plan
has been approved and its provisions have been implemented on
board,

Desiring to ensure the smooth implementation of the provisions of
chapter XI-2 of the Convention and of the Code,

**– bearing in mind
difficulties in
implementing the
ISM Code**

Bearing In Mind the difficulties experienced during implementation
of the International Safety Management (ISM) Code,

**NO EXTENSION OF
ISPS CODE
IMPLEMENTATION
DATE**

1. **Draws** the attention of Contracting Governments to the
   Convention and the industry to the fact that neither chapter
   XI-2 of the Convention nor the Code provide for any extension
   of the implementation dates for the introduction of the special
   measures concerned to enhance maritime security;

2. **Urges** Contracting Governments to take, as a matter of high

priority, any action needed to finalize as soon as possible any legislative or administrative arrangements, which are required at the national level, to give effect to the requirements of the adopted amendments to the Convention (and the Code) relating to the certification of ships entitled to fly their flag or port facilities situated in their territory;

3. **Recommends** that Contracting Governments and Administrations concerned designate dates, in advance of the application date of 1 July 2004 by which requests for:

.1 review and approval of Ship Security Plans;

.2 verification and certification of ships; and

.3 review and approval of Port Facility Security Assessments and of Port Facility Security Plans;

should be submitted in order to allow Contracting Governments, Administrations and Recognized Security Organizations, time to complete the review and approval and the verification and certification process and for Companies, ships and port facilities to rectify any non-compliance;

4. **Invites** Contracting Governments, on and after 1 July 2004, to recognize and accept as valid and as meeting the requirements of chapter XI-2 of the Convention and part A of the Code any:

.1 Ship Security Plans approved, prior to 1 July 2004, pursuant to the provisions of part A of the Code, by Administrations or on their behalf; and

.2 International Ship Security Certificates issued, prior to 1 July 2004, in accordance with the provisions of part A of the Code, by Administrations or on their behalf;

as far as these relate to ships which, on 1 July 2004, were entitled to fly the flag of the State of the Administration which, or on behalf of which, the plan in question was approved or the certificate in question was issued;

5. **Further Recommends** that Contracting Governments and the industry take early appropriate action to ensure that all necessary infrastructure is in place in time for the effective implementation of the adopted measures to enhance maritime security on board ships and ashore.

Conference Resolution 6 (contd)

– Contracting Governments to finalise actions without delay to:

– review and approve SSPs

– verify and certificate ships

– review and approve PFSAs and PFSPs

– Contracting Governments to accept pre-July 2004 Plans and Certificates issued by other Administrations

– industry to set-up early infrastructure

Conference Resolutions

Conference Resolution 7 (adopted on 12 December 2002)

Establishment of Appropriate Measures to Enhance the Security of Ships, Port Facilities, Mobile Offshore Drilling Units on Location and Fixed and Floating Platforms Not Covered by Chapter XI-2 of the SOLAS Convention

ESTABLISHMENT OF APPROPRIATE MEASURES TO ENHANCE THE SECURITY OF SHIPS, PORT FACILITIES, MOBILE OFFSHORE DRILLING UNITS ON LOCATION AND FIXED AND FLOATING PLATFORMS NOT COVERED BY CHAPTER XI-2 OF THE SOLAS CONVENTION

THE CONFERENCE,

Having Adopted amendments to the International Convention for the Safety of Life at Sea, 1974, as amended (hereinafter referred to as "the Convention"), concerning special measures to enhance maritime safety and security,

Recalling that Chapter XI-2 of the Convention applies only to:

(a) the following types of ships engaged on international voyages:

.1 passenger ships including passenger high-speed craft; and

.2 cargo ships, including cargo high speed craft, of 500 gross tonnage and upwards; and

.3 mobile offshore drilling units; and

(b) port facilities serving such ships engaged on international voyages,

Recognizing the important contribution that the implementation of the special measures adopted will make towards the safe and secure operation of ships, for pollution prevention and for the safety and security of those on board and ashore,

Recognizing Also the need to address and establish appropriate measures to enhance the security of ships and of port facilities other than those covered by chapter XI-2 of the Convention,

Recognizing Further that the establishment of such measures will further enhance and positively contribute towards the international efforts to ensure maritime security and to prevent and suppress acts threatening the security in the maritime transport sector,

1. **Invites** Contracting Governments to the Convention to establish, as they may consider necessary, and to disseminate, as they deem fit, appropriate measures to enhance the security of ships and of port facilities other than those covered by chapter XI-2 of the Convention;

2. **Encourages**, in particular, Contracting Governments to establish, as they may consider necessary, and to disseminate,

as they deem fit, information to facilitate the interactions of ships and of port facilities to which chapter XI-2 of the Convention applies with ships which are not covered by chapter XI-2 of the Convention;

3. **Also Encourages** Contracting Governments to establish, as they may consider necessary, and to disseminate as they deem fit, information to facilitate contact and liaison between company and ship security officers and the authorities responsible for the security of port facilities not covered by chapter XI-2 of the Convention, prior to a ship entering, or anchoring off, such a port;

4. **Further Encourages** Contracting Governments, when exercising their responsibilities for mobile offshore drilling units and for fixed and floating platforms operating on their Continental Shelf or within their Exclusive Economic Zone, to ensure that any security provisions applying to such units and platforms allow interaction with those applying to ships covered by chapter XI-2 of the Convention, that serve, or operate in conjunction with, such units or platforms;

5. **Requests** Contracting Governments to inform the Organization of any action they have taken in this respect.

Conference Resolution 7 (contd)

– interaction with ships and port facilities not covered by Ch XI-2

– liaison between CSOs and SSOs with port security authorities prior to ships entering the port

– interaction between drilling units on the Continental Shelf or Exclusive Economic Zone and ships

Conference Resolutions

Conference Resolution 8 (adopted on 12 December 2002)

Enhancement of security in co-operation with the International Labour Organization

(Seafarers. Identity documents and work on the wider issues of port security)

– development of a verifiable Seafarers' ID

Seafarers Identity Documents Convention, 1958 (No 108)

"Improved security for seafarers' identification" – ILO Conference June 2003

ENHANCEMENT OF SECURITY IN CO-OPERATION WITH THE INTERNATIONAL LABOUR ORGANIZATION

(SEAFARERS. IDENTITY DOCUMENTS AND WORK ON THE WIDER ISSUES OF PORT SECURITY)

THE CONFERENCE,

Having Adopted amendments to the International Convention for the Safety of Life at Sea, 1974, as amended (hereinafter referred to as "the Convention"), concerning special measures to enhance maritime safety and security,

Recognizing the important contribution that the implementation of the special measures adopted will make towards the safe and secure operation of ships, for pollution prevention and for the safety and security of those on board and ashore,

Recognizing Also the need to continue the work and establish, as the need arises, further appropriate measures to enhance the security of ships and of port facilities,

Recognizing Further that the development and use of a verifiable Seafarers. Identity Document will further enhance and positively contribute towards the international efforts to ensure maritime security and to prevent and suppress acts threatening the security in the maritime transport sector,

Cognizant of the competencies and work of the International Labour Organization (hereinafter referred to as "the ILO") in the area of development and adoption of the international labour standards,

Recalling the Seafarers' Identity Documents Convention, 1958 (No.108), adopted by the International Labour Conference on 13 May 1958, which entered into force on 19 February 1961,

Recalling Also that the Governing Body of the ILO at its 283rd Session, in March 2002, placed the question of "Improved security for seafarers' identification" as an urgent item on the agenda of the 91st Session of the International Labour Conference, to be held in June 2003, with a view to the adoption of a Protocol to the Seafarers' Identity Documents Convention, 1958 (No. 108),

Recalling Further the long-standing co-operation between the International Maritime Organization (hereinafter referred as "the Organization") and the ILO in the area of international maritime transport,

Noting, with satisfaction, the work undertaken, so far, by the

Conference Resolutions

Governing Body of the ILO and by the International Labour Office on seafarers. identity documents and on port and dockworkers security,

1. **Invites** the ILO to continue the development of a Seafarers' Identity Document as a matter of urgency, which should cover, inter alia, a document for professional purposes; a verifiable security document and a certification information document;

2. **Requests** the Organization to consider the results of the 91st Session of the International Labour Conference on the "Improved Security for Seafarers' Identification" and to take appropriate action, as it deems appropriate;

3. **Invites** States through their tripartite delegations to participate in the 91st Session of the International Labour Conference, in June 2003, and to give favourable consideration to the earliest possible ratification, acceptance, approval or accession to the new ILO instrument concerning seafarers' identification documents, once it is adopted;

4. **Invites** the Organization and the ILO to establish a joint ILO/IMO Working Group to undertake any further work, which may be required, on the wider issue of port security, based on the terms of reference set out in the attached Annex;

5. **Requests** the Secretary-General of the Organization to contribute, with appropriate expertise, to the work of the ILO on the "Improved Security for Seafarers' Identification" and to the proposed joint work of on the wide issue of port security;

6. **Requests** the Secretary-General of the Organization to transmit a copy of this resolution to the Director-General of the International Labour Office.

Conference Resolution 8 (contd)

– ILO to continue the development of Seafarers' ID

– early ratification of Seafarers' ID proposals

– ILO/IMO Working Group

see also Annex (over)

Conference Resolutions

Annex to Conference Resolution 8

IMO/ILO Work on Port Security

(Seafarers. Identity documents and work on the wider issues of Port Security)

– relationship between ship and port security and verifiable ID for those working in these areas

– need to make ID mandatory

– assess impact, benefits and costs of the recommendations

– monitoring of the IMO/ILO Working Group

IMO/ILO WORK ON PORT SECURITY

POSSIBLE TERMS OF REFERENCE

1. The joint IMO/ILO Working Group on Port Security, having regard to the amendments to the International Convention for the Safety of Life at Sea, 1974 and the International Ship and Port Facility Security (ISPS) Code adopted by the December 2002 Conference of Contracting Governments to the International Convention for the Safety of Life at Sea, 1974 for the purpose of introducing mandatory requirements and guidance relating to the enhancement of the safety and security of ships and of port facilities, should:

.1 consider and recommend, for the purpose of enhancing security, safety and the protection of the environment, the form and content of any further guidance, which may be required, on the wider issue of port security including the relationship between ship and port security and the wider security and safety and the protection of the environment considerations relevant to port areas, including the question of verifiable identification of those working within these areas or having access to such areas;

.2 consider the need for any mandatory requirements relating to the above and, if such a need is identified, to recommend the form and content of such requirements; and

.3 prepare and submit a report (including interim work and progress reports) on the aforesaid, together with the relevant reasons and justifications thereto, as well as, an assessment of the impact, benefits and costs of the recommendations, for the consideration of the International Maritime Organization and of the International Labour Organization.

2. The International Maritime Organization and the International Labour Organization will monitor the work of the joint IMO/ILO Working Group on Port Security and, as the need arises, will issue appropriate instructions and guidance to the Working Group.

Conference Resolutions

ENHANCEMENT OF SECURITY IN CO-OPERATION WITH THE WORLD CUSTOMS ORGANIZATION

(CLOSED CARGO TRANSPORT UNITS)

THE CONFERENCE,

Having Adopted amendments to the International Convention for the Safety of Life at Sea, 1974, as amended (hereinafter referred to as "the Convention"), concerning special measures to enhance maritime safety and security,

Recognizing the important contribution that the implementation of the special measures adopted will make towards the safe and secure operation of ships, for pollution prevention and for the safety and security of those on board and ashore,

Recognizing Also the need to address and establish appropriate measures to enhance the security of ships and of port facilities in aspects other than those covered by Chapter XI-2 of the Convention,

Recalling that the Convention on Facilitation of International Maritime Traffic, 1965 already contains requirements related to the provision to administrations of commercial data related to the movement of cargoes by sea,

Recognizing Further the need to include, in due course, in the Convention appropriate requirements to address specifically the security of closed cargo transport units (hereinafter referred to as "closed CTUs") and that such requirements will further enhance and positively contribute towards the international efforts to ensure maritime security and to prevent and suppress acts threatening the security in the maritime transport sector,

Futhermore Recognizing the inter-modal and international nature of closed CTUs movements, the need to ensure security of the complete supply chain and the respective roles of, all those involved,

Recalling Also the role of frontier agencies, in particular Customs Administrations, in controlling the international movement of closed CTUs,

Cognizant of the competencies and work of the World Customs Organization hereinafter referred to as "the WCO") in the area of international maritime transport,

Recalling Further the long-standing co-operation of the International Maritime Organization (hereinafter referred to as "the Organization") with the WCO in the area of international maritime transport,

Conference
Resolution 9
(adopted on
12 December 2002)

Enhancement of
Security in
Co-operation
with the World
Customs
Organization

(Closed Cargo
Transport Units)

– administrative
data: Convention on
Facilitation of
International
Maritime Traffic,
1965

– closed cargo
transport units
(closed CTUs)

– security of
complete supply
chain in inter-modal
and international
traffic

– frontier controls of
closed CTUs

– role of WCO

Conference Resolutions

Noting with satisfaction the signing on 23 July 2002 of a Memorandum of Understanding to strengthen the co-operation between the two Organizations,

1. **Invites** the WCO to consider, urgently, measures to enhance security throughout international movements of closed CTUs;

2. **Requests** the Secretary-General of the Organization to contribute expertise relating to maritime transport and, in particular, to the carriage of closed CTUs. by sea to the discussions at the WCO;

3. **Agrees** that the Convention should be amended, if and when appropriate, to give effect to relevant decisions taken by the WCO and endorsed by the Contracting Governments to the Convention insofar as they relate to the carriage of closed CTUs by sea;

4. **Requests** the Secretary-General of the Organization to transmit a copy of this resolution to the Secretary-General of the WCO.

Conference Resolutions

EARLY IMPLEMENTATION OF LONG-RANGE SHIP'S IDENTIFICATION AND TRACKING

THE CONFERENCE,

Having Adopted amendments to the International Convention for the Safety of Life at Sea, 1974, as amended (hereinafter referred to as "the Convention"), concerning special measures to enhance safety and security,

Recalling that long-range identification and tracking of ships at sea is a measure that fully contributes to the enhancement of the maritime and coastal States security as a whole,

Having Acknowledged that Inmarsat C polling is currently an appropriate system for long-range identification and tracking of ships,

Recognizing the importance of an early implementation of long-range identification and tracking of ships,

Recognizing Also that the equipment installed on board and ashore is available for immediate use and will allow the early implementation of such measures,

1. **Urges** Contracting Governments to take, as a matter of high priority, any action needed at national level to give effect to implementing and beginning the long-range identification and tracking of ships;

2. **Invites** Contracting Governments to encourage ships entitled to fly the flag of their State to take the necessary measures so that they are prepared to respond automatically to Inmarsat C polling, or to other available systems;

3. **Requests** Contracting Governments to consider all aspects related to the introduction of long-range identification and tracking of ships, including its potential for misuse as an aid to ship targeting and the need for confidentiality in respect of the information so gathered.

Early implementation of long-range ship's identification and tracking

– enhancement of security as a whole

– Inmarsat C appropriate system

– readily available for early implementation

– high priority at national level

– ships to respond automatically to Inmarsat C polling

– guard against misuse and confidentiality of ship tracking information

Conference Resolutions

Conference
Resolution 11
(adopted on
12 December 2002)

Human element
related aspects
and shore leave for
seafarers

IMO Resolution
A.907 (22) – long-
term work of the
IMO to 2008

Shore leave: the
general right of
foreign crew to be
allowed ashore

Shore leave:
– human rights of
seafarers

– 'special protection'
for seafarers

– seafarers'
well-being

– essential for crew
changes

– application of
shore leave under
ISPS Code provisions

– feedback on effect
of shore leave
provisions

HUMAN ELEMENT RELATED ASPECTS AND SHORE LEAVE FOR SEAFARERS

THE CONFERENCE,

Having Adopted amendments to the International Convention for the Safety of Life at Sea, 1974, as amended (hereinafter referred to as "the Convention"), concerning special measures to enhance maritime safety and security,

Recognizing that the shipping industry and the smooth transportation of goods are essential to world trade,

Recalling that the Assembly of the International Maritime Organization (hereinafter referred to as "the Organization") adopted Resolution A.907(22) on the long term work programme of the Organization (up to 2008) and that the human element is an important item thereof,

Recalling Also the provisions of the Convention on Facilitation of International Maritime Traffic, 1965, as amended, which has, inter alia, established a general right for foreign crew members to be entitled to shore leave while the ship on which they arrived is in port, provided that the formalities on arrival of the ship have been fulfilled and the public authorities have no reason to refuse permission to come ashore for reasons of public health, public safety or public order;

Recalling Further the generally accepted principles of international human rights applicable to all workers, including seafarers,

Considering that, given the global nature of the shipping industry, seafarers need special protection,

Being Aware that seafarers work and live on ships involved in international trade and that access to shore facilities and shore leave are vital elements of seafarers' general well-being and, therefore, to the realisation of safer seas and cleaner oceans,

Being Aware Also that the ability to go ashore is essential for joining and leaving a ship after the agreed period of service,

1. **Urges** Contracting Governments to take the human element, the need to afford special protection to seafarers and the critical importance of shore leave into account when implementing the provisions of chapter XI-2 of the Convention and the International Ship and Port Facility (ISPS) Code (hereinafter referred to as "the Code");

2. **Encourages** Contracting Governments, Member States of the Organization and non-governmental organizations with consultative status at the Organization to report to the Organization any instances where the human element has been adversely impacted by the implementation of the provisions of chapter XI-2 of the Convention or the Code; and

3. **Requests** the Secretary-General to bring to the attention of the Maritime Safety Committee and the Facilitation Committee of the Organization, any human element related problems, which have been communicated to the Organization as a result of the implementation of Chapter XI-2 of the Convention or the Code

Notes

Notes

INTERNATIONAL MARITIME ORGANIZATION
4 ALBERT EMBANKMENT
LONDON SE1 7SR

Telephone: 020 7735 7611
Fax: 020 7587 3210
Telex: 23588 IMOLDN G

IMO

E

Ref. T2-NAVSEC/2.11

MSC/Circ.1104
15 January 2004

IMPLEMENTATION OF SOLAS CHAPTER XI-2 AND THE ISPS CODE

1   The amendments to the Annex to the International Convention for the Safety of Life at Sea (SOLAS), 1974 and the introduction of the International Ship and Port Facility Security Code (ISPS Code), both adopted by the Conference of SOLAS Contracting Governments on Maritime Security on 12 December 2002, are due to enter into force on 1 July 2004.

2   The urgent need for early action by all parties concerned (Governments, port authorities and the shipping industry) to ensure that the maritime security regime established by the 2002 Conference is implemented by 1 July 2004 is highlighted in both Conference resolution 6 and MSC/Circ.1067 on "Early implementation of measures to enhance maritime security".

3   The importance and significance of IMO's work on maritime security was also recognized by the Council and the Assembly in agreeing that the Organization's theme for the current year should be: "IMO 2004: Focus on maritime security". However, recent surveys carried out on the status of implementation of the security measures introduced by the aforementioned SOLAS amendments and the ISPS Code raise concerns that not enough progress has been achieved so far. This has been reported by Governments and other interested parties (including industry organizations such as ICS, IAPH, BIMCO, IACS, INTERTANKO and INTERCARGO). Given that the purpose of the new measures is to protect shipping against terrorist attacks, the information received gives rise to grave concern also from the point of view of the serious repercussions to ships, shipping companies, port facilities and the international shipborne trade if the situation does not improve by next July and parties concerned are found not in compliance with the measures. It is also worrying from the point of view of the very substance of implementation of the measures if, as a result of last minute bottlenecks, plans are approved and certificates are issued hastily without proper verification.

4   In view of the above, SOLAS Contracting Governments, port authorities, classification societies, recognized security organizations, training institutions and all other parties concerned are invited to redouble their efforts to protect shipping against terrorism by taking action as soon as possible to ensure compliance with the requirements of SOLAS chapter XI-2 and the ISPS Code at as early a stage as possible. Similarly, Administrations are again invited to advise companies and ships operating under their countries' flag to take appropriate steps to increase awareness of the potential dangers so that their crews are extremely vigilant and alert to any security threat they may encounter or be suspicious of, whether they are in port, at offshore terminals or underway.

...Contd

...Contd

5   Pursuant to the foregoing, Member Governments are requested to advise the Organization of the current status of their implementation of the aforementioned security measures and to provide the Secretariat with appropriate progress reports in the run up to the 1 July entry-into-force date. Member Governments are reminded of the mechanism for notifying compliance with SOLAS regulation XI-2/13 (on Communication of information), as described in Circular letter No.2514 dated 8 December 2003.

6   Member Governments and international organizations are further invited to bring this circular to the attention of national Designated Authorities, Administrations and all other parties concerned and responsible for the implementation of IMO's maritime security measures.

7   This circular is issued following consultations between the Secretary-General and the Chairman of the Maritime Safety Committee.

———

MSC/Circ.1104
15 January 2004

INTERNATIONAL MARITIME ORGANIZATION
4 ALBERT EMBANKMENT
LONDON SE1 7SR

Telephone:　020 7735 7611
Fax:　　　　020 7587 3210
Telex:　　　23588 IMOLDN G

IMO

E

Ref. T2-NAVSEC/2.11

MSC/Circ.1097
6 June 2003

GUIDANCE RELATING TO THE IMPLEMENTATION OF SOLAS CHAPTER XI-2 AND THE ISPS CODE

1   The Conference of Contracting Governments to the International Convention for the Safety of Lives at Sea (SOLAS), 1974 (London, 9 to 12 December 2002), adopted amendments to the Annex to the Convention, as amended, in particular new chapter XI-2 on Special measures to enhance maritime security; and, the new International Code for the Security of Ships and Port Facilities (ISPS Code).

2   The Maritime Safety Committee, at its seventy-seventh session (28 May to 6 June 2003), recognizing and considering the need for additional information to assist Contracting Governments and the industry with the implementation of, and compliance with new SOLAS chapter XI-2 and the ISPS Code, directed its Maritime Security Working Group to examine and provide additional guidance on specific aspects of the measures to enhance maritime security.

3   The guidance relating to the implementation of SOLAS chapter XI-2 and the ISPS Code, as approved by the Committee, is given at annex.

4   Reference is also made in this context to MSC/Circ.1067 on Early implementation of measures to enhance maritime security regarding the importance of early action by all parties to ensure that the new security regime is implemented by 1 July 2004.

5   Member Governments and international organizations are invited to bring this circular to the attention of national Designated Authorities, Administrations and all parties concerned and responsible for the implementation of maritime security measures.

***

IMO Guidance: SOLAS Implementation

MSC/Circ.1097

ANNEX

**GUIDANCE RELATING TO THE IMPLEMENTATION OF SOLAS CHAPTER XI-2
AND THE ISPS CODE**

GENERAL

1   The ensuing paragraphs are lifted from the report of the Maritime Security Working Group (MSC 77/WP.15) at MSC 77 and are considered to be of valuable guidance for the implementation of SOLAS chapter XI-2 and the ISPS Code on relevant topics.

Mobile and immobile floating units

2   Paragraphs 3.1.1.1 to .3 of part A of the ISPS Code specify the vessels and mobile offshore drilling units subject to SOLAS chapter XI-2 and ISPS Code requirements. Advice was sought on the position of floating production, storage and offloading units (FPSOs), floating storage units (FSUs) and single buoy moorings (SBMs).

3   The Committee agreed that neither of the two types of floating production, storage and offloading units (FPSOs) and floating storage units (FSUs), were ships subject to the provisions of the ISPS Code, but that they should have some security procedures in place to prevent "contamination" of ships and port facilities subject to the ISPS Code.

4   It was concluded that such units, when attached to a fixed platform, should be covered by the security regime in force for the platform.

5   Such units, when engaged in periodic short voyages between the platform and the coastal State, should not be considered to be ships engaged on international voyages.

6   The Committee also agreed that single buoy moorings (SBMs), attached to an offshore facility would be covered by that facility's security regime and if it was connected to a port facility it would be covered by the port facility security plan (PFSP).

7   In all cases the intention was to provide sufficient security to maintain the integrity of ships and port facilities covered by SOLAS and the ISPS Code.

International Ship Security Certificates (ISSC)

8   The Committee recognized that part B of the ISPS Code was albeit recommendatory, a process all parties concerned needed to go through in order to comply with part A. It was concluded that paragraph 9.4 of part A of the ISPS Code required that in order for an ISSC to be issued, the guidance in part B would need to be taken into account.

9   The Committee further specifically considered that an ISSC would not be issued unless paragraphs 8.1 to 13.8 of part B of the ISPS Code had been taken into account.

MSC/Circ.1097
ANNEX
Page 2

Issue of the International Ship Security Certificate

10   The Committee concluded that a Certificate should only be issued:

.1   when the ship has an approved ship security plan (SSSP); and

.2   there was objective evidence to the satisfaction of the Administration that the ship is operating in accordance with the provisions of the approved plan.

11   Certificates should not be issued in cases where minor deviations from the approved plan or the requirements of SOLAS chapter XI-2 and part A of the ISPS Code existed, even if these deviations did not compromise the ship's ability to operate at security levels 1 to 3.

Subsequent failures or suspensions

12   Any subsequent failure of security equipment or systems, or suspension of a security measure that compromises the ship's ability to operate at security levels 1 to 3 have to be reported immediately, together with any proposed remedial actions, to the Administration or the RSO, if the ISSC was issued by an RSO, and the appropriate authorities responsible for any port facility the ship is using, or the authorities of any coastal State through whose territorial seas the ship has indicated it intends to transit, and instructions requested.

13   Any failure of security equipment or systems, or suspension of a security measure that does not compromise the ship's ability to operate at security levels 1 to 3 have to be reported without delay to the Administration or the RSO, if the ISSC was issued by an RSO, and if so decided by the Administration, for their consideration with details of the equivalent alternative security measures the ship is applying until the failure or suspension is rectified together with an action plan specifying the timing of any repair or replacement.

14   The Administration or the RSO, if the ISSC was issued by an RSO, and if so decided by the Administration, may approve the alternative security measures being taken and the action plan, require amendments to such measures, require additional or alternative measures, speedier repair or replacement or take other appropriate action.

15   The International Ship Security Certificate should be withdrawn or suspended if:

.1   the alternative security measures are not, in fact, in place; or

.2   an approved action plan has not been complied with.

16   Company and Ship Security Officers and Administrations should be aware of the possible cumulative effect of individual failures or suspensions which could impair the ship's ability to operate at security levels 1 to 3.

IMO Guidance: SOLAS Implementation

Records

17   The Committee underlined the importance of maintaining the records required under the ISPS Code.

Training and Certification

18   Guidance on training, drills and exercises on ship security is to be found in 13.1 to13.8 of part B of the ISPS Code. The issue of evidence that Ship Security Officers and ship security personnel had, in fact, received adequate training was discussed by the Committee.

19   As an interim measure, the Committee recommended that the ISSC be accepted as *prima facie* evidence that training has been conducted in accordance with the ISPS Code. The flag State was responsible for deciding how that training was to be conducted, and if any additional certification was required. If a port State control inspection detected a lack of training, further action could be taken. It was anticipated that States would develop and introduce further measures after 1 July 2004, which may include the introduction of individual certificates or other documentary evidence of training.

Reporting requirements and communication of information

20   The Committee agreed that it was essential that the information set out in regulation 13.1.1 to 13.1.5 of SOLAS chapter XI-2 was readily available to the international shipping community.

21   Contracting Governments providing information to the Organization are, therefore, requested to confirm that they are content for the information provided under 13.1.1 to 13.1.5 to be passed by the Organization to a central source for dissemination to the worldwide shipping community.

Inspections Prior to Entering Port

22   SOLAS regulation XI-2/9.2.5 allows inspection of a ship, if the ship is in the territorial sea of the Contracting Government the port of which the ship intends to enter. Clarification was sought from the Committee on the circumstances in which an inspection could be initiated under SOLAS regulation XI-2/9.2.5.3.

23   With regard to the inspection envisaged by SOLAS regulation XI-2/9.2.5.3 the Committee, bearing in mind the requirement for "clear grounds" in regulation XI-2/9.2.4, agreed that this kind of inspection would be expected to be undertaken normally when there was information / intelligence, usually received before arrival of the ship, suggesting that there were "clear grounds" for suspecting that the ship was not in compliance with the provisions or posed a threat to the port facility.

24   Contracting Governments are considered to have the right to carry out inspections of ships, intending to enter their ports, to search for possible suspicious persons, such as terrorists, on board. The inspections would be carried out within the scope of the SOLAS Convention.

Immediate Threat

25   Clarification was also sought on the interpretation of the term "immediate threat" found in SOLAS regulation XI-2/9.3.3.

26   On the question of what was understood to be an "immediate threat" in regulation XI-2/9.3.3, the Committee agreed that this could cover two scenarios: firstly, that the ship did not comply with the provisions of SOLAS chapter XI-2 and part A of the ISPS Code and therefore was considered to be a threat, or secondly, as in paragraph 23 above, intelligence or other information had been received indicating that the ship posed an immediate threat or was under threat itself. The Committee recognized that there may be other scenarios where, under international law, Contracting Governments could take additional measures outside of SOLAS regulation XI-2/9 for national security or defence, even if a ship fully complied with SOLAS chapter XI-2 and part A of the ISPS Code.

Responsibility for the exercise of Control Measures

27   With regard to the responsibility for control measures taken by the Contracting Governments, the Committee recognized that this might indeed differ from State to State, subject to the distribution of responsibilities to the various Government agencies of the country concerned. It was conceivable that all control measures would be undertaken by one control authority while, in other countries, traditional port State control would be conducted by PSC authorities and the security related additional control and compliance measures would be the responsibility of other designated authorities (i.e., immigration, police, navy, etc.).

Ship Identification Numbers

28   The Committee confirmed that the ship identification number (SOLAS regulation XI-1/3) to be permanently marked on the hull of the ship was the prefix "IMO" followed by the 7 digit number in accordance with resolution A.600(15).

Verification of Security Systems

29   In considering the question of how detailed the verification of security systems would have to be, the Committee confirmed that for all technical equipment, specified in the SSP, 100% verification was necessary, while for all operational (non-technical) security measures a sample audit would be sufficient, to the level necessary for the auditor to verify the whole operating system.

Voluntary nature of reporting by ships intending to enter the Territorial Sea

30   The Committee clarified that, with regard to SOLAS regulation XI-2/7, ships operating in, or intending to enter the territorial seas would report to the relevant coastal State on a voluntary basis, triggered by the ship, and that this regulation did not establish a mandatory reporting system.

Declarations of Security

31   With regard to the completion, on request of the ship, of a Declaration of Security (DoS) when interfacing with a port facility or a ship not covered by a security plan, the Committee confirmed its working assumption that, for port facilities not covered by the regulations, the coastal State would have to ensure that a contact point was to be provided ashore, with whom the ship could communicate and who would be empowered to sign the DoS while, for a ship not covered by a security plan, again there should be a designated contact point ashore (in the coastal State) or on the ship designated to sign the DoS.

———

INTERNATIONAL MARITIME ORGANIZATION
4 ALBERT EMBANKMENT
LONDON SE1 7SR

Telephone: 020 7735 7611
Fax: 020 7587 3210
Telex: 23588 IMOLDN G

IMO

E

Ref. T2-NAVSEC/2.11

MSC/Circ.1072
26 June 2003

GUIDANCE ON PROVISION OF SHIP SECURITY ALERT SYSTEMS

1   The Sub-Committee on Radiocommunications and Search and Rescue (COMSAR), at its seventh session (13 to 17 January 2003), taking into account the urgency and importance of implementing SOLAS regulation XI-2/6 on Ship Security Alert Systems adopted by the Conference of Contracting Governments to the SOLAS Convention, 1974 (7-13 December 2002) to be used in the enhancement of Maritime Security, prepared the guidance on provision of ship security alert systems.

2   The Maritime Safety Committee, at its seventy-seventh session (28 May to 6 June 2003), agreed to the proposed guidance regarding Ship Security Alert Systems, as set out in the annex.

3   Member Governments are requested to bring the annexed guidance to the attention of Maritime Administrations, shipmasters, port authorities, port facility security operators, national authorities responsible for security, shipping companies, system manufacturers and designers.

***

...Contd

MSC/Circ.1072

ANNEX

GUIDANCE ON PROVISION OF THE SHIP SECURITY ALERT SYSTEM

1   Regulation 6 of SOLAS chapter XI-2 requires ships to be provided with a ship security alert system. Section A/9 of the International Ship and Port Facility Security (ISPS) Code requires ships to carry a ship security plan. Performance standards for ship security alert systems are given in resolution MSC.147(77). This Circular gives guidance on the design of ship security alert systems provided to comply with the SOLAS regulation.

2   The intent of the ship security alert system is to send a covert signal or message from a ship which will not be obvious to anyone on the ship who is not aware of the alert mechanism. It is of use therefore in circumstances where a ship wishes to inform a person ashore of a problem with a minimum number of the persons onboard aware of the action. The procedures for the security alert are agreed with the ship's Administration as part of the ship security plan and ideally should be individual to the ship. It is not intended that the ship security alert procedures should be to an internationally agreed standard or conform to any particular format for all ships.

3   Possible methods of achieving the alert are as follows:

.1   a system may employ proprietary tracking equipment provided by traffic service providers. The ship then carries a concealed equipment box working over a satellite system on its upper deck which transmits a position report at, typically, 6-hourly intervals. Interruption of power to the equipment or arming of the equipment by means of sensors or manual buttons causes the equipment to transmit a different format of position report. The tracking service providers monitor the transmission reports and inform the Company when the transmission format changes;

.2   a system may utilise modifications of GMDSS equipment.[*] Some GMDSS equipment is not very suitable for modification as it is optimised for "all station" calling and may involve manual setting of frequencies etc and provides confirmation on the ship of messages sent. In these types of systems the ship security alert contains identifiers to ensure that it is not possible to confuse it with a GMDSS distress, urgency or safety alert; and

.3   a system may utilise the exchange of messages containing key words between a ship and, typically, the Company. These messages may be by speech or data communications. Ship equipment which may be used includes cellular phones in coastal areas and satellite services away from coastal areas. It may be possible to use GMDSS VHF/MF/HF equipment in areas where there are coastal facilities for receiving addressed calls.

This list is not intended as exhaustive and is not intended to inhibit future developments.

---

[*] Inmarsat is developing modifications to existing equipment that will allow for this service to be implemented.

MSC/Circ.1072
ANNEX
Page 2

4   The ship security alert system requires two activation points, one of which should be on the bridge. These will typically be fixed or portable telephone handsets, fixed or portable keypads or fixed or portable buttons.

5   Measures should be incorporated in the activation points to avoid their inadvertent operation and the generation of false alerts.

INTERNATIONAL MARITIME ORGANIZATION

IMO

E

MSC/Circ.1073
10 June 2003

T2-NAVSEC/11

MEASURES TO ENHANCE MARITIME SECURITY

DIRECTIVES FOR MARITIME RESCUE CO-ORDINATION CENTRES (MRCCS) ON ACTS OF VIOLENCE AGAINST SHIPS

1   The Maritime Safety Committee, at its seventy-second session (17 to 26 May 2000), approved Directives for Maritime Rescue Co-ordination Centres (MRCCs), (MSC/Circ.967) which, in most incidents of piracy and armed robbery against ships, are the first point of contact between the ship and coastal authorities concerned, following the Master's decision to request assistance.

2   The Maritime Safety Committee, at its seventy-seventh session (28 May to 6 June 2003), modified the text of the exiting Directives to include provisions for the handling by MRCCs of alerts received from ships in response to terrorist acts and other security incidents.

3   The revised text of the Directives is given at annex.

4   Member Governments and international organizations are recommended to bring this circular to the attention of their national MRCCs, shipowners, ship operators, shipping companies, shipmasters and crews.

5   This circular supersedes MSC/Circ.967 dated 6 June 2000.

* * *

MSC/Circ. 1073   - 2 -

ANNEX

DIRECTIVES FOR MARITIME RESCUE CO-ORDINATION CENTRES (MRCCs)

1   Definitions

"Act of violence": For the purposes of this circular, the phrases "act of violence" and "acts of violence against ships" encompass acts of piracy, acts of armed robbery against ships and any other security incident directed against a ship which does not fall into one of the preceding categories. For the purposes of this circular, the "ship" includes all persons on board.

"Piracy" The 1982 United Nations Convention on the Law of the Sea (UNCLOS) (article 101) defines piracy as follows:

"Piracy consists of any of the following acts:
(a) any illegal acts of violence or detention, or any act of depredation, committed for private ends by the crew or the passengers of a private ship or a private aircraft, and directed:
   (i) on the high seas, against another ship or aircraft, or against persons or property on board such ship or aircraft;
   (ii) against a ship, aircraft, persons or property in a place outside the jurisdiction of any State;
(b) any act of voluntary participation in the operation of a ship or of an aircraft with knowledge of facts making it a pirate ship or aircraft;
(c) any act inciting or of intentionally facilitating an act described in sub-paragraph (a) or (b)."

"Security Forces Authority": For the purposes of this circular, and in accordance with the organization of and the decisions by the national Governments, the SFA (Security Forces Authority) is generally a national or regional command of a public agency such as the Navy, Coast Guard or Police in charge of providing the response to security incidents.

"Security incident". SOLAS 1974, as amended, chapter XI-2 defines a security incident as "any suspicious act or circumstance threatening the security of a ship, including a mobile offshore drilling unit and a high speed craft, or of a port facility or of any ship/port interface or any ship to ship activity".

"Overt Security Alert": For the purposes of this circular, an overt security alert uses a communication channel or method which makes no attempt to deny knowledge of its activation and use, for example VHF broadcast.

"Covert Security Alert": For the purposes of this circular, a covert security alert uses a communication channel or method designed to deny knowledge of its activation to perpetrators of the acts of violence, for example a ship security alert system as detailed in the ISPS Code.

IMO Directive: MRCC; Violence Against Ships

2   General

2.1   While all Governments may grant their maritime rescue co-ordination centre(s) (MRCCs)[1], in addition to those of search and rescue (SAR), powers in the application of national regulations and instructions, the response to acts of violence against ships is the only one of these extensions that forms part of the IMO regulations2. In this way, MRCCs are incorporated in the organization that Governments have to set up to deal with acts of violence against ships, which may occur suddenly and anywhere.

2.2   For these reasons, this circular has been drawn up especially for the MRCCs[2], taking into consideration their own situations and normal activities. It should be considered in connection with guidance on maritime security given in chapter XI-2 of the SOLAS Convention, and the International Ship and Port Facility (ISPS) Code, and guidance on piracy and armed robbery against ships given in MSC/Circ.622/Rev.1 for Governments, and MSC Circ.623/Rev.1 aimed at shipping companies, masters and crews.

2.3   MRCCs can expect to receive a ship security alert of an act of violence against a ship in a number of ways. This ship security alert can come directly from the ship or via an alternative source. These alternative sources include, but are not limited to, other ships, an adjacent MRCC, the national SFA, ship operators and flag State administrations.

2.4   The immediate MRCC response to an alert should be determined by whether the alert received by the MRCC is determined to be an overt alert or a covert alert. Determining whether the alert is overt or covert is a critical factor as the response for each is extremely different as shown below:

    .1   Overt Security Alert: For an overt alert communication with the ship or other ships in the vicinity of the ship under threat or attack need not be delayed or disguised, for example a Master of a ship may use an overt alarm to discourage an attack;

    .2   Covert Security Alert: For a covert alert **no attempt is to be made** to contact the ship originating the alert and no communications are to be made with other ships in the vicinity of the ship under threat. A Master of a ship may use a covert alarm to deny those posing the threat or making an attack the knowledge that an alert has been made; and

    .3   Unspecified Security Alert: A security alert is deemed to be unspecified when:

        .1   it is unclear whether the alert is overt or covert; or
        .2   the initial alert is overt and this is subsequently superseded by a declaration that it is a covert alert.

Detailed guidance for these three situations is provided in the operating instructions below.

---

[1] Certain missions, which MRCCs have to carry out, in addition to search and rescue, are however set out in chapter 7 of the IAMSAR Manual, volume II

[2] All the aspects laid down for the MRCC in this circular should be taken as valid for the joint rescue co-ordination centres (JRCC) and, if the national authority so decides, for the maritime rescue sub-centres (MRSC) and joint rescue sub-centres.

MSC/Circ. 1073
- 4 -

2.5 Bilateral agreements between States may be reached for the application of co-operation procedures that might differ from those set out above.

3 Preparatory measures

It is essential that MRCCs are in all respects prepared for situations involving acts of violence against ships. Preparatory measures taken by each MRCC must include actions to:

.1 ensure that the MRCC is in possession of appropriate national instructions giving details of the Security Force Authority (SFA) responsible for the operational application of contingency plans (counter-measures) to deal with situations involving acts of violence against ships;

.2 establish fast and effective methods of communication for use between the MRCC and the SFA in question. These methods of communication should be tested on a regular basis;

.3 If appropriate and feasible, repeat points 3.1 and 3.2 above for each State whose coastal waters are included in the search and rescue region (SRR) of the MRCC;

.4 ensure the MRCC has clear written procedures and instructions on the actions to be taken by operations personnel when dealing with an act of violence against a ship;

.5 establish who is responsible for notifying other Administrations and Contracting Governments of the act of violence in accordance with SOLAS 1974, as amended, chapter XI-2, regulations 6 and 7; and

.6 train the MRCC personnel in:

.1 the risks of an act of violence against a ship in the SRR covered by the MRCC in particular and the phenomenon of acts of violence against ships in general;

.2 the use of the MRCC procedures and instructions relating to acts of violence against ships;

.3 the communications regarding attacks or threats of attack that the MRCC might receive; and

.4 the reports to be sent in the event of an alert and all other actions to be taken.

4 Operating measures

4.1 Action to be taken by MRCCs upon receipt of all types of security alerts:

.1 If the position of the incident is within the SRR of the MRCC, the MRCC should immediately inform the appropriate SFA, using the method of communications set out in 3.2. In addition, if the position is close to the boundaries of the SRR, the MRCC should also inform the appropriate neighbouring MRCC; and

.2   If the position of the incident is outside the SRR of the MRCC, the MRCC should relay the alert to the appropriate MRCC using the normal methods of communication among MRCCs for search and rescue operations or other pre-determined discreet inter-MRCC communication channels as appropriate.

4.2   Operating measures for OVERT security alerts

In the event of receiving an overt security alert, in addition to the actions detailed in paragraph 4.1 above MRCCs should:

.1   maintain contact with the SFA and other parties as detailed in 4.1above;

.2   contact the ship to determine if the security alert is real or false and to ascertain the nature of the current situation;

.3   if no response is received, assume that the act of violence is ongoing and advise the SFA accordingly;

.4   determine the most effective way of issuing a security alert warning for the other ships in the vicinity using appropriate systems and procedures[2] and

.5   place SAR resources on standby if appropriate. Prior to authorizing their dispatch by the MRCC, the SFA should determine the risk to the SAR assets.

4.3   Operating measures for COVERT security alerts

In the event of receiving a covert security alert, in addition to the actions detailed in paragraph 4.1 above, MRCCs should:

.1   maintain contact with the SFA and other parties as detailed in 4.1 above;

.2   under no circumstances should an MRCC receiving a covert security alert acknowledge receipt of the information received. In addition the MRCC must not send any communication or advice to the Master, other persons on board, or ships in the vicinity of the incidents related to that incident unless directed by the SFA;

.3   place SAR resources on standby if appropriate. Prior to authorizing their dispatch by the MRCC, the SFA should determine the risk to the SAR assets; and

.4   assist the SFA by providing operational information as requested by the SFA.

4.4   Operating measures for UNSPECIFIED security alerts

Unspecified alerts should be treated as covert in accordance with paragraph 4.3 above.

5   Additional Actions

5.1   The MRCC should endeavour to keep the ship's Administration informed of the acts of violence committed against this ship and of their consequences.

---

2 e.g Refer to format and drafting guidance in COMSAR/Circ.15 – Joint IMO/IHO/WMO Manual on Maritime Safety Information (MSI)

5.2   If laid down in the national regulations and instructions, the MRCC may also have to report directly:

    .2.1   to the national authority or authorities empowered to deal with the phenomena concerned, if this authority or these authorities are different from the SFA referred to above; and

    .2.2   to the person or body entrusted with the inquiries into the acts of violence within the meaning of this circular.

5.3   The MRCC may be required to supply additional information to the Administration, if the Administration has an obligation to send a report of events to the Organization.

———————

INTERNATIONAL MARITIME ORGANIZATION
4 ALBERT EMBANKMENT
LONDON SE1 7SR

Telephone: 020 7735 7611
Fax: 020 7587 3210
Telex: 23588 IMOLDN G

IMO

E

Ref. T2-NAVSEC2/11

MSC/Circ.1074
10 June 2003

MEASURES TO ENHANCE MARITIME SECURITY

INTERIM GUIDELINES FOR THE AUTHORIZATION OF RECOGNIZED SECURITY ORGANIZATIONS ACTING ON BEHALF OF THE ADMINISTRATION AND/OR DESIGNATED AUTHORITY OF A CONTRACTING GOVERNMENT

1   The Maritime Safety Committee at its seventy-seventh session (28 May to 6 June 2003), bearing in mind the provisions of section 4.3 of Part A and sections 4.3 to 4.7 of part B of the International Ship and Port Facility Security Code (ISPS) on Recognized Security Organization (RSO), developed the attached Interim guidelines for the authorization of recognized security organizations acting on behalf of the administration and/or designated authority of a contracting government.

2   The interim guidelines may be revised, based on the experience gained on the implementation of the new SOLAS chapter XI-2 and the ISPS Code and, in particular, with the designation of RSOs after 1 July 2004.

3   Member Governments and international organizations concerned are recommended to bring this circular to the attention of all parties concerned.

***

MSC/Circ.1074

ANNEX

INTERIM GUIDELINES FOR THE AUTHORIZATION OF RECOGNIZED SECURITY ORGANIZATIONS ACTING ON BEHALF OF THE ADMINISTRATION AND/OR DESIGNATED AUTHORITY OF A CONTRACTING GOVERNMENT

General

1   Under the provisions of SOLAS regulation I/6 and, *inter alia,* SOLAS regulation XI-2/1.16 "Special measures to enhance maritime security", Recognized Security Organization (RSOs) may be delegated specific functions on behalf of the Administration and/or the Designated Authority of the Contracting Government. The following functions may be delegated in whole or in part to RSOs:

    .1   approval of ships security plans;

    .2   verification for ships

    .3   issuance and endorsement of International Ship Security Certificates; and

    .4   development of port facility security assessments.

2   In no instance may the RSO approve, verify, or certify a work product that it has developed (e.g. preparation ship security assessments, preparation ship security plans or of amendments under review).

3   Control in the assignment of such authority is needed in order to promote uniformity of assessments, verification, approval and certification activities required by SOLAS chapter XI-2 or by part A of the International Ship and Port Facility Security (ISPS) Code. Therefore, any delegation of authority to RSO, should:

    .1   determine that the security organization has adequate resources in terms of technical, managerial and operational capabilities to accomplish the tasks being assigned, in accordance with the interim guidelines for RSOs acting on behalf of the Administration and/or Designated Authority as set out in Appendix 1;

    .2   have a formal written agreement between the Administration or Designated Authority and the RSO being authorized;

    .3   specify instructions detailing actions to be followed in the event that a ship is found not in compliance with the relevant provisions of international requirements for which the RSO has been delegated authority;

    .4   provide the RSO with all appropriate instruments of national law giving effect to the provisions of the conventions or specify whether the Administration's and/or Designated Authority's standards go beyond convention requirements in any respect; and

MSC/Circ.1074
ANNEX
Page 2

.5   specify that the RSO maintain records that can provide the Administration and/or Designated Authority with data to assist in interpretation and implementation of specific convention regulations.

Verification and monitoring

4   The Administration and/or Designated Authority should establish a system to ensure the adequacy of work performed by the RSOs authorized to act on its behalf. Such a system should, *inter alia*, include the following items:

.1   procedures for communication with the RSO;

.2   procedures for reporting from the RSO and processing of reports by the Administration and/or Designated Authority;

.3   additional ship and port facility inspections and audits by the Administration and/or Designated Authority or other delegated organizations;

.4   the Administration's and/or Designated Authority's evaluation/acceptance of the certification of the RSO's quality system by an independent body of auditors recognized by the Administration and/or Designated Authority; and

.5   the Administration and/or Designated Authority should monitor and verify the activities related to security delegated to the RSO as appropriate. The Administration and/or Designated Authority maintain the ultimate authority continue or revoke delegations to RSOs.

Appendix 1

**INTERIM GUIDELINES FOR AUTHORIZATION OF RECOGNIZED SECURITY
ORGANIZATIONS ACTING ON BEHALF OF THE ADMINISTRATION
AND/OR DESIGNATED AUTHORITY OF A CONTRACTING GOVERNMENT**

A Security Organization may be recognized by the Administration and/or Designated Authority to perform statutory work on its behalf subject to compliance with the following interim guidelines for which the recognised security organization (RSO) should submit complete information and substantiation.

General

1   The relative size, structure, experience and capability of the RSO commensurate with the type and degree of authority intended to be delegated thereto should be demonstrated.

2   The RSO should be able to document capability and experience in performing security assessments, developing risk assessments, conducting maritime verification, approval and certification activities for ships and/or for port facilities and their ancillary equipment, as appropriate.

Specific Provisions

3   The following should apply for the purpose of delegating authority to perform port facility security assessment and ship verification, and certification services of a statutory nature in accordance with regulatory instruments which require the ability to integrate ship and port interface operational considerations with maritime security threats, and to develop, verify and audit specific requirements:

3.1   The RSO should provide for the publication and systematic maintenance of procedures in the English language for the conduct of activities to ensure compliance with delegated authorities pursuant to SOLAS chapter XI-2. Updating of these procedures should be done on a periodic basis at intervals acceptable to the Administration.

3.2   The RSO should allow participation in the development of its procedures by representatives of the Administration and/or Designated Authority and other parties concerned.

3.3   The RSO should be established with:

   .1   an adequate technical, managerial and support staff capable of developing and maintaining its procedures; and

   .2   a qualified professional staff to provide the required service representing an adequate geographical coverage as required by the Administration and/or Designated Authority.

IMO Guidance: RSO Authorization

3.4   The RSO should be governed by the principles of ethical behaviour, which should be contained in a Code of Ethics and as such recognize the inherent responsibility associated with a delegation of authority to include assurance as to the adequate performance of services as well as the confidentiality of related information as appropriate.

3.5   The RSO should demonstrate the technical, administrative and managerial competence and capacity to ensure the provision of quality services in a timely fashion.

3.6   The RSO should be prepared to provide relevant information to the Administration and/or Designated Authority, as necessary.

3.7   The RSO's management should define and document its policy and objectives for, and commitment to, quality and ensure that this policy is understood, implemented and maintained at all levels in the RSO.

3.8   The RSO should be subject to certification of its quality system by an independent body of auditors recognized by the Administration and/or Designated Authority. The Administration and/or Designated Authority may serve as the auditor.

3.9   The RSO should develop, implement and maintain an effective internal quality system based on appropriate parts of internationally recognized quality standards no less effective than the ISO 9000-2000 series, and which, inter alia, ensures that:

.1   the RSO's procedures are established and maintained in a systematic manner;

.2   the RSO's procedures are complied with;

.3   the requirements of the statutory work for which the RSO is authorized, are satisfied;

.4   the responsibilities, authorities and interrelation of personnel whose work affects the quality of the RSO's services, are defined and documented;

.5   a supervisory system is in place that monitors the actions and work carried out by the RSO;

.6   a system for qualification of assessors, surveyors, and auditors and continuous updating of their knowledge is implemented;

.7   records are maintained, demonstrating achievement of the required standards in the items covered by the services performed, as well as the effective operation of the quality system;

.8   a comprehensive system of planned and documented internal audits of the quality related activities in all locations is implemented;

.9   the RSO has established a process and procedures to assess and monitor at periodic intervals the trustworthiness of its personnel;

.10   the RSO has established processes and procedures to ensure that appropriate measures are in place to avoid unauthorized disclosure of, or access to, security sensitive materials relating to ship security assessments, ship security plans, port facility security assessments and port facility security plans, and to individual assessments or plans; and

.11   a procedure for providing feed back and information, as appropriate, to its customers.

4   The following should, in addition, apply for the purpose of delegating authority to perform certification services of a statutory nature in accordance with regulatory instruments.

.1   the provision and application of proper procedures to assess the degree of compliance of the applicable shipboard maritime security measures and management systems:

.2   the provision of a systematic training and qualification regime for its professional personnel engaged in the maritime security management system certification process to ensure proficiency in the applicable quality and security management criteria as well as adequate knowledge of the technical and operational aspects of maritime security management; and

.3   the means of assessing through the use of qualified professional staff the application and maintenance of the security management system both shore based as well as on board ships intended to be covered in the certification.

Specialized expertise

5   Each RSO shall be able to demonstrate by means of established process, procedures, and relevant documentation the following minimum capabilities following the guidance in paragraph 4.5 of part B of the ISPS Code:

.1   expertise in relevant aspects of security;

.2   appropriate knowledge of ship and port operations, including knowledge of ship design and construction if providing services in respect of ships and port design and construction if providing services in respect of port facilities;

.3   their capability to assess the likely security risks that could occur during ship and port facility operations including the ship/port interface and how to minimize such risks;

.4   their ability to maintain and improve the expertise of their personnel;

.5   their ability to monitor the continuing trustworthiness of their personnel;

.6   their ability to maintain appropriate measures to avoid unauthorized disclosure of, or access to, security-sensitive material;

.7   their knowledge of the requirements of SOLAS chapter XI-2 and part A of the ISPS Code and the guidance contained in part B of the Code and relevant national and international legislation and security requirements;

.8   their knowledge of current security threats and patterns;

IMO Guidance: RSO Authorization

.9   their knowledge of recognition and detection of weapons, dangerous substances and devices;

.10   their knowledge of recognition, on a non-discriminatory basis, of characteristics and behavioural patterns of persons who are likely to threaten security;

.11   their knowledge of techniques used to circumvent security measures; and

.12   their knowledge of security and surveillance equipment and systems and their operational limitations.

———

IMO Guidance: Master as SSO

IMO's FSI Sub-Committee confirms master can be designated as Ship Security Officer (SSO)

The master of a ship can be designated as the Ship Security Officer (SSO) in implementing the provisions of the mandatory ISPS Code, IMO's Flag State Implementation (FSI) Sub-Committee has unanimously decided to recommend to the Maritime Safety Committee (MSC).

The FSI Sub-Committee, which met between 15–19 March 2004 at IMO's London Headquarters, considered the issue following concerns raised by Contracting Governments to SOLAS 1974 and by the shipping industry as to whether the ISPS Code, as drafted, would prevent the master of the ship being designated as the SSO.

Based on information received from the IMO Secretariat, confirmed by the Chairman of the MSC, the Chairman of the Maritime Security Working Group (MSWG) and several delegations which had attended the relevant sessions of the MSWG, the Sub-Committee confirmed that neither the drafting of the definition of the SSO nor the provisions of the ISPS Code relating to his responsibilities, training etc. were aimed at preventing the master from being designated as SSO.

According to the ISPS Code, it is the responsibility of the Company and the Company Security Officer to appoint the SSO. This naturally has to be endorsed by the Administration of the flag State and/or the RSO through the approval of the Ship Security Plan and issuing of the ISSC and/or the relevant training certificate by the Administration as appropriate.

The definition of the SSO should be viewed in conjunction with SOLAS regulation XI-2/8 on "Master's discretion for ship safety and security", which makes it clear that the master has ultimate responsibility for safety and security.

The phrase "accountable to the master" in the definition of SSO is intended to cover those situations, for example on large passenger ships, where the SSO is not the master, by reaffirming that the master has overall responsibility for security. There is no intention of preventing the master from assuming the duties of SSO, as this would be inconsistent with SOLAS regulation XI-2/8.

It is, of course, for the national Administrations to decide if they wish to impose particular restrictions on who may serve as SSOs on ships flying their flag. This should, however, not be imposed by national Administrations on ships not flying their flag through port State control measures, since this is clearly the prerogative of the Contracting Government of the flag State concerned.

Statement issued on the occasion of the meeting of the IMO Flag State Implementation (FSI) Sub-Committee

17 March 2004

No definitions or provisions to restrict Master from SSO role

Company and CSO responsible for appointing SSO

SSO definition clarified

"...accountable to the Master"

Administrations right to impose restrictions on SSO appointments

IMO Guidance: Master as SSO

In view of the limited time available until 1 July 2004, the Sub-Committee considered it appropriate to clarify the issue and invited the MSC to endorse its recommendation that the provisions of the ISPS Code do not prevent the master being appointed as SSO, if so decided by the flag State Administration.

The Sub-Committee was of the view that, by acting in this manner, it provided the industry and all Parties concerned with a clear direction on this issue in the run up to 1 July.

IMO
17 March 2004

European Proposals

In early 2001, the European Commission (EC) produced a landmark in maritime security when it addressed, by way of a White Paper, the subject of cruise passenger security in Europe.

Overview

Subsequently, the EC supported unreservedly the initiative of the IMO that resulted in the amendments to SOLAS 1974 and the ISPS Code. Indeed, from the very early stages of the work to enhance maritime security, the Commission strongly supported the activities of all IMO Committees and Sub-Committees, mainly by co-ordinating positions of the EU Member States. Additionally, since December 2001, the EC has worked closely with the US Coast Guard to establish trans-Atlantic accord in the proposed security measures.

Support for IMO initiative

In supporting the enhancement of maritime security, the Commission sought to follow three lines of approach:

EC line of approach to maritime security

1 – to refrain as much as possible from unilateral action in the domain;
2 – to resort to an international set-up of recommended measures; and
3 – to implement them at a regional (EU) level for enforcement, not only in European ports and on European ships, but also by enforcement in European waters for any foreign ships wishing to trade with Europe.

Accordingly, the Commission planned legislation on the subject based on three elements:
 – a **Regulation** for **ships and port facilities** based on the IMO December 2002 Resolutions;
 – a **Directive** for **ports** security; and
 – a **Directive** on **inter-modal** security.

Planned legislation:
– Regulation
– Directive
– Directive

Proposed Regulation for Ships and Ports

The new EC *Regulation on Enhancing Ship and Port Facility Security* was proposed in May 2003 and deals with the implementation of the IMO December 2002 decisions.

Proposal:

Regulation on Enhancing Ship & Port Facility Security

However, it also provides for an extension, in part, of the ISPS Code and SOLAS amendments to national traffic of Member States in order to achieve the global objective of maritime security, to keep the principle of proportionality between the measures and the potential risks, and to place a particular emphasis on the transport of passengers, including similar measures for the intra-Community Short Sea Shipping Trade.

In explaining their emphasis on intra-community or national passenger transport, the Commission cited three reasons:
1 – local commuters deserve equivalent security as cruise passengers;

– intra-community/ commuter passenger transport

EC Proposals

– distortion of competition
– easier port management

Parliament vote

Proposed Regulation:

– makes Parts of ISPS Code Part B compulsory

– extension to national/domestic traffic

– Class A and other passenger vessels

– compulsory provision by ship of security info

– national focal point for security

– EC-managed inspections

2 – possible distortion of competition between ships on different routes but with the same destination or departure points;
3 – easier port management if all vessels are protected.

On 9 October 2003, the EC's Transport Council gave unanimous agreement to the proposals and on 19 November 2003 the European Parliament voted in favour of the Regulation with a very large majority. The Regulation (at March 2004) is on course for formal adoption within the month.

The Regulation makes compulsory certain provisions from Part B of the ISPS Code which were previously recommendatory. Whilst the Commissioners believe that such action will serve to increase the level of maritime security, they also aim to avoid the differences of interpretation among Member States which may lead to unacceptable distortions of competition, or a weaker protection of EU citizens.

The Regulation also proposes the principle of extension of the security measures to te national traffic of the Member States. This means that Class A passenger ships engaged in international voyages will have to comply with the IMO measures by 1 July 2005. Class A passenger ships are those which are more than 20 nautical miles from any coast during part of their voyage. For other passenger ships and for cargo ships of over 500 GT, the application of security measures by 1 July 2007 will be the subject to the outcome of compulsory security assessments conducted by Member States.

The Regulation also calls for the compulsory provision of security information by any ship prior to its entry into a Member State port. Provisions for facilitating scheduled services on fixed routes are also made, in as much as such facilitation does not compromise the general level of security reached.

Additionally, the Regulation also provides for a single national focal point to be established for the security of ships and port facilities for other Member States and the Commission. An inspection procedure, managed by the EC, is also set to be established.

Directive on Port Security

The Commission has proposed a *Directive on Enhancing Port Security* which was presented to the European Parliament on 10 February 2004.

The Directive seeks to expand the principles of the ISPS Code into the entire port area – including port facilities and all associated security-relevant areas. A security assessment will define the requirements of the security measures.

The Directive also seeks to introduce an appraisal of the efficiency of the port security organisation and its communication links with all parties under the remit of the Port Security Assessment. As a result, a security plan for each port will be derived and will be endorsed by the Port Security Authority nominated for each port and implemented for all ports who wish to handle traffic regulated by the forementioned Regulation.

Directive on Intermodal Transport Security

The Directive, which the Commission is planning to propose by the end of 2004, sets out to achieve homogenous intra-Community traffic under the terms of the proposed new Community Customs code.

At this stage, the Directive is expected to be based on the following principles:
– it should cover all types of shipment (Containers, bulk, etc)
– it should offer a common approach for all surface modes, probably with different implementation rules for each mode
– it should cover intra-Community trade but also incorporate third country trade within European territory.

Full and latest texts of the *Regulation on Enhancing Ship and Port Facility Security* and the *Directive on Enhancing Port Safety* may be found at:

http://europa.eu.int/comm/transport/maritime/security/index_en.htm

---

Proposal

Directive on Enhancing Port Security

– extend ISPS into whole port area

– appraisal of port security organisation

– Port Security Authority

Proposal

Directive on Intermodal Transport Security

– homogenous intra-Community traffic
– all types of cargo types and modes

– third country traffic through Europe

Update and full texts

PROPOSAL ONLY

Regulation of the
European Parliament
and of the Council on
enhancing ship and
port facility security

Brussels
May 2003

Explanatory
Memorandum

REGULATION OF THE EUROPEAN PARLIAMENT AND OF THE
COUNCIL ON ENHANCING SHIP AND PORT FACILITY SECURITY

EXPLANATORY MEMORANDUM
General Introduction

The International Maritime Organisation (IMO) began work on maritime security in February 2002. The Commission therefore considered it preferable to await the outcome of the discussions within the IMO rather than develop unilateral initiatives.

On 12 December 2002, after a five-day Diplomatic Conference, IMO adopted an amendment to the International Convention for the Safety of Life at Sea (SOLAS), and in particular a new chapter entitled "Special measures to enhance maritime security", and an International Ship and Port Facility Security (ISPS) Code .

The purpose of these instruments is to take maritime security issues into account in connection with shipping and port facilities.

IMO's work on maritime security is confined to ships to and port facilities which represent the ship/port interface. The Commission will be presenting a legislative initiative on security in Community ports.

It should be noted that this concerns all of the Member States as flag States and thirteen of them as port States.

The amendment to the SOLAS Convention and Part A of the ISPS Code consist entirely of mandatory provisions; Part B of the ISPS Code is made up of recommendations which the Contracting Governments are requested to implement.

The main provisions of these international instruments are as follows.

The mandatory provisions (the amendment to the SOLAS Convention and Part A of the ISPS Code) are indispensable to enhancing maritime security.

They concern a requirement for ships to be permanently marked with their identification number and fitted with an automatic identification system (AIS) and a ship security alert system for spreading the alarm in the event of hostile action against the ship, and for them to be issued with a continuous synopsis record (CSR), a kind of identity document recording the history of the ship.

Main provisions of
ISPS Code:

They also provide for a set of active and passive security measures based on three security levels (normal, increased, high), their implementation being linked to an overall risk assessment. They include the requirement to appoint people responsible for carrying them out (ship, company and port facility security officers), to prepare a security plan geared to the risk assessment (ship and port facility) and to issue an international ship security certificate, as well as arrangements for personnel training and exercises.

Provision is also made, depending on the potential risk to persons, property and the environment, for the possibility of drawing up a declaration of security between the ship and the host port facility to define the responsibilities of each. Another possibility is that a ship in port or about to enter port can be inspected by the port State authorities for security reasons. The duties and obligations of the various players (Contracting Governments, companies, ships' masters and port facilities) are clearly defined.

Part B of the ISPS Code consists of very detailed recommendations intended to provide guidance in implementing the mandatory provisions.

The Contracting Governments are responsible in particular for designating recognised security organisations (responsible for providing security services to port facilities and ships) and national or regional maritime security contact points, to manage the security levels and to exchange information on security matters. This part of the ISPS Code also contains detailed proposals for both ships and port facilities, regarding assessment of the risks and the security plans to be prepared, and personnel training and exercises. It also shows how and in what cases a declaration of security should be drawn up between the ship and the host port facility.

***

The amendment to the SOLAS Convention and the ISPS Code must enter into force on 1 July 2004. This leaves very little time to complete all the necessary preparations, so some measures will have to be implemented in advance.

These international instruments contain provisions the scope of which has to be defined at Community level. Their application is confined to international shipping, while security has to be seen from a more global perspective that therefore has to embrace certain national modes of transport as well, though maintaining a gradation according to the nature of the risks and their consequences.

Certain provisions of the December 2002 amendment to the SOLAS Convention affect instruments which already form part of Community law, i.e.:
❑ amendments to Regulation 19V of the SOLAS Convention, "Carriage requirements for shipborne navigational systems and

PROPOSAL ONLY

Explanatory Memorandum

Main provisions of ISPS Code contd

Definition of ISPS Code provisions at EC level:

– how they affect existing EC law (AIS)

equipment". These rules relating to the automatic identification system (AIS) will have to be adapted pursuant to Directive 2002/59/EC of the European Parliament and of the Council of 27 June 2002 establishing a Community vessel traffic monitoring and information system;

❏ amendments to Regulations 3 and 5 of Chapter XI of the SOLAS Convention, concerning the identification number and synopsis record of ships. These rules will be taken into account in particular pursuant to Council Directive 95/21/EC of 19 June 1995 concerning port State control of shipping.

***

The Commission therefore considers that steps need to be taken to:

❏ guarantee and monitor at Community level achievement of the main objective of these international instruments, i.e. enhancing ship and port facility security;

❏ ensure harmonised implementation and equal conditions throughout the European Union for access to and monitoring of markets and activities related to the maritime sector.

Accordingly, the Commission:

❏ **will adapt the abovementioned Directives 2002/59/EC and 95/21/EC following the committee procedure, so as to integrate into them relevant provisions of the new Regulations in the SOLAS Convention in addition to those in Chapter XI-2 of SOLAS and the ISPS Code,**

❏ **proposes that the European Parliament and the Council should adopt as soon as possible this Regulation on enhancing ship and port facility security, which transposes Chapter XI-2 of the SOLAS Convention and the ISPS Code, provides a basis for their harmonised interpretation and implementation, as well as Community monitoring, and extends some of their provisions to domestic maritime traffic.**

***

NEED FOR A REGULATION

❏ Implementation of the amendment to the SOLAS Convention and the ISPS Code may vary from one Member State to another since these instruments contain some provisions which though mandatory are open to interpretation and adaptation, and others which are recommendations. There is a need for uniform implementation and uniform monitoring of ships from third countries visiting our shores and putting into our ports.

❏ Member States may adopt national measures of varying scope and applicable on different dates. Failure to harmonise these measures would be potentially damaging to the shipping industry. It could provoke imbalances in the level of security sought and might easily lead to distortions of competition between the Member States.

❏ The objective of enhancing maritime security cannot be achieved by measures confined to international shipping alone; there have to be measures covering domestic traffic as well, and only action at the Community level can guarantee this in a harmonised way.

❏ Finally, provisions need to be adopted which will encourage Member States to promote scheduled maritime traffic within the Community under satisfactory security conditions on fixed routes using dedicated port facilities.

GENERAL PRINCIPLES OF THE PROPOSAL

❏ *As regards achieving the objective of providing a basis for harmonised interpretation and implementation as well as Community monitoring of the special measures to enhance maritime security, by amending the SOLAS Convention and introducing the ISPS Code, the Regulation:*

○ makes mandatory certain provisions of Part B of the ISPS Code, which have the status of recommendations, in order on the one hand to raise the level of security sought and on the other hand to avoid variations in interpretation from one Member State to another. These provisions relate to the security plans and assessments of ships and port facilities, certain responsibilities of the Contracting Governments in the security field, and the company's obligation to supply the master with information on the ship's operators;

○ calls upon Member States to conclude, for the purpose of promoting intra-Community short-sea traffic and in the light of regulation XI-2/11 of the SOLAS Convention, the agreements on security arrangements for scheduled maritime traffic within the Community on fixed routes using dedicated port facilities, without this compromising the general level of security sought. It puts in place a system for checking conformity prior to signature of these agreements;

○ details the arrangements to be made by Member States for ports only occasionally serving international traffic;

○ establishes the system of security checks prior to the entry of ships of whatever origin into a Community port, as well as that of security checks in the port;

○ calls for a single national authority responsible for the security of ships and port facilities, and a timetable for early implementation of some of the measures it contains;

○ provides for a process of inspections to check the arrangements for monitoring the implementation of national plans adopted pursuant to it;

○ entrusts to the Agency set up by Regulation (EC) No 1406/2002 of the European Parliament and of the Council of 27 June 2002 establishing a European Maritime Safety Agency the role of assisting the Commission in the performance of its tasks;

○ lays down a procedure for the adaptation of its provisions.

PROPOSAL ONLY

– need to include domestic traffic

– encourage fixed-route traffic within EC

General Principles of Proposal:

– making parts of ISPS Code Part B mandatory

– utilising dedicated port facilities for some short-sea traffic

– ports with occasional international traffic

– security checks prior to port entry

– single national security authority

– process of monitoring and inspections

– European Maritime Safety Agency

PROPOSAL ONLY

Application to domestic shipping:

– extend ISPS Part A to domestic passenger vessels more than 20 miles from coast

– exemption from security checks for ships on scheduled services

Legal consideration

Synopsis of the Regulation:

Definitions

Scope of the Regulation (vessel types)

❏ *The Commission considers that the overall objective of maritime security can be reached only by applying certain measures to domestic shipping. It considers that in order to maintain uniform conditions of access to the market, these measures have to be taken uniformly in all the Member States, while ensuring that the measures are proportional to the potential risks. Passenger transport therefore takes priority but this must not be allowed to place excessive constraints on scheduled maritime services, provided that the general level of security sought is not compromised. Accordingly, the Regulation:*

○ extends all of the provisions of Chapter XI-2 of the SOLAS Convention and of Part A of the ISPS Code to include passenger ships engaged on domestic voyages during which they are required to be more than twenty nautical miles from the coast, and extends the provisions of the same texts relating to the making of security assessments, the preparation of security plans and the appointment of company and ship security officers to include other ships engaged in domestic traffic;

○ establishes the security arrangements for passenger ships engaged on domestic voyages on scheduled lines, during which they are required to be more than twenty nautical miles from the coast;

○ provides for possible exemption, under strict and constantly verifiable conditions, from the obligation of security checks prior to entry into a port for ships engaged on a scheduled service within a Member State or between two or more Member States.

❏ Legal considerations

The Commission proposes to base the Regulation on Article 80(2) of the EC Treaty, without prejudice to Member States' national security legislation and any measures that might be taken on the basis of Title VI of the Treaty on European Union.

SPECIAL CONSIDERATIONS

Article 1: This article sets out the objectives of the Regulation.

Article 2: This article contains the definitions of the main terms used in the Regulation. Most of them are based on those used in the special measures to enhance maritime security adopted by the IMO Diplomatic Conference on 12 December 2002, amending the SOLAS Convention, and in the ISPS Code.

Article 3: This article defines the common measures and the scope of the Regulation. The special measures to enhance maritime security amending the SOLAS Convention and the ISPS Code apply to the following types of ships engaged on international voyages:

– passenger ships, including high-speed passenger craft;

– cargo ships, including high-speed craft, of 500 gross tonnage and upwards;

– mobile offshore drilling units;
– port facilities serving international traffic.

This Regulation extends all of the measures in the IMO documents to passenger ships engaged on domestic voyages during which they are required to be more than twenty nautical miles from the coast, and to the port facilities serving them.

It also extends the provisions of the special measures to enhance maritime security in the SOLAS Convention and the ISPS Code concerning the making of security assessments, the preparation of security plans and the appointment of company and ship security officers to include other ships engaged in domestic traffic (passenger ships, including high-speed passenger craft; cargo ships, including high-speed craft, of 500 gross tonnage and upwards) and to the port facilities serving them.

Part B of the ISPS Code contains a set of recommendations for the implementation of IMO's mandatory instruments (special measures to enhance maritime security amending the SOLAS Convention and Part A of the ISPS Code), of which Member States must take the utmost account.

To raise the level of security of shipping in the Community and to avoid variations in interpretation from one Member State to another, which could cause, amongst other things, distortions of competition, this Regulation is intended to make the following sections of Part B of the ISPS Code mandatory:

❏ 1.12 on continuous checking of the relevance of ship security plans, and their revision;
❏ 1.16 on the security assessments of port facilities, and their periodical revision;
❏ 4.1 on protection of the confidentiality of security plans and assessments;
❏ 4.5 on the minimum competency of the recognised security organisations which can be authorised by Member States to assess the security of port facilities and, on behalf of the competent administrations of the Member States, to approve and verify the ship security plans and certify ships' conformity with regard to security;
❏ 4.8 on the establishment by Member States of the security level for ships and port facilities;
❏ 4.14, 4.15 and 4.16 on the establishment of central or regional contact points with regard to port facility security plans and the security information to be supplied to ship, company and port facility security officers;
❏ 4.18 on identification documents for government officials appointed to inspect security measures;
❏ 4.24 on ships' application of the safety measures recommended by the State in whose territorial waters they are sailing;

PROPOSAL ONLY

– extends all ISPS Code to domestic passenger ships and their ports

– extends special measures to other domestic traffic

Part B sections to become mandatory:

– ship security plans

– port facility security assessments
– confidentiality of plans

– minimum competency levels of RSOs

– establishment of Security Levels

– establishment of central or regional contact points

– ID documents for officials

❏ 4.28 on observance of the new requirements generated by security tasks when ships' crews are selected;

❏ 4.41 on the communication of information between States when entry into port is denied or the ship is expelled from port;

❏ 4.45 on the treatment of ships from a State which is not party to the Convention;

❏ 6.1 on the company's obligation to furnish the master with information on the ship's operators;

❏ 8.3 to 8.10 on the minimum standards to be observed with regard to assessment of the security of the ship;

❏ 9.2 on the minimum standards to be observed with regard to assessment of the ship security plan;

❏ 13.6 and 13.7 on the frequency of security training, drills and exercises for ships' crews and for company and ship security officers;

❏ 15.3 and 15.4 on the minimum standards to be observed with regard to the assessment of the security of a port facility;

❏ 16.3 and 16.8 on the minimum standards to be observed with regard to the security plan of a port facility;

❏ 18.5 and 18.6 on the frequency of security training and exercises in port facilities and for port facility security officers.

Article 4: This article confirms the obligation for each Member State to communicate to the International Maritime Organisation the information requested under regulation 13 (communication of information) of the special measures to enhance maritime security in the SOLAS Convention, and creates this obligation towards the Commission and the other Member States. This information concerns the national authorities responsible for ship and port facility security, the existence of approved port facility security plans, the contact points available at all times to receive and act upon the various types of alert and maritime security information and to give appropriate advice or assistance, the authorisation of recognised security organisations, agreements on other security arrangements and any equivalent security arrangements.

Article 5: This article gives Member States the possibility of concluding amongst themselves the bilateral or multilateral agreements provided for in regulation 11 (concerning alternative security arrangements) of the special measures to enhance maritime security in the SOLAS Convention, and in particular those necessary for promoting scheduled short-sea shipping within the Community on fixed routes between port facilities located within their territories.

The third indent of paragraph 2 allows the Commission to evaluate the draft agreements before they are concluded, under the safeguard procedure.

Paragraph 4 allows Member States to adopt security arrangements for passenger ships engaged on a scheduled domestic service during which they are required to be more than twenty nautical miles from the coast,

EC Regulation: Ship & Port

and for the port facilities serving them, without the general level of security being compromised. In the inspections provided for in article 10 the Commission will assess the monitoring of these measures.

PROPOSAL ONLY

Article 6: This article makes provision for port facilities in ports which only occasionally serve international maritime traffic, where it might be disproportionate too apply all the security rule in this Regulation on a permanent basis. In the light of the security assessments it will carry out, each Member State will draw up a list of the ports concerned and alternative measures providing an adequate level of protection. It will communicate all this information to the Commission, and only the list to the other Member States.

Ports occasionally serving international traffic

Article 7: This article introduces the obligation for any ship declaring its intention to enter a port of a Member State to provide in advance the information concerning its International Ship Security Certificate and the security level it is currently operating and the level at which it has operated previously, as well as any other practical security-related information.
The article requires Member States to appoint a "competent authority for port security" with the task of coordinating, for each Community port, the application of the security measures laid down by this Regulation for ships and port facilities.
Finally, Member States are required to keep a record of the procedure followed for each ship.

Provision of ship entry information in advance

Article 8: This article provides for the possibility of exempting from these security checks prior to entry into a port ships engaged on scheduled services within a Member State or between two or more Member States. This exemption is tied to a requirement for the shipping company to keep at the disposal of the authorities of the Member States concerned a list of the ships involved and all the information normally required in each case.
The list of companies and ships involved is sent to the Commission by each Member State concerned.

Exemption for ships on scheduled services

Article 9: Security checks in port are normally carried out by the competent security authorities of the Member States.
However, the presence of the International Ship Security Certificate on board the ship may also be checked by the port State control inspectors as provided for by Council Directive 95/21/EC of 19 June 1995 concerning port State control, as amended by Directive 2001/106/EC of the European Parliament and of the Council of 19 December 2001. This Article therefore provides for complementarity of action by the administrations concerned when different administrations are involved.

ISSC checks by port State control

Article 10: This article sets out Member States' obligations as regards administration, monitoring and provision of resources necessary for

EC Regulation: Ship & Port

PROPOSAL ONLY

achieving the objectives of the Regulation, and requires them to adopt a national plan for implementing its provisions.

Single national authority for ship and port facility security

It provides for the setting up of a single national authority responsible for ship and port facility security, which will be the Commission's contact point for implementation of the Regulation.

In paragraph 3 it sets out a timetable for the early implementation of certain measures, in accordance with resolution 6 adopted by the IMO Diplomatic Conference on 12 December 2002, in order for the security system to be up and running by 1 July 2004, the date fixed by IMO.

Timetable of application

This timetable covers the following measures:
- the appointment of a single national authority, as described in the previous paragraph, by 1 January 2004;
- the making of ship and port facility security assessments and the appointment of ship, company and port facility security officers by 1 March 2004;
- the approval of the ship and port facility security plans by 1 May 2004;
- the issuing of the international ship security certificates by 1 June 2004.

Inspections and monitoring of national systems

In paragraphs 4 to 6 it sets out a process whereby inspections supervised by the Commission are put in place to check the effectiveness of procedures for monitoring the implementation of each national system.

Paragraph 7 confers on the Agency created by Regulation (EC) No 1406/2002 of the European Parliament and of the Council of 27 June 2002 establishing a European Maritime Safety Agency, and in accordance with its rules, the role of assisting the Commission in its tasks.

Possible further amendments

Article 11: This article regulates the possibility for the Commission, following the regulatory procedure, to implement further amendments of the SOLAS Convention and of the ISPS Code, and in the light of experience to make mandatory provisions of Part B of the ISPS Code in addition to those which this Regulation already makes mandatory, or to establish a harmonised system for applying those Part B provisions which have been made mandatory.

Exercise of Powers

Article 12: The Commission is assisted by a committee acting in accordance with the regulatory procedure (Article 5 of Council Decision 1999/468/EC of 28 June 1999 laying down the procedures for the exercise of implementing powers conferred on the Commission) and the safeguard procedure (Article 6 of that Decision). This committee is that established by Article 3 of Regulation (EC) No 2099/2002 of the European Parliament and of the Council of 5 November 2002 establishing a Committee on Safe Seas and the Prevention of Pollution from Ships (COSS).

Penalties for infringement

Article 13: Calls upon Member States to institute effective, proportionate and dissuasive penalties for infringement of this Regulation.

EC Regulation: Ship & Port

Article 14: In order to keep to the 1 July 2004 time limit set by IMO for implementing the provisions of the special measures to enhance maritime security amending the SOLAS Convention and the ISPS Code, and to assist with gradual and ordered implementation, this Regulation will enter into force on the twentieth day following its publication in the Official Journal of the European Union.

It will be applicable as from 1 July 2004, apart from the provisions of Article 10(3), which will enter into force and be applicable on the dates specified by that article. Article 10(3) concerns:

- the appointment of a single national authority by 1 January 2004;
- the making of ship and port facility security assessments and the appointment of ship, company and port facility security officers by 1 March 2004;
- the approval of the ship and port facility security plans by 1 May 2004;
- the issuing of the international ship security certificates by 1 June 2004.

Annex 1: This annex contains Chapter XI-2 (Special measures to enhance maritime security) of the SOLAS Convention.

Annex 2: This annex contains Part A of the ISPS Code.

Annex 3: This annex contains Part B of the ISPS Code.

Timetable of application

Annexes

PROPOSAL ONLY

Regulation of the European Parliament and of the Council on Enhancing Ship and Port Facility Security

PROPOSAL FOR A REGULATION OF THE EUROPEAN PARLIAMENT AND OF THE COUNCIL
on enhancing ship and port facility security
(Text with EEA relevance)

THE EUROPEAN PARLIAMENT AND THE COUNCIL OF THE EUROPEAN UNION,
Having regard to the Treaty establishing the European Community, and in particular Article 80(2) thereof,
Having regard to the proposal from the Commission,
Having regard to the opinion of the European Economic and Social Committee,
Having regard to the opinion of the Committee of the Regions, Acting in accordance with the procedure laid down in Article 251 of the Treaty,
Whereas:

(1) Malicious acts and terrorism are among the greatest threats to the ideals of democracy and freedom and to the values of peace, which are the very essence of the European Union.

(2) The security of European Community shipping and of citizens using it in the face of threats of intentional unlawful acts should be ensured at all times.

(3) On 12 December 2002 the Diplomatic Conference of the International Maritime Organisation (IMO) adopted amendments to the International Convention for the Safety of Life at Sea (SOLAS) and an International Ship and Port Facility Security Code (ISPS). These instruments are intended to enhance the security of ships used in international trade and associated port facilities; they comprise mandatory provisions, the scope of some of which in the Community should be clarified, and recommendations, some of which should be made mandatory within the Community.

Treaty of the EU

(4) Without prejudice to the rules of the Member States in the field of national security and measures which might be taken on the basis of Title VI of the Treaty on European Union, the security objective described in recital 2 should be achieved by adopting appropriate measures in the field of maritime transport policy establishing joint standards for the interpretation, implementation and monitoring within the Community of the provisions adopted by the Diplomatic Conference of the International Maritime Organisation (IMO) on 12 December 2002. Implementing powers should be conferred on the Commission to adopt detailed implementing provisions.

Fundamental rights in EU

(5) This Regulation respects the fundamental rights and observes the principles recognised in particular by the Charter of Fundamental Rights of the European Union.

(6) Security should be enhanced not only for ships used in international shipping and the port facilities which serve them, but also for ships operating domestic services within the Community and their port facilities, in particular passenger ships, on account of the number of human lives which such trade puts at risk.

(7) Part B of the ISPS Code comprises a number of recommendations which should be made mandatory within the Community in order to make uniform progress towards achievement of the security objective described in recital 2.

(8) In order to contribute to the recognised and necessary objective of promoting intra-Community short-sea traffic, the Member States should be asked to conclude, in the light of regulation XI-2/11 of the SOLAS Convention, the agreements on security arrangements for scheduled maritime traffic within the Community on fixed routes using dedicated port facilities, without this compromising the general standard of security sought after.

(9) Permanently applying all the security rules provided for in this Regulation to port facilities situated in ports which only occasionally serve international shipping might be disproportionate. The Member States should determine, on the basis of the security assessments which they are to conduct, which ports are concerned and which alternative measures provide an adequate level of protection.

(10) Member States should vigorously monitor compliance with the security rules by ships intending to enter a Community port, whatever their origin. For each Community port, the Member State concerned should appoint a "competent authority for port security" responsible for coordinating the application of the security measures laid down in this Regulation as they apply to ships and port facilities. This authority must require each ship intending to enter the port to provide in advance information concerning its international ship security certificate and the levels of safety at which it operates and has previously operated, and any other practical information concerning security.

(11) Member States should be permitted to grant exemptions from the systematic requirement to provide the information referred to in the previous recital in the case of intra-Community or domestic scheduled shipping services, provided the companies operating such services are able to provide such information at any time on request by the competent authorities of the Member States.

(12) Security checks in the port may be carried out by the competent security authorities of the Member States, but also, as regards the international ship security certificate, by inspectors acting in the

PROPOSAL ONLY

Extension to domestic shipping

Part B recommendations made mandatory

Scheduled traffic on fixed routes

Ports which occasionally serve international traffic

'Competent authority for port security'

Exemptions for scheduled services

Security checks

EC Regulation: Ship & Port

PROPOSAL ONLY

Security checks under port State control

Single competent authority to co-ordinate security measures

European Maritime Safety Agency

Committee on Safe Seas and the Prevention of Pollution from Ships (COSS)

Reaching objectives – cross-Community

framework of port State control, as provided for in Council Directive 95/21/EC of 19 June 1995 on port State control, as amended by Directive 2001/106/EC of the European Parliament and of the Council of 19 December 2001. Where different administration are concerned, provision must therefore be made for them to complement each other.

(13) In view of the number of parties involved in the implementation of security measures, each Member State should appoint a single competent authority responsible for coordinating and monitoring the application of shipping security measures at national level. Member States should put in place the necessary resources and draw up a national plan for the implementation of this Regulation in order to achieve the security objective described in recital 2, in particular by establishing a timetable for the early implementation of certain measures in accordance with the terms of Resolution 6 adopted by the Diplomatic Conference of the IMO on 12 December 2002. The effectiveness of the checks on the implementation of each national system should be the subject of inspections supervised by the Commission.

(14) The European Maritime Safety Agency set up by Regulation (EC) No 1406/2002 of the European Parliament and of the Council of 27 June 2002 should assist the Commission as necessary in its inspection tasks and in keeping and monitoring relevant data supplied by the Member States.

(15) The measures needed to implement this Regulation should be adopted in accordance with Council Decision 1999/468/EC of 28 June 1999 laying down the procedures for the exercise of implementing powers conferred on the Commission. These tasks should be assigned to the Committee on Safe Seas and the Prevention of Pollution from Ships (COSS) set up by Article 3 of Regulation (EC) No 2099/2002 of the European Parliament and of the Council of 5 November 2002 establishing a Committee on Safe Seas and the Prevention of Pollution from Ships (COSS). A procedure should be defined for the adaptation of this Regulation to take account of developments in international instruments and, in the light of experience, to make mandatory further provisions of Part B of the ISPS Code not initially made mandatory by this Regulation.

(16) Since the objectives of the proposed action, namely the introduction and application of appropriate measures in the field of maritime transport policy, cannot be sufficiently achieved by the Member States and can therefore, by reason of the European scale of this Regulation, be better achieved at Community level, the Community may adopt measures in accordance with the principle of subsidiarity set out in Article 5 of the Treaty. In

the principle of proportionality set out in that Article, this Regulation is limited to the basic joint standards required to achieve the objectives of ship and port facility security and does not go beyond what is necessary for that purpose,

HAVE ADOPTED THIS REGULATION:

Article 1
Objectives

1. The main objective of this Regulation is to introduce and implement Community measures aimed at enhancing the security of ships used in international trade and domestic shipping and associated port facilities in the face of threats of intentional unlawful acts.

2. The Regulation is also intended to provide a basis for the harmonised interpretation and implementation and Community monitoring of the special measures to enhance maritime security adopted by the Diplomatic Conference of the International Maritime Organisation (IMO) on 12 December 2002, which amended the International Convention for the Safety of Life at Sea (SOLAS) and established the International Ship and Port Facility Security Code (ISPS).

Article 2
Definitions

For the purposes of this Regulation:

1. "special measures to enhance maritime security of the SOLAS Convention" means the amendments inserting the new Chapter XI-2 into the Annex to the International Convention for the Safety of Life at Sea, 1974 (SOLAS Convention) of the International Maritime Organisation (IMO), as amended, set out in Resolution 1 adopted by the Diplomatic Conference of the IMO on 12 December 2002 and attached as Annex 1 to this Regulation,

2. "ISPS Code" means the International Ship and Port Facility Security Code adopted by the Diplomatic Conference of the International Maritime Organisation on 12 December 2002,

3. "Part A of the ISPS Code" means the Preamble and the mandatory requirements forming Part A of the ISPS Code concerning the provisions of Chapter XI-2 of the Annex to the International Convention for the Safety of Life at Sea, 1974, as amended, set out in Resolution 2 adopted by the Diplomatic Conference of the International Maritime Organisation (IMO) on 12 December 2002 and attached as Annex 2 to this Regulation,

4. "Part B of the ISPS Code" means the guidance forming Part B of the ISPS Code regarding the provisions of chapter XI-2 of the Annex to the International Convention for the Safety of Life at Sea,

PROPOSAL ONLY

Objectives

Definitions:

– special measures to enhance maritime security of the SOLAS Convention

– ISPS Code

– Part A of the ISPS Code

– Part B of the ISPS Code

EC Regulation: Ship & Port

Definitions contd

1974, as amended, and Part A of the ISPS Code, set out in Resolution 2 adopted by the Diplomatic Conference of the International Maritime Organisation (IMO) on 12 December 2002 and attached as Annex 3 to this Regulation,

– maritime security

5. "maritime security" means the combination of measures and human and material resources intended to protect shipping against intentional unlawful acts,

– single national authority

6. "single national authority" means the national authority responsible for the security of ships and of port facilities designated by each Member State,

– competent authority for port security

7. "competent authority for port security" means the authority designated for each Community port by the single national authority of the Member State concerned to coordinate the application of the security measures laid down in this Regulation as they apply to ships and port facilities,

– international shipping

8. "international shipping" means any maritime transport service from a port of a Member State to a port outside that Member State, or conversely;

– domestic shipping

9. "domestic shipping" means any transport service in sea areas from a port of a Member State to the same port or another port within that Member State,

– scheduled services

10. "scheduled service" means a series of sailings organised in such a way as to provide a service linking two or more ports:
(a) either on the basis of a published timetable;
(b) or with a regularity or frequency such as to constitute a recognisable systematic service,

– port facility

11. "port facility" means a location where the ship/port interface takes place; this includes areas such as anchorages, waiting berths and approaches from seaward, as appropriate,

– ship/port interface

12. "ship/port interface" means the interactions that occur when a ship is directly and immediately affected by actions involving the movement of persons or goods or the provision of port services to or from the ship.

Joint measures and scope

Article 3
Joint measures and scope

1. In respect of international shipping, Member States shall apply in full the special measures to enhance maritime security of the SOLAS Convention and Part A of the ISPS Code, as defined in Article 2 above, in accordance with the conditions and with respect to the ships, companies and port facilities referred to therein.

2. In respect of domestic shipping, the requirements of paragraph 1 above shall apply in exactly the same way to Class A passenger ships within the meaning of Article 4 of Council Directive 98/18/EC of 17 March 1998 on safety rules and standards for passenger ships operating domestic services and to the companies which own an operate them and to the port facilities serving them. The requirements of the special measures to enhance maritime security of the SOLAS Convention and the ISPS Code relating to the carrying-out of security assessments, the preparation of a security plan, and the designation of company and ship security officers shall apply to other ships as defined in Regulation 2, paragraph 1.1 (application / types of ship) of the special measures to enhance maritime security of the SOLAS Convention operating domestic services. The same requirements shall apply to the port facilities which serve them.

PROPOSAL ONLY

– extension to domestic shipping

– special measures concerning security assessments, plans and security officers for ships on domestic traffic

3. When implementing the provisions required pursuant to paragraphs 1 and 2 above, Member States shall take fully into account the recommendations contained in Part B of the ISPS Code, as defined in Article 2(4) above.

4. Member States shall conform to the following paragraphs of Part B of the ISPS Code as if they were mandatory:
   - 1.12 (revision of ship security plans),
   - 1.16 (port facility security assessment),
   - 4.1 (protection of the confidentiality of security plans and assessments),
   - 4.5 (minimum competencies of recognised security organisations),
   - 4.8 (setting the security level),
   - 4.14, 4.15, 4.16 (contact points and information on port facility security plans),
   - 4.18 (identification documents),
   - 4.24 (ships' application of the security measures recommended by the State in whose territorial waters they are sailing),
   - 4.28 (manning level),
   - 4.41 (communication of information when entry into port is denied or the ship is expelled from port),
   - 4.45 (ships from a State which is not party to the Convention),
   - 6.1 (company's obligation to provide the master with information on the ship's operators),
   - 8.3 to 8.10 (minimum standards for the ship security assessment),
   - 9.2 (minimum standards for the ship security plan),
   - 13.6 and 13.7 (frequency of security drills and exercises for ships' crews and for company and ship security officers),
   - 15.3 to 15.4 (minimum standards for the port facility security assessment),
   - 16.3 and 16.8 (minimum standards for the port facility security plan),

– ISPS Code Part B measures to be mandatory

– 18.5 and 18.6 (frequency of security drills and exercises in port facilities and for port facility security officers).

Periodic review

5. The periodic review of the port facility security plans provided for in paragraph 1.16 of Part B of the ISPS Code shall be carried out each time a component changes either the nature or the intended use of a port facility, and at the latest three years after the plan was drawn up or last reviewed.

Promulgation of refused entry information

6. Each Member State shall communicate to the Commission and the other Member States the contact details of the contact officials referred to in paragraph 4.16 of Part B of the ISPS Code and the information provided for in paragraph 4.41of Part B of the ISPS Code when a ship is expelled from or refused entry to a Community port.

Communication of information

Article 4
Communication of information

Each Member State shall communicate to the International Maritime Organisation, the Commission and the other Member States the information required pursuant to Regulation 13 (Communication of information) of the special measures to enhance maritime security of the SOLAS Convention.

Intra-Community and domestic shipping

Article 5
Intra-Community and domestic shipping

1. For the purposes of this Regulation, Regulation 11 (Alternative security agreements) of the special measures to enhance maritime security of the SOLAS Convention may apply to scheduled intra-Community shipping operating on fixed routes and using specific associated port facilities.

2. To that end, Member States may conclude among themselves, each acting on its own behalf, the bilateral or multilateral agreements provided for in the said Regulation, and in particular such agreements as are necessary to promote intra-Community short sea shipping.
The Member States concerned shall notify the draft agreements to the Commission.
The Commission shall examine whether the draft agreements guarantee an adequate level of protection, in particular as regards the requirements of paragraph 2 of the above-mentioned Regulation 11, and whether they are in accordance with Community law. If the draft agreements do not meet these criteria, the Commission shall within four months adopt a decision in accordance with the procedure referred to in Article 12(3); in such cases, the Member States concerned shall adapt the drafts accordingly before concluding the agreements.

3. The periodic review of such agreements provided for in paragraph 4 of Regulation 11 of the special measures to enhance maritime security must take place at intervals of no more than three years.

4. Member States may adopt such security arrangements for passenger ships operating domestic scheduled services as referred to in the first subparagraph of Article 3(2) of this Regulation, and for the port facilities serving them, without the general level of security thereby being compromised.

The Member State concerned shall communicate such measures and the outcome of periodic reviews thereof to the Commission by 1 July of each year.

The conditions of application of such measures shall be subject to the Commission inspections provided for in Article 10(4)–(7) of this Regulation under the procedures defined therein.

Article 6
Occasional international shipping
1. Each Member State shall draw up the list of ports concerned, in the light of the port facility security assessments carried out, and establish the scope of the measures taken to apply the provisions of paragraph 2 of Regulation 2 (extent of application to port facilities which occasionally serve international voyages) of the special measures to enhance maritime security of the SOLAS Convention.

2. Each Member State shall communicate the said list and the measures taken to the Commission by 1 July 2004 at the latest.

3. Each Member State shall communicate the said list to the other Member States by the same date.

Article 7
Security checks prior to entry into a Community port
1. When a ship which is subject to the requirements of the special measures to enhance maritime security of the SOLAS Convention and of the ISPS Code or of Article 3 of this Regulation announces its intention to enter a port of a Member State, the competent authority for port security of that Member State shall require that the information referred to in paragraph 2.1 of Regulation 9 (Ships intending to enter a port of another Contracting Government) of the special measures to enhance maritime security of the SOLAS Convention be provided. The said authority shall analyse the information provided and, where necessary, apply the procedure provided for in paragraph 2 of that Regulation.

2. The information referred to in the preceding paragraph shall be provided:

        (a) at least twenty-four hours in advance; or
        (b) at the latest, at the time the ship leaves the previous port, if the voyage time is less than twenty-four hours; or
        (c) if the port of call is not known or it is changed during the voyage, as soon as this information is available.

3. A report shall be kept of the procedure followed in respect of each ship.

PROPOSAL ONLY

Intra-Community and domestic shipping contd

Ports handling occasional international traffic

Security checks prior to entry into a Community port

PROPOSAL ONLY

Exemptions from
security checks prior
to entry into port

Article 8
Exemptions from security checks prior to entry into a port

1. Member States may exempt scheduled services performed between ports located on their territory from the requirement laid down in Article 7 where the following conditions are met:

    (a) the company operating the scheduled services referred to above keeps and updates a list of the ships concerned and sends it to the competent authority for security at the port concerned,

    (b) for each voyage performed, the information referred to in paragraph 2.1 of Regulation 9 of the special measures to enhance maritime security of the SOLAS Convention is kept available for the competent authority for port security upon request. The company must establish an internal system to ensure that, upon request 24 hours a day and without delay, the said information can be sent to the competent authority.

2. When an international scheduled service is operated between two or more Member States, any of the Member States involved may request of the other Member States that an exemption be granted to that service. All Member States involved shall collaborate in granting an exemption to the service concerned in accordance with the conditions laid down in paragraph 1.

3. Member States shall periodically check that the conditions laid down in paragraphs 1 and 2 are being met. Where at least one of these conditions is no longer being met, Member States shall immediately withdraw the privilege of the exemption from the company concerned.

4. Member States shall draw up a list of companies and ships granted exemption under this Article, and shall update that list. They shall communicate the list and updates thereof to the Commission

Article 9
Security checks in Community ports

1. Certificate verification, as defined in paragraph 1.1 of Regulation 9 (Control of ships in port) of the special measures to enhance maritime security of the SOLAS Convention, shall be carried out in the port either by the competent authority for port security defined in Article 2(7) of this Regulation or by the inspectors defined in Article 2(5) of Council Directive 95/21/EC of 19 June 1995 on port State control of shipping, as last amended by Directive 2001/106/EC of the European Parliament and of the Council of 19 December 2001.

2. Where the inspector performing port State control does not belong to the competent authority for port security defined in Article 2(7) of this Regulation and where he believes that there are clear grounds for believing that the ship is not in compliance with the requirements of the special measures to enhance maritime security of the SOLAS Convention and of the ISPS Code, he shall immediately refer the matter to the

competent authority for port security, which shall take the measures provided for in paragraphs 1.2 and 1.3 of Regulation 9 of the special measures to enhance maritime security of the SOLAS Convention.

Article 10
Implementation and conformity checking

1. Member States shall carry out the administrative and control tasks required pursuant to the provisions of the special measures to enhance maritime security of the SOLAS Convention and of the ISPS Code. They shall ensure that all necessary means are allocated and effectively provided for the implementation of the provisions of this Regulation.

2. In accordance with Regulation 13 of the special measures to enhance maritime security of the SOLAS Convention, Member States shall designate the national authority responsible for ship and port facility security. This single national authority shall be the Commission's correspondent for the application of this Regulation.

3 Each Member States shall adopt a national plan for the implementation of this Regulation. Each Member State shall take every measure to ensure the early implementation of:
- the appointment of a single national authority, as described in the previous paragraph, by 1 January 2004;
- the making of ship and port facility security assessments and the appointment of ship, port facility and company security officers by 1 March 2004;
- the approval of the ship and port facility security plans by 1 May 2004;
- the issuing of the international ship security certificates by 1 June 2004.

4. Six months after the date of application of this Regulation, the Commission, in cooperation with the authority referred to in paragraph 2 above, shall start a series of inspections to verify the means of monitoring implementation of the national plans adopted pursuant to this Regulation. These inspections shall take account of the data supplied by the authority referred to in paragraph 2 above, including the monitoring reports. The procedures for conducting such inspections shall be adopted in accordance with the procedure referred to in Article 12(2).

5. The officials mandated by the Commission to conduct such inspections in accordance with paragraph 4 above shall exercise their powers upon production of an authorisation in writing issued by the Commission and specifying the subject-matter, the purpose of the inspection and the date on which it is to begin. The Commission shall in good time before inspections inform the Member States concerned by the inspections.
With a view to verifying the effective implementation of the national plans, such inspections may be extended, as necessary, to the departments

PROPOSAL ONLY

Implementation and conformity checking:

– designation of national authority

– adoption of national plan

– monitoring of national plans

– inspectors' authorisation

responsible for monitoring port facilities, companies and ships. In such cases, the inspections shall be carried out without advance notice.

The Member State concerned shall submit to such inspections and shall ensure that bodies or persons concerned also submit to those inspections.

– inspection reports

6. The Commission shall communicate the inspection reports to the Member State concerned, which shall indicate the measures taken to remedy any shortcomings within three months of receipt of the report. The report and the answer of the authority referred to in paragraph 2 shall be communicated to the Committee referred to in Article 12(1).

– EMSA role

7. The European Maritime Safety Agency set up by Regulation (EC) No 1406/2002 of the European Parliament and of the Council of 27 June 2002 shall, in accordance with its rules, assist the Commission in its inspection tasks and in keeping and monitoring the data supplied by the Member States pursuant to Articles 3(6), 4, 5, 6, 8 and 10 of this Regulation.

Adaptions

Article 11
Adaptations

In accordance with the procedure provided for in Article 12(2), provisions may be adopted in order:
- to apply, for the purposes of this Regulation, subsequent amendments to the international instruments referred to herein,
- in the light of experience, to extend the obligations provided for in Article 3(4) of this Regulation to other paragraphs of Part B of the ISPS Code, or to define harmonised arrangements for their application.

Committee procedure

Article 12
Committee procedure

1. The Commission shall be assisted by the Committee on Safe Seas and the Prevention of Pollution from Ships (COSS) created by Article 3 of Regulation (EC) No 2099/2002 of 5 November 2002 of the European Parliament and of the Council establishing a Committee on Safe Seas and the Prevention of Pollution from Ships (COSS).

2. Where reference is made to this paragraph, Articles 5 and 7 of Council Decision 1999/468/EC of 28 June 1999 laying down the procedures for the exercise of implementing powers conferred on the Commission shall apply, having regard to the provisions of Article 8 thereof.

The period laid down in Article 5(6) of Decision 1999/468/EC shall be set at one month.

3. Where reference is made to this paragraph, Articles 6 and 7 of Decision 1999/468/EC shall apply having regard to the provisions of Article 8 thereof.

EC Regulation: Ship & Port

Article 13
Penalties
Penalties for breaching the provisions of this Regulation shall be effective, proportionate and dissuasive.

Article 14
Entry into force
This Regulation shall enter into force on the twentieth day following that of its publication in the Official Journal of the European Union. It shall apply from 1 July 2004, apart from the provisions of Article 10(3), which shall enter into force and apply on the dates specified therein.
This Regulation shall be binding in its entirety and directly applicable in all Member States.
Done at Brussels, [...]
For the European Parliament
The President
For the Council
The President

PROPOSAL ONLY

Penalties

Entry into Force

EC Regulation: Ship & Port

PROPOSAL ONLY

ANNEXE 1
Amendments to the
Annex to SOLAS
1974, as Amended

ANNEXE 1
AMENDMENTS TO THE ANNEX TO THE
INTERNATIONAL CONVENTION FOR THE SAFETY
OF LIFE AT SEA, 1974 AS AMENDED

CHAPTER XI-2 SPECIAL MEASURES TO ENHANCE MARITIME SECURITY

Regulation 1
Definitions

1 For the purpose of this chapter, unless expressly provided otherwise:

Definitions:

– bulk carrier
   .1 Bulk carrier means a bulk carrier as defined in regulation IX/1.6.

– chemical tanker
   .2 Chemical tanker means a chemical tanker as defined in regulation VII/8.2.

– gas carrier
   .3 Gas carrier means a gas carrier as defined in regulation VII/11.2.

– high-speed craft
   .4 High-speed craft means a craft as defined in regulation X/1.2.

– mobile offshore drilling unit
   .5 Mobile offshore drilling unit means a mechanically propelled mobile offshore drilling unit, as defined in regulation IX/1, not on location.

– oil tanker
   .6 Oil tanker means an oil tanker as defined in regulation II-1/2.12.

– company
   .7 Company means a Company as defined in regulation IX/1.

– ship/port interface
   .8 Ship/port interface means the interactions that occur when a ship is directly and immediately affected by actions involving the movement of persons, goods or the provisions of port services to or from the ship.

– port facility
   .9 Port facility is a location, as determined by the Contracting Government or by the Designated Authority, where the ship/port interface takes place. This includes areas such as anchorages, waiting berths and approaches from seaward, as appropriate.

– ship to ship activity
   .10 Ship to ship activity means any activity not related to a port facility that involves the transfer of goods or persons from one ship to another.

– designated authority
   .11 Designated Authority means the organization(s) or the administration(s) identified, within the Contracting Government, as responsible for ensuring the implementation of the provisions of this chapter pertaining to port facility security and ship/port interface, from the point of view of the port facility.

– ISPS Code
   .12 International Ship and Port Facility Security (ISPS) Code means the International Code for the Security of Ships and of Port Facilities consisting of Part A (the provisions of which shall be treated as mandatory) and part B (the provisions of which shall be treated as recommendatory), as adopted, on 12 December 2002, by resolution 2 of the Conference of Contracting Governments to the International Convention for the Safety of Life at Sea, 1974 as may be amended by the Organization, provided that:

      .1 amendments to part A of the Code are adopted, brought into force and take effect in accordance with article VIII of the present Convention concerning the amendment procedures applicable to the Annex other than chapter I; and

.2 amendments to part B of the Code are adopted by the Maritime Safety Committee in accordance with its Rules of Procedure.

.13 Security incident means any suspicious act or circumstance threatening the security of a ship, including a mobile offshore drilling unit and a high speed craft, or of a port facility or of any ship/port interface or any ship to ship activity.

.14 Security level means the qualification of the degree of risk that a security incident will be attempted or will occur.

.15 Declaration of security means an agreement reached between a ship and either a port facility or another ship with which it interfaces specifying the security measures each will implement.

.16 Recognized security organization means an organization with appropriate expertise in security matters and with appropriate knowledge of ship and port operations authorized to carry out an assessment, or a verification, or an approval or a certification activity, required by this chapter or by part A of the ISPS Code.

2 The term "ship", when used in regulations 3 to 13, includes mobile offshore drilling units and high-speed craft.

3 The term "all ships", when used in this chapter, means any ship to which this chapter applies.

4 The term "Contracting Government", when used in regulations 3, 4, 7, 10, 11, 12 and 13 includes a reference to the "Designated Authority".

Regulation 2
Application
1 This chapter applies to:
.1 the following types of ships engaged on international voyages:
.1.1 passenger ships, including high-speed passenger craft;
.1.2 cargo ships, including high-speed craft, of 500 gross tonnage and upwards; and
.1.3 mobile offshore drilling units; and
.2 port facilities serving such ships engaged on international voyages.

2 Notwithstanding the provisions of paragraph 1.2, Contracting Governments shall decide the extent of application of this chapter and of the relevant sections of part A of the ISPS Code to those port facilities within their territory which, although used primarily by ships not engaged on international voyages, are required, occasionally, to serve ships arriving or departing on an international voyage.

2.1 Contracting Governments shall base their decisions, under paragraph 2, on a port facility security assessment carried out in accordance with the provisions of part A of the ISPS Code.

2.2 Any decision which a Contracting Government makes, under

PROPOSAL ONLY
Definitions contd.
– security incident
– security level
– declaration of security
– recognised security organisation
– ship
– all ships
– contracting government
Application:
– ship types
– ports occasionally handling international traffic

EC Regulation: Ship & Port

PROPOSAL ONLY

Application contd.

paragraph 2, shall not compromise the level of security intended to be achieved by this chapter or by part A of the ISPS Code.

3 This chapter does not apply to warships, naval auxiliaries or other ships owned or operated by a Contracting Government and used only on Government non-commercial service.

4 Nothing in this chapter shall prejudice the rights or obligations of States under international law.

Obligations of Contracting Governments

Regulation 3
Obligations of Contracting Governments with respect to security
1 Administrations shall set security levels and ensure the provision of security level information to ships entitled to fly their flag. When changes in security level occur, security level information shall be updated as the circumstance dictates.

2 Contracting Governments shall set security levels and ensure the provision of security level information to port facilities within their territory, and to ships prior to entering a port or whilst in a port within their territory. When changes in security level occur, security level information shall be updated as the circumstance dictates.

Requirements for Companies and Ships

Regulation 4
Requirements for Companies and ships
1 Companies shall comply with the relevant requirements of this chapter and of part A of the ISPS Code, taking into account the guidance given in part B of the ISPS Code.

2 Ships shall comply with the relevant requirements of this chapter and of part A of the ISPS Code, taking into account the guidance given in part B of the ISPS Code, and such compliance shall be verified and certified as provided for in part A of the ISPS Code.

3 Prior to entering a port or whilst in a port within the territory of a Contracting Government, a ship shall comply with the requirements for the security level set by that Contracting Government, if such security level is higher than the security level set by the Administration for that ship.

4 Ships shall respond without undue delay to any change to a higher security level.

5 Where a ship is not in compliance with the requirements of this chapter or of part A of the ISPS Code, or cannot comply with the requirements of the security level set by the Administration or by another Contracting Government and applicable to that ship, then the ship shall notify the appropriate competent authority prior to conducting any ship/port interface or prior to entry into port, whichever occurs earlier.

Regulation 5
Specific responsibility of Companies

The Company shall ensure that the master has available on board, at all times, information through which officers duly authorised by a Contracting Government can establish:

Specific responsibilities of a Company

.1 who is responsible for appointing the members of the crew or other persons currently employed or engaged on board the ship in any capacity on the business of that ship;

.2 who is responsible for deciding the employment of the ship; and

.3 in cases where the ship is employed under the terms of charter party(ies), who are the parties to such charter party(ies).

Regulation 6
Ship security alert system

Ship Security Alert System

1 All ships shall be provided with a ship security alert system, as follows:

.1 ships constructed on or after 1 July 2004;

.2 passenger ships, including high-speed passenger craft, constructed before 1 July 2004, not later than the first survey of the radio installation after 1 July 2004;

.3 oil tankers, chemical tankers, gas carriers, bulk carriers and cargo high speed craft, of 500 gross tonnage and upwards constructed before 1 July 2004, not later than the first survey of the radio installation after 1 July 2004; and

.4 other cargo ships of 500 gross tonnage and upward and mobile offshore drilling units constructed before 1 July 2004, not later than the first survey of the radio installation after 1 July 2006.

2 The ship security alert system, when activated, shall:

.1 initiate and transmit a ship-to-shore security alert to a competent authority designated by the Administration, which in these circumstances may include the Company, identifying the ship, its location and indicating that the security of the ship is under threat or it has been compromised;

.2 not send the ship security alert to any other ships;

.3 not raise any alarm on-board the ship; and

.4 continue the ship security alert until deactivated and/or reset.

3 The ship security alert system shall:

.1 be capable of being activated from the navigation bridge and in at least one other location; and

.2 conform to performance standards not inferior to those adopted by the Organization.

4 The ship security alert system activation points shall be designed so as to prevent the inadvertent initiation of the ship security alert.

5 The requirement for a ship security alert system may be complied with by using the radio installation fitted for compliance with the requirements of Ch. IV, provided all requirements of this regulation are complied with.

EC Regulation: Ship & Port

Ship Security Alert System Contd.

6 When an Administration receives notification of a ship security alert, that Administration shall immediately notify the State(s) in the vicinity of which the ship is presently operating.

7 When a Contracting Government receives notification of a ship security alert from a ship which is not entitled to fly its flag, that Contracting Government shall immediately notify the relevant Administration and, if appropriate, the State(s) in the vicinity of which the ship is presently operating.

Threats to Ships

Regulation 7
Threats to ships
1 Contracting Governments shall set security levels and ensure the provision of security level information to ships operating in their territorial sea or having communicated an intention to enter their territorial sea.

2 Contracting Governments shall provide a point of contact through which such ships can request advice or assistance and to which such ships can report any security concerns about other ships, movements or communications.

3 Where a risk of attack has been identified, the Contracting Government concerned shall advise the ships concerned and their Administrations of:
   .1 the current security level;
   .2 any security measures that should be put in place by the ships concerned to protect themselves from attack, in accordance with the provisions of part A of the ISPS Code; and
   .3 security measures that the coastal State has decided to put in place, as appropriate.

Master's discretion for ship safety and security

Regulation 8
Master's discretion for ship safety and security
1 The master shall not be constrained by the Company, the charterer or any other person from taking or executing any decision which, in the professional judgement of the master, is necessary to maintain the safety and security of the ship. This includes denial of access to persons (except those identified as duly authorized by a Contracting Government) or their effects and refusal to load cargo, including containers or other closed cargo transport units.

2 If, in the professional judgement of the master, a conflict between any safety and security requirements applicable to the ship arises during its operations, the master shall give effect to those requirements necessary to maintain the safety of the ship. In such cases, the master may implement temporary security measures and shall forthwith inform the Administration and, if appropriate, the Contracting Government in whose port the ship is operating or intends to enter.

EC Regulation: Ship & Port

Any such temporary security measures under this regulation shall, to the highest possible degree, be commensurate with the prevailing security level. When such cases are identified, the Administration shall ensure that such conflicts are resolved and that the possibility of recurrence is minimised.

Regulation 9
Control and compliance measures
1 Control of ships in port

Control and compliance measures:

  1.1 For the purpose of this chapter, every ship to which this chapter applies is subject to control when in a port of another Contracting Government by officers duly authorised by that Government, who may be the same as those carrying out the functions of regulation I/19. Such control shall be limited to verifying that there is onboard a valid International Ship Security Certificate or a valid Interim International Ships Security Certificate issued under the provisions of part A of the ISPS Code (Certificate), which if valid shall be accepted, unless there are clear grounds for believing that the ship is not in compliance with the requirements of this chapter or part A of the ISPS Code.

– verifying ISSC

  1.2 When there are such clear grounds, or where no valid Certificate is produced when required, the officers duly authorized by the Contracting Government shall impose any one or more control measures in relation to that ship as provided in paragraph 1.3. Any such measures imposed must be proportionate, taking into account the guidance given in part B of the ISPS Code.

– no ISSC

  1.3 Such control measures are as follows: inspection of the ship, delaying the ship, detention of the ship, restriction of operations including movement within the port, or expulsion of the ship from port. Such control measures may additionally or alternatively include other lesser administrative or corrective measures.

– control measures

2 Ships intending to enter a port of another Contracting Government

– information from ships on port entry

  2.1 For the purpose of this chapter, a Contracting Government may require that ships intending to enter its ports provide the following information to officers duly authorized by that Government to ensure compliance with this chapter prior to entry into port with the aim of avoiding the need to impose control measures or steps:

    .1 that the ship possesses a valid Certificate and the name of its issuing authority;

    .2 the security level at which the ship is currently operating;

    .3 the security level at which the ship operated in any previous port where it has conducted a ship/port interface within the timeframe specified in paragraph 2.3;

    .4 any special or additional security measures that were taken by the ship in any previous port where it has conducted a ship/port interface within the timeframe specified in paragraph 2.3;

PROPOSAL ONLY

**Control and
compliance
measures contd.**

**– information from
ships on port entry
contd.**

.5 that the appropriate ship security procedures were maintained during any ship to ship activity within the timeframe specified in paragraph 2.3; or

.6 other practical security related information (but not details of the ship security plan), taking into account the guidance given in part B of the ISPS Code.

If requested by the Contracting Government, the ship or the Company shall provide confirmation, acceptable to that Contracting Government, of the information required above.

2.2 Every ship to which this chapter applies intending to enter the port of another Contracting Government shall provide the information described in paragraph

2.1 on the request of the officers duly authorized by that Government. The master may decline to provide such information on the understanding that failure to do so may result in denial of entry into port.

2.3 The ship shall keep records of the information referred to in paragraph 2.1 for the last 10 calls at port facilities.

2.4 If, after receipt of the information described in paragraph 2.1, officers duly authorised by the Contracting Government of the port in which the ship intends to enter have clear grounds for believing that the ship is in non-compliance with the requirements of this chapter or part A of the ISPS Code, such officers shall attempt to establish communication with and between the ship and the Administration in order to rectify the non-compliance. If such communication does not result in rectification, or if such officers have clear grounds otherwise for believing that the ship is in non-compliance with the requirements of this chapter or part A of the ISPS Code, such officers may take steps in relation to that ship as provided in paragraph 2.5. Any such steps taken must be proportionate, taking into account the guidance given in part B of the ISPS Code.

2.5 Such steps are as follows:

.1 a requirement for the rectification of the non-compliance;

.2 a requirement that the ship proceed to a location specified in the territorial sea or internal waters of that Contracting Government;

.3 inspection of the ship, if the ship is in the territorial sea of the Contracting Government the port of which the ship intends to enter; or

.4 denial of entry into port.

Prior to initiating any such steps, the ship shall be informed by the Contracting Government of its intentions. Upon this information the master may withdraw the intention to enter that port. In such cases, this regulation shall not apply.

3 Additional provisions

3.1 In the event:

.1 of the imposition of a control measure, other than a lesser administrative or corrective measure, referred to in paragraph 1.3; or

.2 any of the steps referred to in paragraph 2.5 are taken, an officer duly authorized by the Contracting Government shall forthwith inform in writing the Administration specifying which control measures have been imposed or steps taken and the reasons thereof. The Contracting Government imposing the control measures or steps shall also notify the recognized security organization, which issued the Certificate relating to the ship concerned and the Organization when any such control measures have been imposed or steps taken.

3.2 When entry into port is denied or the ship is expelled from port, the authorities of the port State should communicate the appropriate facts to the authorities of the State of the next appropriate ports of call, when known, and any other appropriate coastal States, taking into account guidelines to be developed by the Organization. Confidentiality and security of such notification shall be ensured.

3.3 Denial of entry into port, pursuant to paragraphs 2.4 and 2.5, or expulsion from port, pursuant to paragraphs 1.1 to 1.3, shall only be imposed where the officers duly authorized by the Contracting Government have clear grounds to believe that the ship poses an immediate threat to the security or safety of persons, or of ships or other property and there are no other appropriate means for removing that threat.

3.4 The control measures referred to in paragraph 1.3 and the steps referred to in paragraph 2.5 shall only be imposed, pursuant to this regulation, until the noncompliance giving rise to the control measures or steps has been corrected to the satisfaction of the Contracting Government, taking into account actions proposed by the ship or the Administration, if any.

3.5 When Contracting Governments exercise control under paragraph 1 or take steps under paragraph 2:

.1 all possible efforts shall be made to avoid a ship being unduly detained or delayed. If a ship is thereby unduly detained, or delayed, it shall be entitled to compensation for any loss or damage suffered; and

.2 necessary access to the ship shall not be prevented for emergency or humanitarian reasons and for security purposes.

Regulation 10
Requirements for port facilities

1 Port facilities shall comply with the relevant requirements of this chapter and part A of the ISPS Code, taking into account the guidance given in part B of the ISPS Code.

2 Contracting Governments with a port facility or port facilities within their territory, to which this regulation applies, shall ensure that:

PROPOSAL ONLY

Control and compliance measures contd.

Additional provisions

Requirements for port facilities

.1 port facility security assessments are carried out, reviewed and approved in accordance with the provisions of part A of the ISPS Code; and

.2 port facility security plans are developed, reviewed, approved and implemented in accordance with the provisions of part A of the ISPS Code.

3 Contracting Governments shall designate and communicate the measures required to be addressed in a port facility security plan for the various security levels, including when the submission of a Declaration of Security will be required.

Alternative security agreements

**Regulation 11
Alternative security agreements**

1 Contracting Governments may, when implementing this chapter and part A of the ISPS Code, conclude in writing bilateral or multilateral agreements with other Contracting Governments on alternative security arrangements covering short international voyages on fixed routes between port facilities located within their territories.

2 Any such agreement shall not compromise the level of security of other ships or of port facilities not covered by the agreement.

3 No ship covered by such an agreement shall conduct any ship-to-ship activities with any ship not covered by the agreement.

4 Such agreements shall be reviewed periodically, taking into account the experience gained as well as any changes in the particular circumstances or the assessed threats to the security of the ships, the port facilities or the routes covered by the agreement.

Equivalent security arrangements

**Regulation 12
Equivalent security arrangements**

1 An Administration may allow a particular ship or a group of ships entitled to fly its flag to implement other security measures equivalent to those prescribed in this chapter or in part A of the ISPS Code, provided such security measures are at least as effective as those prescribed in this chapter or part A of the ISPS Code. The Administration, which allows such security measures, shall communicate to the Organization particulars thereof.

2 When implementing this chapter and part A of the ISPS Code, a Contracting Government may allow a particular port facility or a group of port facilities located within its territory, other than those covered by an agreement concluded under regulation 11, to implement security measures equivalent to those prescribed in this chapter or in Part A of the ISPS Code, provided such security measures are at least as effective as those prescribed in this chapter or part A of the ISPS Code. The Contracting Government, which allows such security measures, shall communicate to the Organization particulars thereof.

Regulation 13

Communication of information

1 Contracting Governments shall, not later than 1 July 2004, communicate to the Organization and shall make available for the information of Companies and ships:

.1 the names and contact details of their national authority or authorities responsible for ship and port facility security;

.2 the locations within their territory covered by the approved port facility security plans.

.3 the names and contact details of those who have been designated to be available at all times to receive and act upon the ship-to-shore security alerts, referred to in regulation 6.2.1;

.4 the names and contact details of those who have been designated to be available at all times to receive and act upon any communications from Contracting Governments exercising control and compliance measures, referred to in regulation 9.3.1; and

.5 the names and contact details of those who have been designated to be available at all times to provide advice or assistance to ships and to whom ships can report any security concerns, referred to in regulation 7.2; and thereafter update such information as and when changes relating thereto occur. The Organization shall circulate such particulars to other Contracting Governments for the information of their officers.

2 Contracting Governments shall, not later than 1 July 2004, communicate to the Organization the names and contact details of any recognized security organizations authorized to act on their behalf together with details of the specific responsibility and conditions of authority delegated to such organizations. Such information shall be updated as and when changes relating thereto occur. The Organization shall circulate such particulars to other Contracting Governments for the information of their officers.

3 Contracting Governments shall, not later than 1 July 2004 communicate to the Organization a list showing the approved port facility security plans for the port facilities located within their territory together with the location or locations covered by each approved port facility security plan and the corresponding date of approval and thereafter shall further communicate when any of the following changes take place:

.1 changes in the location or locations covered by an approved port facility security plan are to be introduced or have been introduced. In such cases the information to be communicated shall indicate the changes in the location or locations covered by the plan and the date as of which such changes are to be introduced or were implemented;

.2 an approved port facility security plan, previously included in the list submitted to the Organization, is to be withdrawn or has

EC Regulation: Ship & Port

PROPOSAL ONLY

Communication of information contd.

been withdrawn. In such cases, the information to be communicated shall indicate the date on which the withdrawal will take effect or was implemented. In these cases, the communication shall be made to the Organization as soon as is practically possible; and

.3 additions are to be made to the list of approved port facility security plans. In such cases, the information to be communicated shall indicate the location or locations covered by the plan and the date of approval.

4 Contracting Governments shall, at five year intervals after 1 July 2004, communicate to the Organization a revised and updated list showing all the approved port facility security plans for the port facilities located within their territory together with the location or locations covered by each approved port facility security plan and the corresponding date of approval (and the date of approval of any amendments thereto) which will supersede and replace all information communicated to the Organization, pursuant to paragraph 3, during the preceding five years.

5 Contracting Governments shall communicate to the Organization information that an agreement under regulation 11 has been concluded. The information communicated shall include:

.1 the names of the Contracting Governments which have concluded the agreement;

.2 the port facilities and the fixed routes covered by the agreement;

.3 the periodicity of review of the agreement;

.4 the date of entry into force of the agreement; and

.5 information on any consultations which have taken place with other Contracting Governments; and thereafter shall communicate, as soon as practically possible, to the Organization information when the agreement has been amended or has ended.

6 Any Contracting Government which allows, under the provisions of regulation 12, any equivalent security arrangements with respect to a ship entitled to fly its flag or with respect to a port facility located within its territory, shall communicate to the Organization particulars thereof.

7 The Organization shall make available the information communicated under paragraph 3 to other Contracting Governments upon request.

ANNEXE 2
See Page 1 [ISPS Code, Part A Mandatory]

ANNEXE 3
See Page 30 [ISPS Code, Part B Guidance]

PROPOSAL ONLY
Commission of the
European
Communities

Proposal

Directive on
Enhancing Port
Security
Brussels, Feb 2004

Explanatory
Memorandum

Why are ports
at risk?

DIRECTIVE OF THE EUROPEAN PARLIAMENT AND OF THE COUNCIL ON ENHANCING PORT SECURITY

EXPLANATORY MEMORANDUM

General Introduction

The communication on Maritime Security (COM(2003) 229 final) which incorporated a proposal for ship and ship/port interface security, currently going through the legislative process and referred to in this document as Regulation (EC) Nr. .../..., identified port security as a necessary second step which should secure both the port and the interface between the port and the hinterland. The need for protection extends to people working in or passing through ports, infrastructure and equipment, including means of transport. This proposal builds on to that earlier communication.

Why are Ports at Risk?

Ports are an essential link within the total transport chain, linking up maritime with landside trade and passenger flows. Ports are often the focal point for shipments of dangerous cargo, for major chemical and petrochemical production centres, and/or situated near cities. It is clear that terrorist attacks in ports can easily result in serious disruptions to transport systems and trigger knock-on effects on the surrounding industry as well as directly harming people in the port and the neighbouring population. It is within this context that the Commission is proposing to develop a comprehensive port security policy.

International Focus

Work in the IMO has led to the development of amendments to SOLAS and the ISPS Code. The Commission has proposed a regulation aimed at incorporating these measures into binding community law (COM(2003) 229 final). The legislative process is currently ongoing.

IMO-ILO
Code of Practice

Although an IMO-ILO Working Group is currently working on a Code of Practice on Port Security, it appears unrealistic to expect results soon. It is to be noted that such a code would not be legally binding. In the light of this the Commission believes that the EU should go ahead with an own port security scheme. This proposal complements the work of the IMO-ILO.

Port Security
Directive need

Need for a Port Security Directive

The SOLAS amendments, ISPS Code and the proposed regulation, will enhance maritime security by developing security measures on

---

[1] In this context "port facility" means a location where the ship/port interface takes place; this includes areas such as anchorages, waiting berths and approaches from seaward, as appropriate". "Ship/port interface" means the interactions that occur when a ship is directly and immediately affected by actions involving the movement of persons or goods or the provision of port services to or from the ship.

EC Directive: Port Security

ships and in port facilities[1] Regulation (EC) Nr. .../... stops at that part of the port which represents the ship/port interface, i.e. the terminal[1]. There is a dual purpose to this proposal: to enhance security in those areas of ports not covered by Regulation (EC) Nr. .../... and to ensure that security measures implemented in application of Regulation (EC) Nr. .../... benefit from enhanced security in adjacent port areas. This proposal does not create new obligations in areas already covered by Regulation (EC) Nr. .../....

The Commission therefore considers that this directive achieves the following:

- Guaranteeing and monitoring at Community level the achievement of a sufficient level of port security, by complementing and supporting the security measures applying to the ship/port interface.
- Ensuring harmonised implementation and equal conditions throughout the European Union so as not to create differences for the commercial port users.
- Ensuring that necessary security measures covering the entire port can be implemented as far as possible by relying on already existing tools introduced by Regulation (EC) Nr. .../..., thereby achieving maximum security results through minimum additional burden for the ports.

Against the background of the significant variety of Community ports (large-small, privately-publicly owned, etc.), as well as in view of the diverse activities co-existing within Community-ports (cargo handling, industry, warehousing, transport, environmental areas, conurbations, and many more) a directive is the most appropriate legal instrument to introduce the required flexibility while establishing the necessary common port security level throughout the Community.

It is recognised that a number of port security regimes are already being applied in Member States. This directive allows existing security measures and structures to be maintained provided they comply with the rules of the directive.

Accordingly, the Commission:
- Proposes that the European Parliament and the Council should adopt as soon as possible this directive on enhancing Port Security. The proposal complements the security measures introduced by the regulation on enhancing ship and port facility security (Regulation (EC) Nr. .../...) by ensuring that, as a result, the entire port is covered by a security regime. This new proposal covers any port housing one or more of the port facilities which are covered by Regulation (EC) Nr. .../....

---

[1] Although it would theoretically be possible for Member States to interpret 'port facility' extensively so as to include the entire port, thus extending application of the ISPS Code to the entire port, it is understood that such interpretation is unlikely to be given

EC Directive: Port Security

CONTENT OF THE PORT SECURITY DIRECTIVE

The measures required for enhancing port security would follow these principles:

- Port security complements maritime and ship/port interface security and ensures that these security measures are reinforced by security measures in the entire port area;
- A port security assessment decides what measures are required, where and when;
- Security levels distinguish between normal, heightened or imminent threats;
- A port security plan outlines all measures and details for enhancing port security;
- A port security authority is responsible for the identifying and implementing appropriate port security measures by means of the above mentioned assessment and plan;
- A port security officer coordinates development and implementation of the port security plan;
- A port security committee provides advice to the responsible authority;
- Training and control will support implementation of the required measures.

GENERAL PRINCIPLES OF THE PROPOSAL

- The proposal relies on the same security structures and bodies (security assessments, officers, etc.) as Regulation (EC) Nr. .../... so as to ensure a comprehensive security regime for the entire maritime logistics chain from the vessel to the ship/port interface to the entire port to the port/hinterland interface. This approach allows a simplification of procedures as well as synergies in security. In particular, the proposed directive:
- calls upon Member States to define the boundaries of their ports for the purpose of this directive;
- calls upon Member States to ensure that proper port security assessments and port security plans are developed;
- calls upon Member States to determine and communicate the security levels in use and changes thereto;
- calls upon Member States to designate a port security authority for every port or for groups of ports. This is this public authority that will be responsible for the appropriate identification and implementation of port security measures;
- establishes the need to appoint a port security officer for each individual port to ensure proper coordination when port security assessments and plans are established, updated and followed up;
- establishes the general requirement of an advisory security committee, bringing together representatives of all relevant operational and government functions in a port;
- puts forward minimum requirements for security assessments and plans;
- calls for the appointment of focal points in the Member States to

EC Directive: Port Security

provide the necessary communication both to other member states and to the Commission;
- provide for inspection procedures to monitor the implementation of port security measures;
- lays down a procedure for the adaptation of its provisions.

LEGAL CONSIDERATIONS
The Commission proposes to base the directive on Article 80(2) of the EC Treaty, without prejudice to member states' national security legislation and any measures that might be taken on the basis of Title VI of the Treaty on European Union.

Legal considerations

SPECIAL CONSIDERATIONS
Article 1: This article sets out the subject-matter of the directive.
Article 2: This article sets out the scope of the directive.
Article 3: This article contains the definitions of the main terms used in the directive.
Article 4: This article imposes upon Member States the obligation to closely co-ordinate the port security measures with those taken in application of the Regulation on maritime and port facility security.
Article 5: This article imposes upon Member States the obligation to designate a port security authority. This port security authority will be responsible for the identification and implementation of appropriate port security measures.
Article 6: This article contains the obligation for Member States to ensure that port security assessments are performed for all their ports covered by this directive. Such assessments will take into account the specificities of different sections of the port, as well as the security assessments developed for port facilities within the port boundaries as a result of the provisions of the regulation on maritime security. The detailed requirements of a port security assessment are contained in Annex I.
Article 7: This article contains the obligation for Member States to ensure that port security plans are established for all their ports covered by this directive. Such plans will take into account the specificities of different sections of the port, as well as the security plans in place for the port facilities within the port boundaries as a result of the provisions of the regulation on maritime security. The detailed requirements of a port security plan are contained in Annex II. This Article also encompasses the need for adequate training and exercises. For this purpose it refers to Annex III, containing basic training requirements.
Article 8: The directive imposes the use of three distinct security levels. Member States are required to introduce such system of levels to their relevant ports, determine and communicate the security levels in use in the different parts of their ports and any changes thereto. Communication will be based on a 'need-to-know' basis.
Article 9: Article 9 contains the obligation to designate a port security officer for each port covered by this directive, who should have sufficient local knowledge and authority to adequately ensure and coordinate the establishment, update and follow up of port security assessments and

Special
Considerations

Articles:
1 – subject matter
2 – scope
3 – definitions
4 – co-ordinate port measures
5 – designate port security authority

6 – port security assessments

7 – port security plans

8 – security levels

9 – port security officer

EC Directive: Port Security

plans in their respective ports.

Article 10: Recognising the need for optimal cooperation between the operational and public authority functions in a port, this article provides for the establishment of an advisory port security committee regrouping these port security stakeholders.

Article 11: This article contains the requirement to review regularly port security assessments.

Article 12: Article 12 provides for the possibility for Member States to appoint recognised port security organisations, provided these organisations comply with the conditions set out in Annex IV.

Article 13: This article provides for the setting up of a focal point for port security, which will be the Commission's contact point for implementation of this directive.

Article 14: This article encompasses the obligation of Member States to establish an adequate and regular control system concerning port security plans and their implementation. This article also contains the process whereby inspections supervised by the Commission are put in place to check the effectiveness of port security implementation monitoring and measures.

Article 15: This article indicates that provisions may be adopted in order to define harmonised procedures for the application of the details related to the Annexes to this directive. Such adaptations will be guided by the Committee procedure, as defined in Article 14.

Article 16: The Commission is assisted by the same committee set up by Regulation (EC) Nr. .../.... This committee acts in accordance with the regulatory procedure (Articles 5 and 7 of Council Decision 1999/468/EC of 28 June 1999 laying down the procedures for the exercise of implementing powers conferred on the Commission).

Article 17: These articles are concerned with the confidentiality of security related information, in particular of inspection reports and answers of Member States.

Article 18: This article calls upon Member States to institute effective, proportionate and dissuasive penalties for infringement of this directive.

Article 19: This article contains the obligation upon Member States to bring into force the laws, regulations and administrative provisions necessary to comply with this directive and this not later than one year from the date of its entrance into force.

Article 20: Contains the entry into force details.

Article 21: Deals with the addressees of this directive.

Annex I: Contains the detailed requirements for establishing a port security assessment.

Annex II: Contains the detailed requirements for establishing a port security plan.

Annex III: Contains the basic training requirements.

Annex IV: Contains the detailed conditions to be fulfilled by a recognised port security organisation.

PROPOSAL FOR A
DIRECTIVE OF THE EUROPEAN PARLIAMENT AND OF THE COUNCIL
ON ENHANCING PORT SECURITY
(Text with EEA relevance)

PROPOSAL ONLY

Directive of the European Parliament and of the Council on Enhancing Port Security

THE EUROPEAN PARLIAMENT AND THE COUNCIL OF THE EUROPEAN UNION,

Having regard to the Treaty establishing the European Community, and in particular Article 80(2) thereof,

Having regard to the proposal from the Commission,

Having regard to the opinion of the European Economic and Social Committee,

Having regard to the opinion of the Committee of the Regions,

Acting in accordance with the procedure laid down in Article 251 of the Treaty,

Whereas:

(1) Unlawful acts and terrorism are among the greatest threats to the ideals of democracy and freedom and to the values of peace, which are the very essence of the European Union.

(2) The security of people, infrastructure and equipment, including means of transport, in ports as well as in relevant adjacent areas should be protected against unlawful acts and their devastating effects. Such protection would benefit transport users, the economy and society as a whole.

(3) On Day/Month/2003 the European Parliament and the Council of the European Union adopted Regulation (EC) Nr. .../.... on maritime security. The maritime security measures imposed by this regulation constitute only part of the measures necessary to achieve an adequate level of security throughout maritime linked transport chains.
This regulation is limited in scope to security measures onboard vessels and the immediate ship/port interface.

(4) In order to achieve the fullest protection possible for maritime and port industries, port security measures should be introduced. They should extend beyond the ship/port interface and cover the entire port thus both protecting the port areas and ensuring that security measures taken in application of Regulation (EC) Nr. .../.... benefit from enhanced security in adjacent areas. These measures should apply to all those ports in which one or more port facilities are situated which are covered by Regulation (EC) Nr. .../.... .

Extend measures beyond ship/port interface

(5) Without prejudice to the rules of the Member States in the field of national security and measures which might be taken on the basis of Title VI of the Treaty on the European Union, the security objective described in recital 2 should be achieved by adopting appropriate measures in the field of port policy establishing joint standards for establishing a sufficient port security level throughout Community ports.

– Community-wide port security level

EC Directive: Port Security

PROPOSAL ONLY

– defining port
boundaries

– preventative and
remedial measures

– recognition of
individual
responsibilities

– effectiveness
checks

– focal point
between Member
States and EC

– fundamental rights

– ongoing update

– principle of
subsidarity

(6) Member States should rely upon detailed security assessments to identify the exact boundaries of the security-relevant port area, as well as the different measures required to ensure appropriate port security. Such measures shall be different according to the security level in place and will reflect differences in the risk profile of different subareas in the port.

(7) Member States should establish port security plans which thoroughly transpose the findings of the port security assessment. The efficient working of security measures also requires clear task divisions between all parties involved as well as regular exercise of measures. The retention of task divisions and exercise procedures in the format of the port security plan is considered to contribute strongly to the effectiveness of both preventive and remedial port security measures.

(8) Member States should ensure that responsibilities in port security are clearly recognised by all parties involved. Member States shall monitor the compliance with security rules and establish a clear responsible authority for all its ports, approve all security assessments and plans for its ports, set and communicate security levels, ensure that measures are well communicated, implemented and coordinated, and provide for enhancing the effectiveness of security measures and alertness by means of a platform for advice within the port community.

(9) Member States should approve assessments and plans and monitor the implementation in their ports. The effectiveness of the implementation monitoring should be the subject of inspections supervised by the Commission.

(10) Member States should ensure that a focal point takes up the role of contact point between the Commission and Member States.

(11) This directive respects the fundamental rights and observes the principles recognised in particular by the Charter of Fundamental Rights of the European Union.

(12) The measures needed to implement this directive should be adopted in accordance with Council Decision 1999/468/EC of 28 June 1999 laying down the procedures for the exercise of implementing powers conferred on the Commission. A procedure should be defined for the adaptation of this directive to take account of developments in international instruments and, in the light of experience, to adapt or complement the detailed provisions of the Annexes to this directive, without widening the scope of this directive.

(13) Since the objectives of the proposed action, namely the balanced introduction and application of appropriate measures in the field of maritime transport and port policy, cannot be sufficiently achieved by the Member States and can therefore, by reason of the European scale of this directive, be better achieved at Community level, the Community may

EC Directive: Port Security

adopt measures in accordance with the principle of subsidiarity set out in Article 5 of the Treaty. In accordance with the principle of proportionality set out in that Article, this directive is limited to the basic joint standards required to achieve the objectives of port security and does not go beyond what is necessary for that purpose,

HAVE ADOPTED THIS DIRECTIVE:

Article 1

Subject-matter

1. The main objective of this directive is to introduce and implement Community measures aimed at enhancing port security in the face of threats of intentional unlawful acts. It shall also ensure that security measures taken in application of Regulation (EC) Nr..../.... benefit from enhanced security in adjacent port areas.

Subject matter

2. The measures referred to in paragraph 1 shall consist of:
   a) The setting of common basic rules on port security measures;
   b) The setting up of an implementation mechanism for these rules;
   c) The setting up of appropriate compliance monitoring mechanisms.

Article 2

Scope

1. This directive addresses security measures which need to be observed by or affect people, infrastructure and equipment, including means of transport, in ports as well as in adjacent areas where these have a direct or indirect impact on security in the port.

Scope:
– people
– means of transport
– port areas

2. The measures laid down in this directive shall apply to any port located in the territory of a Member State in which one or more port facilities are situated which are covered by Regulation (EC) Nr. .../....

– all Community ports

3. Member States shall identify for each port the boundaries for the purposes of this directive, appropriately taking into account the information from the port security assessment.

– port boundaries

4. Where the boundaries of a port facility within the meaning of Regulation (EC) Nr..../.... have been defined by the Member State as effectively covering the port, the relevant provisions of Regulation (EC) Nr. .../.... take precedence over those of this directive.

Article 3

Definitions

For the purpose of this directive:

1. "port" or "seaport" means an area of land and water made up of such works and equipment as to permit principally, the reception of ships, their loading and unloading, the storage of goods, the receipt and delivery of these goods, and the embarkation and disembarkation of passengers.

Definitions:
– port
– seaport

2. "ship/port interface" means the interactions that occur when a ship is

– ship/port interface

EC Directive: Port Security

PROPOSAL ONLY

Definitions contd:

– port facility

– focal point for maritime security

– port security authority

Co-ordination with Ship & Port Security Regulation

Port Security Authority

Port Security Assessment

directly and immediately affected by actions involving the movement of persons, goods or the provisions of port services to or from the ship.

3. "port facility" means a location where the ship/port interface takes place; this includes areas such as anchorages, waiting berths and approaches from seaward, as appropriate.

4. "focal point for maritime security" means the body designated by each Member State to serve as contact point for the Commission and other Member States and to facilitate, follow and inform on the application of the maritime security measures laid down in this directive, as well as of those laid down in Regulation (EC) Nr. .../....

5. "port security authority" means the authority responsible for security matters in a given port.

Article 4
Coordination with measures taken in application of Regulation (EC) Nr. .../....
Member States shall ensure that port security measures introduced by this directive are closely coordinated with measures taken in application of Regulation (EC) Nr. .../.....

Article 5
Port security authority
1. Member States shall designate a port security authority for each port covered by this directive. A port security authority may be appointed for more than one port.
2. The port security authority shall be responsible for the identification and implementation of appropriate port security measures by means of port security assessments and plans.
3. Member States may appoint a 'competent authority for maritime security' under Regulation (EC) Nr. .../.... as port security authority.

Article 6
Port security assessment
1. Member States shall ensure that port security assessments are made for the ports covered by this directive. These assessments should take due account of the specificities of different sections of a port and shall take into account the assessments for port facilities within their boundaries as carried out in application of Regulation (EC) Nr. .../.... . Port security assessments have to be approved by the Member State.

2. Each port security assessment shall be performed according to the detailed requirements provided in Annex I to this directive.

3. Port security assessments may be made by a recognised port security organisation, as referred to in Article 12.

EC Directive: Port Security

Article 7
Port security plan

1. Member States shall ensure that, as a result of port security assessments, port security plans are developed, maintained and updated. Port security plans should adequately address the specificities of different sections of a port and shall integrate the security plans for port facilities within their boundaries established in application of Regulation (EC) Nr. .../.... . Port security plans must to be approved by the Member State. They can only be implemented once that approval has been given.

2. Port security plans shall identify, for each of the different security levels referred to in Article 8:
   a) the procedures to be followed;
   b) the measures to be put in place;
   c) the actions to be undertaken.

3. Each port security plan shall be established in accordance with the detailed requirements provided in Annex II to this directive.

4. Port security plans may be developed by a recognised port security organisation as referred to in Article 12.

5. Member States shall ensure that the implementation of port security plans is coordinated with other control activities carried out in the port.

6. Member States shall ensure that adequate training and exercises are performed, taking into account the basic training requirements listed in Annex III.

Article 8
Security levels

1. Member States shall introduce a system of port security levels.
2. There shall be 3 security levels, as defined in Regulation (EC) Nr. .../....:
   - Security level 1 means the level for which minimum appropriate protective security measures shall be maintained at all times;
   - Security level 2 means the level for which appropriate additional protective security measures shall be maintained for a period of time as a result of heightened risk of security incident;
   - Security level 3 means the level for which further specific protective security measures shall be maintained for a limited period of time when a security incident is probable or imminent, although it may not be possible to identify the specific target.

3. Member States shall determine the security levels in use. At each security level, a Member State may determine that different security measures are to be implemented in different parts of the port depending on the outcome of the port security assessment.

4. Member States shall communicate the security level in force for each

Port Security Plan

Security Levels

EC Directive: Port Security

port as well as any changes thereto. Security levels should be made known on a 'need-to-know' basis in accordance with the port security plan.

Port Security Officer

Article 9
Port security officer
1. A port security officer shall be designated for each port. Each port shall have a different port security officer. Small adjacent ports may have a shared security officer.

2. The port security officers shall fulfil the role of point of contact for port security related issues and should have sufficient authority and local knowledge to adequately ensure and coordinate the establishment, update and follow-up of port security assessments and port security plans.

3. Where the port security officer is not the same as the port facility(ies) security officer(s) under Regulation (EC) Nr. .../.... , close cooperation between them must be ensured.

Port Security Committee

Article 10
Port security committee

1. Member States shall ensure that port security committees are established to provide practical advice in the ports covered by this directive, unless the specificity of a port renders such committees superfluous.

2. The membership of the port security committee may vary between ports, but should always reflect the operational and public authority functions in a port. It shall function on a 'need to know basis'.

Reviews of port security assessments and plans

Article 11
Reviews
1. Member States shall ensure that port security assessments and port security plans are reviewed every time security-relevant changes occur. They must be reviewed at least every five years. Upon review the port security assessments and port security plans must be approved by the Member State. A reviewed plan can only be implemented once that approval has been given.

2. Reviews of port security assessments and port security plans may be developed by a recognised port security organisation, as referred to in Article 12.

Recognised port security organisation

Article 12
Recognised port security organisation
Member States may appoint recognised port security organisations for the purposes specified in this directive. Recognised port security organisations must fulfil the conditions set out in Annex IV.

EC Directive: Port Security

Article 13
Focal point for port security

Member States shall appoint for port security aspects the focal point appointed under Regulation (EC) Nr. .../.... for maritime and port facility security.

The focal point for port security shall communicate to the Commission the list of ports concerned by this directive.

The focal point for port security shall establish and maintain a list of the contact details of the authorities for port security, as well as the port security officers. This list shall be communicated to the Commission and updated upon changes.

Article 14
Implementation and conformity checking

1. Member States shall set up a system ensuring adequate and regular supervision of the port security plans and their implementation.

2. Six months after the date referred to in Article 19, the Commission, in co-operation with the focal points referred to in Article 13, shall start a series of inspections, including inspections of a suitable sample of ports, to monitor the application by Member States of this directive. These inspections shall take account of the data supplied by the focal points, including monitoring reports. The procedures for conducting such inspections shall be adopted in accordance with the procedure referred to in Article 16 (2).

3. The officials mandated by the Commission to conduct such inspections in accordance with paragraph 2 shall exercise their powers upon production of an authorisation in writing issued by the Commission and specifying the subject-matter, the purpose of the inspection and the date on which it is to begin. The Commission shall in good time before inspections inform the Member States concerned of the inspections.

The Member State concerned shall submit to such inspections and shall ensure that bodies or persons concerned also submit to those inspections.

4. The Commission shall communicate the inspection reports to the Member State concerned, which within three months of receipt of the report shall indicate sufficient details of the measures taken to remedy any shortcomings. The report and the answers shall be communicated to the Committee referred to in Article 16.

Article 15
Adaptations

The provisions of Annexes I to IV may be amended in accordance with the procedure referred to in Article 16 (2), without broadening the scope of this directive.

Article 16
Committee procedure

PROPOSAL ONLY

Focal point for port security

Implementation and conformity checking

Adaptations

1. The Commission shall be assisted by the committee set up by Regulation (EC) Nr..../.... and comprising representatives of the Member States, chaired by a Commission representative.

2. Where reference is made to this paragraph, Articles 5 and 7 of Decision 1999/468/EC shall apply, having regard to the provisions of Article 8 thereof.
The period laid down in Article 5(6) of Decision 1999/468/EC shall be set at one month.

Article 17
Confidentiality and dissemination of information

1. In applying this directive, the Commission shall take, in accordance with the provisions of Commission Decision 2001/844/EC, ECSC, Euratom, appropriate measures to protect information subject to the requirement of confidentiality to which it has access or which is communicated to it by Member States. The Member States shall take equivalent measures in accordance with relevant national legislation.

2. Any personnel carrying out security inspections, or handling confidential information related to this directive, must have an appropriate level of security vetting by the Member State of which the personnel concerned has the nationality.

3. Without prejudice to the public right of access to documents as laid down in Regulation (EC) Nr. 1049/2001 of the European Parliament and of the Council, the inspection reports and the answers of the Member States referred to in Article 14 (4) shall be secret and not be published. They shall only be available to the relevant authorities, which shall communicate them only to interested parties on a need-to-know basis, in accordance with applicable national rules for dissemination of sensitive information.

4. Member States shall as far as possible and in accordance with applicable national law treat as confidential information arising from inspection reports and answers of Member States when it relates to other Member States.

5. Unless it is clear that the inspection reports and answers shall or shall not be disclosed, Member States or the Commission shall consult with the Member State concerned.

Article 18
Sanctions

The Member States shall ensure that effective, proportionate and dissuasive sanctions are introduced for infringements of the national provisions adopted pursuant to this directive.

EC Directive: Port Security

Article 19

Implementation

1. Member States shall bring into force the laws, regulations and administrative provisions necessary to comply with this directive not later than [...] [one year from the date of its entry into force]. They shall forthwith inform the Commission thereof.

When Member States adopt those provisions, they shall contain a reference to this directive or be accompanied by such a reference on the occasion of their official publication. Member States shall determine how such reference is to be made.

2. Member States shall communicate to the Commission the text of the main provisions of national law which they adopt in the field covered by this directive.

Article 20

Entry into force

This directive shall enter into force on the twentieth day following that of its publication in the Official Journal of the European Union.

Article 21

Addressees

This Directive is addressed to the Member States.

Done at Brussels,

For the European Parliament
The President

For the Council
The President

Implementation

Entry into force

Addresses

EC Directive: Port Security

PROPOSAL ONLY

ANNEX I

Port Security
Assessment:

– elements

– aspects

ANNEX I
Port security assessment

The port security assessment is the basis for the work on the port security plan and its eventual implementation. The port security assessment shall at least look into the following elements:
– Identification and evaluation of important assets and infrastructure it is important to protect;
– Identification of possible threats to the assets and infrastructure and the likelihood of their occurrence, in order to establish and prioritise security measures;
– Identification, selection and prioritisation of counter-measures and procedural changes and their level of effectiveness in reducing vulnerability; and
– Identification of weaknesses, including human factors in the infrastructure, policies and procedures.

For this purpose the assessment shall at least cover the following aspects:
– identify all areas which are relevant for port security, thus also identifying the port boundaries. This includes port facilities which are already covered by Regulation (EC) Nr. .../.... and whose risk assessment will serve as a basis;
– identify security issues deriving from the interface between port facility and other port security measures;
– identify risk groups among personnel working in a port;
– subdivide, if useful, the port according to the likelihood of becoming a target of intentional unlawful acts. Areas will not only be judged upon their direct profile as a potential target, but also upon their potential role of passage when neighbouring areas are targeted;
– identify risk variations, e.g. those based on seasonality;
– identify the specific characteristics of each sub-area, such as location, accesses, power supply, communication system, ownership and users and other elements considered security-relevant;
– identify potential threat scenarios for each identified sub-area. A sub-area, infrastructure, cargo, baggage, people or transport equipment within this area can be a direct target of an identified threat, or it can be part of a wider area developed in the threat scenario;
– identify the specific consequences of a threat scenario. Consequences can impact on one or more sub-areas. Both direct and indirect consequences should be identified. Special attention should be given to the risk of human casualties;
– identify the possibility of cluster effects of acts of unlawful interference;
– identify the vulnerabilities of each sub-area;
– identify all organisational aspects relevant to overall port security, including the division of all security-related authorities, existing rules and procedures;
– identify vulnerabilities of the overarching port security related to organisational, legislative and procedural aspects;

ISPS Code

EC Directive: Port Security

- identify measures, procedures and actions aimed at reducing critical vulnerabilities.

Specific attention should be paid to the need for, and the means of, access control or restrictions to the entire port or to specific parts of a port, including identification of passengers, port employees or other workers, visitors and ship crews, area or activity monitoring requirements, cargo and luggage control. Measures, procedures and actions should be in line with the perceived risk, which may vary between port areas;

- identify an organisational structure supporting the enhancement of port security;
- identify how measures, procedures and actions should be reinforced in the event of an increase of security level;
- identify specific requirements for dealing with established security concerns, such as 'suspect' cargo, luggage, bunker, provisions or persons, unknown parcels, known dangers (e.g. bomb). These requirements should analyse desirability conditions for either clearing it on site or clearing it upon transport towards a secure area;
- identify measures, procedures and actions aimed at limiting and mitigating consequences;
- identify task divisions allowing for the appropriate and correct implementation of the measures, procedures and actions identified;
- pay specific attention, where appropriate, to the relationship with other security plans (e.g. port facility security plans) and other already existing security measures.

Attention should also be paid to the relationship with other response plans (e.g. oil spill response plan, port contingency plan, medical intervention plan, nuclear disaster plan, etc.);

- identify communication requirements for the implementation of the measures and procedures;
- pay specific attention to measures to protect security-sensitive information from disclosure. Identify the need-to-know requirements of all those directly involved as well as, where appropriate, the general public.

PROPOSAL ONLY

ANNEX II

Port Security Plan

– aspects

– tasks

ANNEX II
Port security plan

The port security plan sets out the port's security arrangements. It will be based on the findings of the port security assessment. It will clearly set out detailed measures. It will contain a control mechanism allowing, where necessary, for appropriate corrective measures
to be taken.

The port security plan will be based on the following general aspects:
- Define all areas relevant for port security. Depending on the port security assessment, measures, procedures and actions may vary from sub-area to sub-area. Indeed, some sub-areas may require stronger preventive measures than others.
  Special attention should be paid to the interfaces between sub-areas, as identified in the port security assessment;
- Ensure coordination between security measures for areas with different security characteristics;
- Provide, where necessary, for varying measures both with regard to different parts of the port, changing security levels, and specific intelligence.

Based on these general aspects the port security plan shall attribute tasks and specify work
plans in the following fields:
- access requirements. For some areas, requirements will only enter into force when security levels exceed minimal thresholds. All requirements and thresholds should be comprehensively included in the port security plan;

- ID, luggage and cargo control requirements. Requirements may or may not apply to sub-areas; requirements may or may not apply in full to different sub-areas. Persons entering or within a sub-area may be liable to control. The port security plan will appropriately respond to the findings of the port security assessment, which is the tool by which the security requirements of each sub-area and at each security level will be identified. When dedicated identification cards are developed for port security purposes, clear procedures should be established for the issue, the use/control and the return of such documents. Such procedures should take into account the specificities of certain groups of port users allowing for dedicated measures in order to limit the negative impact of access control requirements. Categories should at least include seafarers, authority officials, people permanently working in the port, people regularly working or visiting the port, residents living in the port and people occasionally working or visiting the port;

- liaison with cargo control, baggage and passenger control authorities. Where necessary, the plan is to provide for the linking up of the information and clearance systems of these authorities, including

EC Directive: Port Security

possible pre-arrival clearance systems.

– procedures and measures for dealing with suspect cargo, luggage, bunker, provisions or persons, including identification of a secure area; as well as for other security concerns and breaches of port security;

– monitoring requirements for sub-areas or activities within sub-areas. Both the need for and possible technical solutions will be derived from the port security assessment;

– signposting. Areas with any requirements (access and/or control), should be properly signposted. Control and access requirements shall appropriately take into account all relevant existing law and practices. Monitoring of activities should be appropriately indicated if national legislation so requires;

– communication and security clearance. All relevant security information must be properly communicated according to security clearance standards included in the plan. In view of the sensitivity of some information, communication will be based on a need-to-know basis, but it will include where necessary procedures for communications addressed to the general public. Security clearance standards will form part of the plan and are aimed at protecting security sensitive information against unauthorised disclosure.

– reporting of security incidents. With a view to ensure a rapid response the port security plan should set out clear reporting requirements to the port security officer of all security incidents and/or to the competent authority for port security.

– integration with other preventive plans or activities. The plan should specifically deal with integration with other preventive and control activities in force in the port.

– integration with other response plans and/or inclusion of specific response measures, procedures and actions. The plan should detail the interaction and coordination with other response and emergency plans. Where necessary conflicts and shortcomings should be resolved.

– training and exercise requirements.

– operational port security organisation and working procedures. The port security plan will detail the port security organisation, its task division and working procedures. It will also detail the coordination with port facility and ship security officers, where appropriate. It will delineate the tasks of the port security committee, if this exists.

– procedures for adapting and updating the port security plan.

PROPOSAL ONLY

ANNEX III

Basic training
requirements

ANNEX III
Basic training requirements

Various types of exercises which may include participation of port facility security officers, in conjunction with relevant authorities of Member States, company security officers, or ship security officers, if available, should be carried out at least once each calendar year with no more than 18 months between the exercises. Requests for the participation of company security officers or ships security officers in joint exercises should be made bearing in mind the security and work implications for the ship. These exercises should test communication, coordination, resource availability and response. These exercises may be:

(1) full scale or live;
(2) tabletop simulation or seminar; or
(3) combined with other exercises held such as emergency response or other port State authority exercises.

ANNEX IV

Conditions to be
fulfilled by a
recognised port
security organisation

ANNEX IV
Conditions to be fulfilled by a recognised port security organisation

A recognised port security organisation should be able to demonstrate:

(1) expertise in relevant aspects of port security;
(2) an appropriate knowledge of port operations, including knowledge of port design and construction;
(3) an appropriate knowledge of other security relevant operations potentially affecting port security;
(4) the capability to assess the likely port security risks;
(5) the ability to maintain and improve the port security expertise of its personnel;
(6) the ability to monitor the continuing trustworthiness of its personnel;
(7) the ability to maintain appropriate measures to avoid unauthorised disclosure of, or access to, security-sensitive material;
(8) knowledge of relevant national and international legislation and security requirements;
(9) the knowledge of current security threats and patterns;
(10) the knowledge of recognition and detection of weapons, dangerous substances and devices;
(11) the knowledge of recognition, on a non-discriminatory basis, of characteristics and behavioural patterns of persons who are likely to threaten port security;
(12) the knowledge of techniques used to circumvent security measures;
(13) the knowledge of security and surveillance equipment and systems and their operational limitations.
(14) A recognised port security organisation which has made a port security assessment or review of such an assessment for a port is not allowed to establish or review the port security plan for the same port.

Notes

Notes

US Maritime Strategy

Under the provisions of the United States Maritime Transportation Security Act of 2002, the U.S. Coast Guard (USCG) is appointed as the lead federal agency for Maritime Homeland Security.

U.S. Coast Guard Maritime Strategy for Homeland Security

Accordingly, the USCG has developed a maritime strategy to fight global terrorism that sets to balance their responsibility for upholding the principles of America's security – as laid down in the National Security Strategy and the National Strategy for Homeland Security - with the imperatives of preserving fundamental liberties and economic well-being.

Executive Summary

The U.S. Coast Guard Maritime Strategy for Homeland Security sets out strategic objectives as follows (in order of priority):

Strategic objectives

- ❏ Prevent terrorist attacks within, and terrorist exploitation of, the U.S. Maritime Domain
- ❏ Reduce America's vulnerability to terrorism within the U.S. Maritime Domain.
- ❏ Protect U.S. population centres, critical infrastructure, maritime borders, ports, coastal approaches, and the boundaries and seams between them
- ❏ Protect the U.S. Marine Transportation System while preserving the freedom of the U.S. Maritime Domain for legitimate pursuits
- ❏ Minimize the damage and recover from attacks that may occur within the U.S. Maritime Domain as either the lead federal agency or a supporting agency.

The Coast Guard's homeland security mission is to protect the U.S. Maritime Domain and the U.S. Marine Transportation System and deny their use and exploitation by terrorists as a means for attacks on U.S. territory, population, and critical infrastructure.

Protection of U.S. Maritime Domain

Additionally, the U.S. Coast Guard (USCG) will prepare for and, in the event of attack, conduct emergency response operations. And, when directed, as the supported or supporting commander, the Coast Guard will conduct military homeland defence operations in its traditional role as a military service.

Conduct military homeland defence operations

To achieve its strategic objectives the Coast Guard's Maritime Strategy comprises six elements:

Basic Elements

- ❏ Increase Maritime Domain Awareness
- ❏ Conduct Enhanced Maritime Security Operations
- ❏ Close Port Security Gaps
- ❏ Build Critical Security Capabilities and Competencies
- ❏ Leverage Partnerships to Mitigate Security Risks
- ❏ Ensure Readiness for Homeland Defence Operations

Ref: *www.uscg.mil/news/reportsandbudget/Maritime_strategy/ USCG_Maritme_Strategy.pdf*

www document

US Maritime Strategy

Strategic Elements	USCG NEAR TERM INITIATIVES
1. Increase Maritime Domain Awareness	* Establish Maritime Intelligence Fusion Center at each Area to leverage interagency information sharing . * Co-chair with Navy a Joint Maritime Surveillance Working Group. * Install SIPRNET at each COTP and Group. * Install GCCS in all command centres. * Expand sensor capability with RESCUE-21, PAWSS, Deepwater, and state-of-the-art port surveillance system.
2. Conduct Enhanced Security Operations	* Commission MSSTs and enhance boarding team capabilities. * Evaluate arming all HH-60/65s. * Conduct robust exercise plan to test effectiveness of an expanded layered defence. * Acquire new small boat fleet. * Increase acquisition of WPB-87 Coastal Patrol Boat. * Deploy HC-130J with advanced C2 and sensor systems for increased maritime surveillance capability.
3. Close Port Security Gaps	* Conduct and update Port Security Assessments on ports, vessels and facilities using Port Security Risk Assessment Tool methodology. * Conduct follow-on detailed vulnerability assessments on ports most at risk. * Plan and conduct port-level counter-terrorism exercises. * Field bio-terrorism response policy. * Establish Port Security Committees in each port with participation from all key stakeholders.
4. Build Critical Security Capabilities and Competencies	* Expand, train and commission MSSTs. * Expand security-training infrastructure to include Operational Intelligence and MLE Schools and Fast Boat Center of Excellence. * Modernize via Deepwater upgraded C4ISR capabilities in 37 existing major cutters, all WPBs, selected HC-130s, all HH60Js, all HH65s and 12 command centres, and add new MPAs and UAVs. * Develop skill sets in workforce to leverage increased technological capability being fielded.
5. Leverage Partnerships to Mitigate Security Risks	* Conduct port vulnerability assessments. * Establish and exercise specialized HAZMAT Response Teams and other critical capabilities from existing first responder type organizations. * Pursue efforts to increase cargo security and enhance the security and validity of mariner documentation at international level.

US Maritime Strategy

* Field Deepwater to increase operational capability and DOD compatibility.
* Prepare to conduct operations as a supported and supporting commander to U.S. NORTHCOM.
o Prepare, equip, and train forces to conduct both HLS and HLD operations and to transition smoothly between missions.
o Procure CBRNE personal protective equipment for field personnel deemed at risk.
o Develop training programs to ensure safety and effectiveness of Coast Guard personnel pursuing HLS and HLD missions.

6. Ensure Readiness for Homeland Defence

Maritime Domain: The U.S. Maritime Domain encompasses all U.S. ports, inland waterways, harbours, navigable waters, Great Lakes, territorial seas, contiguous waters, customs waters, coastal seas, littoral areas, the U.S. Exclusive Economic Zone, and oceanic regions of U.S. national interest, as well as the sealanes to the United States, U.S. maritime approaches, and the high seas surrounding America.

Maritime Domain Awareness (MDA): Maritime Domain Awareness is comprehensive information, intelligence, and knowledge of all relevant entities within the U.S. Maritime Domain - and their respective activities - that could affect America's security, safety, economy, or environment

Maritime Homeland Security (MHLS): Maritime homeland security is the concerted national effort lead by the U.S. Coast Guard to secure the homeland associated with or in the U.S Maritime Domain from terrorist attacks

Maritime Safety and Security Teams (MSST): Maritime Safety and Security Teams are U.S. Coast Guard mobile units established for maritime homeland security missions in response to the terrorist attacks of 2001. These 100-person units are modelled after the Coast Guard's existing Port Security Units and Law Enforcement Detachments to provide a fast-deployment capability for homeland security. Like all Coast Guard units, MSSTs are multi-mission capable, and can conduct search and rescue and law enforcement missions, as well as maritime security tasking. MSSTs will deploy in support of National Security Special Events, such as OpSail, as well as for severe weather recovery operations, protection of military load-outs, enforcement of security zones, defence of critical waterside facilities in strategic ports, and interdiction of illegal activities

Maritime Transportation Security Act of 2002: Landmark legislation passed by the 107th Congress to increase the security efforts of the Coast Guard and other agencies in the U.S. Maritime Domain

GLOSSARY OF TERMS

US Maritime Domain

US Maritime Domain Awareness

Maritime Homeland Security

Maritime Safety & Security Teams (MSST)

Maritime Transportation Security Act 2002

US Maritime Strategy

National Distress and Response System (NDRS)

National Distress and Response System (NDRS): The National Distress and Response System is the replacement communications and distress reporting system for the U.S. Coast Guard. Once fielded this new communications system will serve as the means for Coast Guard operational commanders to exercise command and control over all Coast Guard units conducting all missions along the 95,000-mile U.S. coastline out to 20 miles offshore, as well as, in the ports and interior waterways including the Great Lakes. Additionally, NDRS serves as the emergency reporting system for the public and commercial mariners for them to contact the Coast Guard if in distress. This system is also designated as "Rescue 21."

National Strike Force (NSF):

National Strike Force (NSF): The National Strike Force is a U.S. Coast Guard capability composed of three mobile units established for rapid response to oil discharges and hazardous substance releases. With highly specialized equipment, NSF units support Federal On-Scene Coordinators and Coast Guard incident commanders to reduce the environmental damage from oil discharges and hazardous substance releases. Since the NSF also has a CBRNE capability (that was used in the aftermath of the bio-terrorism attacks on the U.S. Capital), the NSF has a major role in homeland security preparedness and recovery operations in the U.S. Maritime Domain

Ports and Waterways Safety System (PAWSS)

Ports and Waterways Safety System (PAWSS): The Ports and Waterways Safety System is a U.S. Coast Guard project to provide an integrated system of vessel traffic centres, communications, information management capabilities, remote sensors, and associated facilities for vessel traffic management in selected U.S. ports and waterways to provide safe operations and protect the environmental. PAWSS capabilities can directly support Coast Guard maritime security operations for tasking such as surveillance, detection, and command and control

Sea Marshals

Sea Marshals: Sea Marshals are a U.S. Coast Guard capability to intercept and board incoming ships to the United States prior to the ships arrival in U.S. ports, principally to deter and prevent the ship itself from being used a means to conduct a terrorist attack in the port. Upon boarding a vessel Sea Marshals meet with the ship's captain to explain their purpose and check cargo manifests and crew lists. They stand guard in critical areas of the ships, including the bridge, keeping a watchful eye for suspicious behaviour. Ships carrying hazardous materials or those hailing from countries that the United States has identified as having terrorist links or unfriendly relations with the United States are given the highest priority. Other vessels are boarded randomly, both in port and at sea

U.S. Maritime Domain

U.S. Maritime Domain: See Maritime Domain

US Maritime Security Act

The U.S. **Maritime Transportation Security Act of 2002 (MTSA)**, is designed to protect the ports and waterways of the United States from a terrorist attack. The Act represents landmark legislation that encompasses the ISPS Code and amendments to SOLAS 1974.

Maritime Security Act of 2002 (MTSA)

In addition, on Oct. 22, 2003, the US Coast Guard published maritime security final rules that revised temporary interim rules (TIR) published on July 1, 2003.

The following summarizes significant changes and clarifications in the final rules.

Summary

AUTOMATIC IDENTIFICATION SYSTEM (AIS)

AIS

The TIR required the installation of AIS equipment on commercial vessels on international voyages and certain commercial vessels, (including fishing, towing, and passenger vessels over 65' in length), when operating in a Vessel Traffic Service Area or a Vessel Movement Reporting Service Area.

To ease the immediate cost burden on industry, the Coast Guard amended the AIS requirement so that only SOLAS certificated fishing vessels over 300 GT and small passenger vessels certificated to carry over 150 passengers must carry an AIS. However, the Coast Guard will be evaluating approaches with better cost-benefit rationale for all vessels operating in U.S. waters to carry AIS and will be soliciting additional public comment regarding costs and possible alternatives.

FERRY SYSTEM

Ferries and passenger vessels

In the final rule, the Coast Guard clarified the requirements, reiterating that ferries and other passenger vessels will not be required to implement "airport-like" passenger screening and that other procedures will be permitted, including increased security patrols and monitoring as well as random screenings of persons, baggage, and vehicles.

FOREIGN VESSEL SECURITY PLANS

Foreign Vessel Security Plans

The final rule clarifies that foreign flag SOLAS vessel owners do not have to submit security plans to the Coast Guard for approval. Non-SOLAS foreign vessels will be required to have either Coast Guard-approved security plans, comply with an alternative security plan (i.e. ISPS Code compliant), or comply with measures specified in a bilateral or multilateral agreement. With a stringent and thorough boarding program, the Coast Guard will examine and enforce the vessel's compliance with international security regulations. Vessels not in compliance may be denied entry into U.S. ports.

US Maritime Security Act

Cargo Screening Requirements

CARGO SCREENING REQUIREMENTS

The final rules amend cargo-screening requirements, mandating the checking of cargo for evidence of tampering, but no longer require the screening of cargo for dangerous substances. The Department of Homeland Security will explore enhanced solutions, including the development of comprehensive cargo screening guidelines.

Alternative Security Program (ASP)

ALTERNATIVE SECURITY PROGRAM (ASP)

The final rules allow more flexibility for non-SOLAS vessels and all facilities to participate in an ASP, if they wish. This program was strongly endorsed by several organizations because it allows security measures to be tailored to the unique needs of each industry segment.

Vessel Security Plans

VESSEL SECURITY PLANS

Security plans are required for all vessels, exemptions are as follows:
- Passenger vessels that do not carry more than 150 passengers, regardless of how many are overnight passengers
- Non-self propelled Mobile Offshore Drilling Units and other industrial vessels (e.g., dredges)

Facility Security Plans

FACILITY SECURITY PLANS

Facilities are required to develop individual security plans, exemptions are as follows:
- Facilities that only service passenger vessels when those vessels are not carrying passengers
- Public Access Facilities that are used by the public primarily for purposes such as recreation, entertainment, retail, or tourism, and not for receiving certain passenger vessels subject to the regulations. Owners and operators of public access facilities will be responsible for implementing appropriate security measures in accordance with the Area Security Plan
- Shipyards

Security Assessment Tools

SECURITY ASSESSMENT TOOLS

The final rule provides industry with the flexibility to use their own security assessment tools, but also includes a list of tools that may be used. This list includes the Transportation Security Administration Maritime Self Assessment Risk Model (TMSARM) a no-cost, user-friendly, web-based, vulnerability-self-assessment tool designed by TSA specifically to meet the requirements of MTSA.

The TSA tool can be found on the web at:
http://www.tsa.gov/public/interapp/editorial/editorial_0826.xml

US Maritime Security Act

PART 104 - VESSEL SECURITY

Subpart A– General § 104.100 Definitions.
Except as specifically stated in this subpart, the definitions in part 101 of this subchapter apply to this part.

§ 104.105 Applicability.
(a) This part applies to the owner or operator of any:
(1) Mobile Offshore Drilling Unit (MODU), cargo, or passenger vessel subject to SOLAS, 1974;
(2) Foreign commercial vessel greater than 100 gross register tons not subject to SOLAS;
(3) Commercial vessel greater than 100 gross register tons subject to 46CFR subchapter I, except commercial fishing vessels inspected under 46 CFR part 105;
(4) Vessel subject to 46 CFR subchapter L;
(5) Passenger vessel subject to 46 CFR subchapters H or K;
(6) Other passenger vessel carrying more than 12 passengers that is engaged on an international voyage;
(7) Barge subject to 46 CFR subchapters D or O;
(8) Barge subject to 46 CFR subchapter I that carries Certain Dangerous Cargoes in bulk, or that is engaged on an international voyage;
(9) Tankship subject to 46 CFR subchapters D or O; and
(10) Towing vessel greater than 8 meters in registered length that is engaged in towing a barge or barges subject to this part.

(b) An owner or operator of any vessel not covered in paragraph (a) of this section is subject to parts 101 through 103 of this subchapter.

(c) Foreign vessels that have on board a valid International Ship Security Certificate (ISSC) that attests to the vessel's compliance with SOLAS Chapter XI–2 and the ISPS Code, and having taken into account the relevant provisions in the ISPS Code, part B, will be deemed to be in compliance with this part, except for §§ 104.240, 104.255, 104.292, and 104.295 as appropriate.

(d) Except pursuant to international treaty, convention, or agreement to which the U.S. is a party, this part does not apply to any foreign vessel that is not destined for, or departing from, a port or place subject to the jurisdiction of the U.S. and that is in:
(1) Innocent passage through the territorial sea of the U.S.; or
(2) Transit through the navigable waters of the U.S. that form a part of an international strait.

§ 104.240 Maritime Security (MARSEC)
Level coordination and implementation.
(a) The vessel owner or operator must ensure that, prior to entering a port, all measures are taken that are specified in the Vessel Security

---

Maritime Security Act of 2002 (MTSA)

Extract from the Regulations

Application

Vessel types

ISPS Code-compliant foreign vessels

Vessels on passage

MARSEC (Security) Level requirements

Plan (VSP) for compliance with the MARSEC Level in effect for the port.

Action on increase in MARSEC Level

(b) When notified of an increase in the MARSEC Level, the vessel owner or operator must ensure:

(1) If a higher MARSEC Level is set for the port in which the vessel is located or is about to enter, the vessel complies, without undue delay, with all measures specified in the VSP for compliance with that higher MARSEC Level;

(2) The COTP is notified as required by § 101.300(c) when compliance with the higher MARSEC Level has been implemented; and

(3) For vessels in port, that compliance with the higher MARSEC Level has taken place within 12 hours of the notification.

MARSEC Levels 2 & 3

(c) For MARSEC Levels 2 and 3, the Vessel Security Officer must brief all vessel personnel of identified threats, emphasize reporting procedures, and stress the need for increased vigilance.

(d) An owner or operator whose vessel is not in compliance with the requirements of this section must inform the COTP and obtain approval prior to entering any port, prior to interfacing with another vessel or with a facility or to continuing operations.

MARSEC Level 3

(e) For MARSEC Level 3, in addition to the requirements in this part, a vessel owner or operator may be required to implement additional measures, pursuant to 33 CFR part 6, 160 or 165, as appropriate, which may include but are not limited to:

(1) Arrangements to ensure that the vessel can be towed or moved if deemed necessary by the Coast Guard;

(2) Use of waterborne security patrol;

(3) Use of armed security personnel to control access to the vessel and to deter, to the maximum extent practical, a TSI; or

(4) Screening the vessel for the presence of dangerous substances and devices underwater or other threats.

Declaration of Security

§ 104.255 Declaration of Security (DoS).

(a) Each vessel owner or operator must ensure procedures are established for requesting a DoS and for handling DoS requests from a facility or other vessel.

– at MARSEC Level 1

(b) At MARSEC Level 1, the Master or Vessel Security Officer (VSO), or their designated representative, of any cruise ship or manned vessel carrying Certain Dangerous Cargoes, in bulk, must complete and sign a DoS with the VSO or Facility Security Officer (FSO), or their designated representative, of any vessel or facility with which it interfaces.

(1) For a vessel-to-facility interface, prior to arrival of a vessel to a facility, the FSO and Master, VSO, or their designated

representatives must coordinate security needs and procedures, and agree upon the contents of the DoS for the period of time the vessel is at the facility. Upon a vessel's arrival to a facility and prior to any passenger embarkation or disembarkation or cargo transfer operation, the FSO or Master, VSO, or designated representatives must sign the written DoS.

(2) For a vessel engaging in a vessel-to-vessel interface, prior to the interface, the respective Masters, VSOs, or their designated representatives must coordinate security needs and procedures, and agree upon the contents of the DoS for the period of time the vessel is at the facility. Upon the vessel-to-vessel interface and prior to any passenger embarkation or disembarkation or cargo transfer operation, the respective Masters, VSOs, or designated representatives must sign the written DoS.

(c) At MARSEC Levels 2 and 3, the Master, VSO, or designated representative of any vessel required to comply with this part must sign and implement a DoS prior to any vessel-to-vessel interface.

– at MARSEC Level 2

(d) At MARSEC Levels 2 and 3, the Master, VSO, or designated representative of any vessel required to comply with this part must sign and implement a DoS with the FSO of any facility on which it calls prior to any cargo transfer operation or passenger embarkation or disembarkation.

– at MARSEC Levels 2 & 3

(e) At MARSEC Levels 1 and 2, VSOs of vessels that frequently interface with the same facility may implement a continuing DoS for multiple visits, provided that:
(1) The DoS is valid for the specific MARSEC Level;
(2) The effective period at MARSEC Level 1 does not exceed 90 days; and
(3) The effective period at MARSEC Level 2 does not exceed 30 days.

– at MARSEC Levels 1 & 2

(f) When the MARSEC Level increases beyond the level contained in the DoS, the continuing DoS becomes void and a new DoS must be signed and implemented in accordance with this section.
(g) The COTP may require at any time, at any MARSEC Level, any manned vessel subject to this part to implement a DoS with the VSO or FSO prior to any vessel-to-vessel or vessel-to-facility interface when he or she deems it necessary.

§ 104.292 Additional requirements – passenger vessels and ferries
(a) At all Maritime Security (MARSEC) Levels, the vessel owner or operator must ensure security sweeps are performed, prior to getting underway, after any period the vessel was unattended.

Passenger Vessels & Ferries – additional requirements

(b) As an alternative to the identification checks and passenger screening requirements in § 104.265 (e)(1), (e)(3), and (e)(8), the owner or operator of a passenger vessel or ferry may ensure security

– passenger screening

US Maritime Security Act

Passenger Vessels & Ferries

– passenger screening

measures are implemented that include:
(1) Searching selected areas prior to embarking passengers and prior to sailing; and
(2) Implementing one or more of the following:
(i) Performing routine security patrols;
(ii) Providing additional closed-circuit television to monitor passenger areas; or
(iii) Securing all non-passenger areas.

– vehicle screening

(c) Passenger vessels certificated to carry more than 2000 passengers, working in coordination with the terminal, may be subject to additional vehicle screening requirements in accordance with a MARSEC Directive or other orders issued by the Coast Guard.

MARSEC Level 2 additional measures

(d) At MARSEC Level 2, a vessel owner or operator must ensure, in addition to MARSEC Level 1 measures, the implementation of the following:
(1) Search selected areas prior to embarking passengers and prior to sailing;
(2) Passenger vessels certificated to carry less than 2000 passengers, working in coordination with the terminal, may be subject to additional vehicle screening requirements in accordance with a MARSEC Directive or other orders issued by the Coast Guard; and
(3) As an alternative to the identification and screening requirements in § 104.265(e)(3), intensify patrols, security sweeps and monitoring identified in paragraph (b) of this section.

MARSEC Level 3 additional measures

(e) At MARSEC Level 3, a vessel owner or operator may, in addition to MARSEC Levels 1 and 2 measures, as an alternative to the identification checks and passenger screening requirements in § 104.265(e)(3), ensure that random armed security patrols are conducted, which need not consist of vessel personnel.

Cruise Ships

– additional requirements

§ 104.295 Additional requirements – cruise ships

(a) At all MARSEC Levels, the owner or operator of a cruise ship must ensure the following:
(1) Screen all persons, baggage, and personal effects for dangerous substances and devices;
(2) Check the identification of all persons seeking to board the vessel; this check includes confirming the reason for boarding by examining joining instructions, passenger tickets, boarding passes, government identification or visitor badges, or work orders;
(3) Perform security patrols; and
(4) Search selected areas prior to embarking passengers and prior to sailing.

(b) At MARSEC Level 3, the owner or operator of a cruise ship must ensure that security briefs to passengers about the specific threat are provided.

US Maritime Security Act

Useful Internet links to further information on the US Maritime Security Act 2002:

For complete text of the Act:

www.uscg.mil/d9/wwm/mso/chicago/index05.htm

For United States Coast Guard:

www.uscg.mil/USCG.shtm

For Department of Homeland Security:

www.dhs.gov/dhspublic/

For Department of Transportation:

www.dot.gov/

For US Maritime Administration (MARAD)

http://marad.dot.gov/index.html

For American Association of Port Authorities:

www.aapa-ports.org

WWW Links

Notes

Notes

ISPS Code Keyword Index

IMPORTANT NOTE:
Due to the abbreviated and non-legislative content of the IMO Guidance, European Proposals and US Maritime Strategy sections, the keyword index covers ONLY the ISPS Code and SOLAS Amendments sections of this publication i.e. Pages i to 125. It is designed solely to assist in identifying and referencing items of major significance in the ISPS Code and associated SOLAS amendments. For the purposes of simplicity and layout, duplicate entries of a keyword within a single page and/or within a single section or sub-section may be represented by a page reference to the first or any of the entries only. Consequently, readers are strongly advised not to rely on the keyword index as their only source of reference but to use it as a guide to areas of likely relevance and further reading.

ISPS Code Keyword Index

ISPS Code Keyword Index

ISPS Code Keyword Index

ISPS Code Keyword Index

Notes

ISPS Code

Notes

Advertisers Index

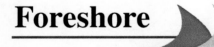

Foreshore

Publications

Foreshore Publications produces other titles
which may be of use to the mariner
or those involved with Port Management and Operations.

Check on our website for the latest publications
or to purchase further copies of this book.

www.foreshorebooks.com